A History of
Britain's Transport

A History of
Britain's Transport

Jeremy Black

PEN & SWORD
TRANSPORT

First published in Great Britain in 2024 by
Pen & Sword Transport
An imprint of Pen & Sword Books Limited
Yorkshire – Philadelphia

Copyright © Jeremy Black 2024

ISBN 978 1 03610 956 1

Typeset by Mac Style
Printed in the UK by CPI Group (UK) Ltd, Croydon, CR0 4YY.

Pen & Sword Books Limited incorporates the imprints of After
the Battle, Atlas, Archaeology, Aviation, Discovery, Family History,
Fiction, History, Maritime, Military, Military Classics, Politics,
Select, Transport, True Crime, Air World, Frontline Publishing, Leo
Cooper, Remember When, Seaforth Publishing, The Praetorian Press,
Wharncliffe Local History, Wharncliffe Transport, Wharncliffe True
Crime and White Owl.

For a complete list of Pen & Sword titles please contact

PEN & SWORD BOOKS LIMITED
47 Church Street, Barnsley, South Yorkshire, S70 2AS, England
E-mail: enquiries@pen-and-sword.co.uk
Website: www.pen-and-sword.co.uk
or
PEN AND SWORD BOOKS
1950 Lawrence Rd, Havertown, PA 19083, USA
E-mail: uspen-and-sword@casematepublishers.com
Website: www.penandswordbooks.com

For
Rob Kenny
Who is as thoughtful and agreeable as he is a brilliant transporter.

Contents

Contents

Preface

The Importance of Culture

'…a dirty inn;
The meat was very tough and bad,
and mother stormed like any mad,
But forced "half pleased to be content",
We munched our meat and on we went.'

A motorway service station in 2024? No, Mary Montagu-Douglas-Scott reaching Worksop in 1780,[1] when every journey would have taken longer and all the facilities have been far worse. So also for voyages by sea, Jonathan Swift complaining from the port of Holyhead on Anglesey, very much an island, en route to Dublin in September 1727:

'Lo here I sit at Holyhead
With muddy ale and mouldy bread
…
I'm fastened both by wind and tide
…
the Captain swears the sea's too rough
He has not passengers enough.
And thus the Dean [Swift] is forced to stay
Till others come to help the pay.'

Britain, 2023–4: the destruction of ULEZ (Ultra-low-emission zone) cameras in London, prolonged rail strikes, and the disputes over the hopelessly over-budget HS2 train scheme, much of which was cancelled in 2021 and 2023, separately and together underline the contention that is transport. It is not sadly simply a story of technological proficiency and improvement through time. Instead, far more is involved, and the history is not solely one of success. In some respects, notably with the number of potholes, it is precisely the opposite.

Transport both frames our lives and is moulded by them. This book draws on our interest in transport history, the routes, vehicles and experiences. Transport history is national history and social history, the blood and beat of everyday experience and special moments, the making of routes, the source and means of our engagement with worlds greater than our own background. There is longevity, and it echoes in our culture, throughout our culture. In Neil Humphreys' detective story *Lost Women* (2023), one character remarks: 'You do know there are haulage firms from Barking to the Dartford Crossing right? We tend to stick our supply chains near rivers and ports. I heard the Romans did the same round here.'[2]

We cover here all the types of transport, and for both passengers and freight. The latter includes information. Messages and documents sent by runner or horsed courier transported information, as electronic means do today, and the post, telegraphy, radio and broadcasting have all done. We begin with the walking and packhorses that predominated for much of national history. Both tend to be underrated, and yet they reflected a reaction to landscape that captured the dominant role of the latter for much of the transport history of the country. Moreover, walking continues to be crucial as a means to work, play and much else; even if packhorses have long since ceased to be of significance, and, although veterinary surgeons grew from horse and cow doctors, the role of horse-care is as one with the Medes and the Persians of Antiquity. So also with once timeless scenes such as Thomas Gainsborough's *The Harvest Wagon* (1767) and his *Peasants Going to Market* (*c.* 1770), the latter one in which packhorses are used.

We move on to the changes brought by improvements to road transport, from the Romans to medieval bridgebuilders and, then, subsequently, to the turnpiking that began in the late seventeenth century and then flourished in the eighteenth century. In parallel, transport by water, whether river or coast-hugging, canal or sea-crossing, developed across the same long timespan, with change present alongside the continuities that are most obvious.

The situation then speeds up. We have the age of rail, and, within a century of the beginning of steam locomotion on both land and sea, there is the internal combustion engine and then powered flight. Forms overlap, as well as emphases being sequential, and that takes us to the present, a time when we can clearly see the contentious and politicised nature of much discussion about usage, cost, taxation, and government support.

In discussing change, it is appropriate to be sceptical about the notion of transport revolutions, for example the medieval shift to the horse[3] or the sixteenth-century appearance of the coach and the impact of four-wheeled wagons.[4] This notion has been over-used, not least due to the tendency to underplay both the length of time taken and the extent to which other forms of transport continued. In practice, moreover, there is the question of how far infrastructure affected demand, or how much demand caused that infrastructure. What were the drivers of change in transport, and how far was it a matter of contexts, such indeed that any focus on the machinery of transport is misleading?

This template provides us with a chronological account, which is the structure adopted in this book, but it is also necessary to note the significant presence of thematic considerations. These include an emphasis on freight as well as passengers. Evidence is greater for the latter, including for traffic on vehicles that carried both. In comparative terms, there is relatively little material, whether correspondence or diaries, for those who moved freight, but far far more for passengers. Yet, it is necessary to appreciate that freight was not only an economic consideration but also political and social, national, regional and local, in its resonances. On a longstanding basis, the transport system enabled the movement to ports for export of goods that were of great consequence for neighbourhoods far from the coast, whether wool, cloth, wheat or coal. Thus, on 7 May 1735, *Wye's Letter*, the leading newsletter, reported: 'The price of wheat rises considerably on account of the great demand thereof from abroad, not less than one thousand quarters of wheat meal were yesterday shipped off for Spain.' If exported from London, goods had to be moved there, as with grain that year.[5] Moreover, in many senses, the movement of freight was more important, and remains so especially if we include energy, information and opinion as part of the equation.

There is also the judgmental issue of avoiding the assumption that later means better, and vice versa. This assumption is central to the teleology of progressivist accounts of history, and they tend to be to the fore in long-term treatments of topics, not least if there is an attempt to offer an organising account or, at least, explanation.

In addition, there is the need to reconcile, or arbitrate in space and significance, between the atypical and the typical. This is a particular problem if there is a tendency to focus on 'great' individuals, for example the bridgebuilder Thomas Telford, or works, such as the Grand Union Canal, and/or to follow the modern device of centring a chapter on a specific story about such a work, for example the construction of the M1. Instead, transport involves routes; facilities such as inns, stables, ports, stations, and airports; personnel; vehicles; supplies such as fuel, food and water; information systems such as maps and timetables; economic demand, social context and political oversight.

Separately, the geographical perspective comes to the fore. Britain is distinctive for having more sea coast per square mile of land than other major European countries. It also had plentiful accessible, near-surface, coal. In analysis, the national and the regional have to be distinguished, and that remains the case despite the emphasis on national transport policy, circumstances and institutions, for example National Highways. There are questions of preponderance in the British coverage. Furthermore, for much of the history of the British Isles, it was also the case that the identity of at least part was bound up with that stemming from conquest from overseas.[6] Thus, 'domestic transport,' in so far as the term has validity, was a matter not only of transport within the British Isles, but also between them and areas from which they had been conquered. Indeed, these might be much closer than transport within the British Isles, as when comparing in the late eleventh century cross-Channel transport between England and Normandy with that between England and Ireland. Trade links offer an important variation on this theme, one that could also have an overlap.[7]

There are also issues of preponderance between England and other parts of the British Isles. One context is that of population, which leads to a focus on England, and indeed ensures that each of northern and southern England deserves more attention than Scotland, still more Wales. There is also the contexts of economic significance, transport provision, and transport innovation, each of which even more clearly leads to a focus on England.

Within that, there has generally been a stress on London with the rare exception of the early days of rail. A Swiss visitor in 1726 was able to assume, mistakenly, that turnpikes had replaced the old road system in large part because he based his account on the London area where indeed turnpiking was furthest advanced, but far from universal:

'The journey on the high roads of England, and more especially near London, is most enjoyable and interesting. These roads are magnificent, being wide, smooth and well kept. Contractors have the care of them, and cover them when necessary with that fine gravel so common in this country. The roads are rounded in the shape of an ass's back, so that the centre is higher than the sides, and the rain flows off into the ditches with which the roads are bordered on either side. It is the custom here, as it is in France, for the poor peasants to be forced to make and keep up the high roads at their own expense and care. In this country everyone who makes use of roads is obliged to contribute to the expense of keeping them up.'[8]

There are also methodological issues, those relating to the methods we should adopt when discussing and explaining transport history, and these issues are often linked to conceptual points, the ways in which we understand circumstance and change. In particular, there is the question of silences, experiences and methods about which we know little, and the degree to which these are related to contemporary and current-day assumptions about importance. These silences and assumptions relate to those travelling, to the routes taken, and to what was transported. If an obvious point, the views of animals, such as the horses in Gainsborough's painting *Returning from Market* (*c.*1780) or cattle being ferried across a river, as both motive force and cargo, are not present. So also for illiterate humans, other than indirectly, a point also true of their experiences, with legal records in particular being relevant in trying to recover their stories. It is not known what the convicts who built the bridge over the Severn at Montford in 1790–2 thought of their task, which ranked as an achievement for Thomas Telford.

Aside from silences, there are the many journeys for which sources are non-existent or scarce, notably the walking that provided most of the very local journeys that were those taken by the majority of the population.

Both walking and very local journeys continue to be much underrated in contemporary accounts of transport. For example, the focus on urban cycling can be at the expense of the concerns of city walkers. This is true of the provision of cycleways, but also of illegal cycling through traffic signals and on pavements.

Contemporary accounts also tend to neglect 'vertical transport,' but that is central to the building up that is important both to housing density and to office and other work. Walking upstairs or, earlier, ladders was/is central, but the lift has transformed the situation, or, rather situations, just as it also played a role, alongside the escalator, in allowing subterranean travel, notably by tube in London. Lifts have also played an important role in other aspects of the infrastructure of transport, particularly multi-level carparks, whether sub-surface or surface.

There was a gender dimension for most of transport history, whether in attitudes to chaperoning, which were affected by cycling, or the hesitant willingness of trade unions to accept female lorry drivers. In the early nineteenth century, women and girls were not generally expected to ride horses, but men and boys did. In going to Box Hill for their outing in Jane Austen's *Emma* (1815), the gentlemen go on horseback and the women by carriage, a journey delayed by a lame carriage horse. *Emma* is of course a novel, but novels helped define what was seen as normative including aspirationally normative. As a result, the cultural presentation of transport is an important aspect of this book. This was not only the case in famous works but also in genre fiction, such as detective novels.

Social artifice could play a role. In Austen's *Pride and Prejudice* (1813), Mrs Bennet suggests to her daughter Jane that when she goes to the Bingleys at Netherfield for dinner, she should not take the carriage, but rather 'go on horseback, because it seems likely to rain; and then you must stay all night,' which would develop the desired social links. Jane Bennet goes on horseback, but gets wet through. As a reminder that all was not artifice, Austen's good friend Anne Lefroy died when she fell from a bolting horse onto hard ground. There was scant protection for such accidents.

Social bias was also at stake, not least with the differential impact on surviving sources of, for example, attitudes towards costs and 'improvements.' Thus, in Bristol, turnpike riots, for example in 1749, and the rebuilding of Bristol Bridge using tolls in the 1760s, which led to the Bristol Bridge riots of 1793 (with several fatalities), underlined the extent to which all changes have winners and losers. In 1754, William, 2nd Viscount Barrington, the Secretary-at-War, opposing in Parliament the opposition proposal for a smaller army, referred to hostility to turnpikes:

> 'the licentiousness of the capital, the mutinous miners and colliers, the smugglers, the destroyers of turnpikes, all the outlaws that increase of riches and licence produces and encourages, all were to be kept in awe.'[9]

Moreover, there was an ongoing level of discontent with toll-based models, especially either when first introduced or later if the need for the toll appeared to have passed and it was now seen as a monopoly charge. So also in 1798 with the deadly riot in London against the new Thames River Police which was designed to prevent the theft of cargo.

In 1799, Patrick Colquhoun, a Scottish merchant and statistician, who was the Superintending Magistrate of the Thames River Police, referred to the 'inconceivable' number of those 'who with their families, find their way to the Metropolis from the most remote quarters of Great Britain and Ireland.'[10] More generally, many travelled, generally for work, including drovers, recruits, would-be servants, servants accompanying masters, and so on. However, the travel of the affluent dominated attention. Even so, there were tensions over expectations. Social bias remains a major issue, as in present-day concerns about rail rather than bus, and long-range train to London rather than local services. In practice, the latter in each case is underrated in national discussion.

Social emulation was important to travel styles, as the novelist Tobias Smollett noted in *The Adventures of Ferdinand, Count Fathom* (1753), in the case of doctors:

> 'a walking physician was considered as an obscure pedlar.... A chariot [carriage] was not now set up for the convenience of a man sinking under the fatigue of extensive practice, but as a piece of furniture every way as necessary as a large periwig.'

Austen commented on the social significance of particular carriages. Linked to that, but also more general, is the question of relative standards, how they varied by individual, and how they changed through time. In *Pride and Prejudice*, Darcy, responding to Elizabeth Bennet's observation that Hunsford was nearly fifty miles from Longbourn and therefore not 'an easy distance,' observed, 'And what is fifty miles of good road.' Little more than half a day's journey. Yes, I call it a *very* easy distance.' As a wealthy man, Darcy would have enjoyed access to faster carriages.

Transport had a host of local cultures, each borne of places and practices. In *Metroland* (1980), Julian Barnes captures not only a sense of past rail glories,[11] but also the specific experiences of the young:

> 'The tricks of travel were learned early. How to fold a full-size newspaper vertically so that you could turn over in the width of one page. How to pretend you hadn't seen the sort of women you were expected to stand up for. Where to stand in a full train to get the best chance of a seat when it began to empty. Where to get on a train so that you got off at just the right spot. How to use the no-exit tunnels for short-cuts. How to use your season ticket beyond its permitted range.'[12]

In a point of lasting relevance, Barnes also noted that journeys that might appear similar, if not identical, could be very different in the experience they offered:

> 'The termitary of Kilburn; the grimy, lost stations between Baker Street and Finchley Road; the steppe-like playing-fields at Northwick Park; the depot at Neasden, full of idle, aged rolling-stock; the frozen faces of passengers glimpsed in the windows of fast Marylebone trains.'[13]

Very differently, there is the hazard of visual evidence, whether paintings and drawings or, more recently, paintings and then film. By their nature, these records are atypical. They relate also to daylight, while it is also very difficult from them to understand the impact of bad weather. Sources are a particular problem prior to the sixteenth century, but that should not mean that that long age is ignored. As evidence of selectivity, visual evidence is scarcely to the fore for strikes, but can over-estimate shipwrecks.

Inclusion and omission are issues. For example, the security of transport tends to attract attention as far as passengers are concerned. In 1728, Daniel Defoe suggested the stationing of troops in order to protect transport. Pedestrians in London were at stake in the garroting scare of 1862 which was noted in *Punch* with 'The Song of the Garroter':

'So meet me by moonlight alone,
kind stranger, I beg and entreat,
And I'll make all your money my own,
And leave you half dead in the street.'

Security was also highly significant with regard to freight. In practice, ports faced particular problems from well-organised gangs of thieves. Improvements in security could be important to transport. To speed up unloading times and improve security, Parliament passed the West India Dock Act in 1799 so that West India produce 'might be effectually secure from loss by theft or other causes and the public revenue greatly benefited.' In 1802, the West India Dock Company, which had been granted a 21-year monopoly on the trade and thus a source of finance equivalent to a Turnpike Act, opened the enclosed West India Docks on the Isle of Dogs, with an import dock and an export dock lined with five-storey warehouses, enclosed by walls and a ditch, overseen by an armed watch. Other enclosed docks followed. Theft affected other means of transport as well, Heathrow acquiring the nickname 'Thiefrow,' while lorry hijacks of whisky were frequent, and such hijacks have become common for electrical goods.

The rush of adverse news at present can lead to a failure to understand, even note, the similarly contentious nature of the earlier situation. Thus, a stress on new turnpikes and river improvements in the early eighteenth century can lead to a failure to note the number of projects that did not win parliamentary approval. So on for later. Contention then and on other occasions could be a matter of rivalry within a more general commitment to change, as with the attempt by York in 1790 to prevent the construction of a bridge at Selby that, in contrast, was backed by Ripon. In part, this was an aspect of the longstanding opposition between those interests that wanted free river passage and those who wanted what could be obstacles to such passage, notably weirs for millraces and bridges. The former factor contributed to the longstanding emphasis on ferries and fords which were less disruptive than bridges for river transport as well as less expensive to build. A stress on roads, however, had the consequence of an emphasis on bridges. There were also disputes between those in favour of change and those against.

Social issues could be highlighted by transport problems. Under the headline 'The Lord Lieutenant and the North Devon Railway', *Trewman's Exeter Flying Post* of 3 January 1856 reported at length a clash between the mores of aristocratic society and the notion of public responsibility:

'Express trains will not do the bidding of Lords Lieutenant. Railways are not managed as were coaches; – the times of arrival and departure, as advertised, are kept as regularly as possible; and a railway superintendent would as soon think of keeping a train back to accommodate a peer of the realm as he would of ending off a train too soon to baulk a director. It was his misfortune to be in the down express from Bristol last Saturday afternoon week, which did not happen to reach Taunton until after the time it was due at Exeter. The North Devon train is advertised to leave the station at 3.30, – half an hour after the arrival of the express. The superintendent having ascertained by telegraph that the express was much behind its time, started the North Devon train at 3.45.'

Hugh, 2nd Earl Fortescue complained about the failure to delay the latter, despite the large number of passengers on it. The paper asked, Does Lord Fortescue mean to say that these should have been detained an hour and a half to suit his Lordship's convenience?' The elderly Fortescue (1783–1861), had been a reformist Whig but his attitude was now unacceptable. Some stations, such as Badminton in Gloucestershire, were constructed for the convenience of landownders, in this case the Duke of Beaufort. Arthur Conan Doyle noted in the character of the litigious Frankland in *The Hound of the Baskervilles* (1901) that the social dimension of travel could be very varied, even in the same person:

'I have established a right of way through the centre of old Middleton's park.... We'll teach these magnates that they cannot ride roughshod over the rights of the commoners, confound them! And I've closed the wood where the Fernworthy folk used to picnic. These infernal people seem to think that there are no rights of property, and that they can swarm where they like with their papers and their bottles.'

The experience of travel was different socially, but in many other respects, whatever their background, travellers had to face similar circumstances. Tobias Smollett, an active traveller, began his novel *The Adventures of Sir Launcelot Greaves* (1760): 'It was on the great northern road from York to London, about the beginning of the month of October, and the hour of eight in the evening, that four travellers were, by a violent shower of rain, driven for shelter into a little public-house on the side of the highway.'

Growing up in outer suburbia in the late 1950s and early 1960s, I can recall the very varied nature of transport, including the 'rag-and-bone' man going round with his horse and cart calling out for rubbish, the more modern council rubbish collectors, the electric milk floats delivering dairy products,[14] ice cream vans providing their cheery song, trolley-buses waiting to be scrapped while internal-combustion-engine buses crisscrossed the region, a steam train still to Little Stanmore, the tube (there an overground 'underground') to Edgware and Stanmore, the family car, the coach to school, and being a paperboy on foot, like the postman, although some paperboys used bicycles.

It has been very enjoyable as well as useful to discuss this subject with a number of colleagues and friends. I owe a particular debt to Steve Bodger, Lester Crook, Grayson Ditchfield, Dorian Gerhold, Bill Gibson, David Griffiths, Murray Pittock and Nigel Ramsay, for commenting on all or part of an earlier draft of this book. Jonathan Barry, David Bates, George Bernard, John Blair, Ron Fritze, Crawford Gribben, Levi Roach, Nigel Saul, Mark Stoyle, Henry Summerson and Tim Tatton-Brown helped with particular points. They are not responsible for any errors that remain. This book is dedicated to Rob Kenny, a linchpin of transport.

Chapter 1

The Major Sweep

The legendary Belinus the Great, a ruler of the Britons in Geoffrey of Monmouth's fanciful twelfth century *History of the Kings of Britain*, was a great and successful warrior, but also able to legislate in his peaceful later years. Geoffrey had Belinus enforce peace and security on the roads, in doing so extending the Molmutine Laws of his fictional father who had taken legal care of the roads leading to temples. Roads were seen as part of benign and necessary royal activity and good government.

The very long age covered in this chapter might appear to be a constant one for transport, with no dramatic change in routes or vehicles, and nothing to compare with the many that have come since. For this chapter, horses and carts move along long-established tracks, while the masters of ships hugging the coast anxiously scan the horizon for storms in the offing. And so, across the centuries in a pre-modern prelude to the transformative pressures of recent centuries.

Well, yes, but also no. There was of course a fundamental continuity in the technology of travel, the props of propulsion, the packaging of passage. The dark, the glutinous mud of rain-soaked lowlands, the crossing of fords when rivers were swollen with heavy rains or snow-melt, worrying about the health of horses, sleeping on straw or the ground; all these, and much more, were there for centuries, indeed millennia. And yet, there were also changes, and important ones. Some changes are readily apparent, notably Roman roads and medieval bridges; others less so.

And for the latter, let us start with the most famous journey of our long period – a fictional one, for such are often the iconic experiences, and one toward the end of the period. According to Geoffrey Chaucer (*c*.1343–1400), Comptroller of the Customs for London and then Clerk of the King's Works, the pilgrims of his fictional *Canterbury Tales* (*c*.1387) have the Tabard Inn in Southwark, south of the River Thames, as their meeting place for their journey to Canterbury. *The Prologue*, which I and many others had to study as a schoolchild, refers to an annual pattern of spring pilgrimage to Thomas Becket's tomb at Canterbury, and the *Tales* consist of the stories Chaucer provides for his very different pilgrims. A key point, indeed a 'silence' of this source, is that England is essentially internally peaceful at this juncture and that there are the resources available for such activity. There is scant sense of menace for the travellers, although going in a group provides not only company but also security and assistance against brigands, accidents and poor health. The problems with international travel led to the system of pilgrimage 'equivalents' so that two to St Davids equalled one to Rome.

The absence of menace, indeed, was (and remains) a central variable in transport. There is of course the safety offered by various forms of transport. This is a point to which we will revert, and one that should be considered alongside variations in the safety that was enjoyed, not least in proportional terms. More significantly, however, there is the question of the stability of the country and the ability of government to provide security, both for passengers and for freight. This is an important variable for the transport history of every country, but one that can be neglected owing to a focus on technology. Instead, it is important to appreciate that most of us do not think about how transport might be improved by modern technology (which itself is a varying and contested perspective). Instead, we focus on how transport can be safely, reliably and promptly fulfilled with the present one. Moreover, many in the past put any concern about safety from accidents alongside that of security from attack.

Transport, both routes and vehicles, and for passengers and freight, was rendered especially hazardous by political and social instability. Irrespective of the more general provisions of the law, roads in the sense of highways were long a particular legal category and practice, in that they were protected spaces with travellers protected by public law and were not on private property.[1] The main roads were the 'king's highway' and under his special protection.

There is of course the theft and violence that is seen even under stable government systems, for example the Great Train Robbery of 1963, a successful stopping and attack on the valuables on a mail train. Under a very different stable system, Edward I (r. 1272–1307), by the Statute of

Winchester of 1285, ordered the clearing of land beside the highways to 200 feet on each side in order to make ambushes more difficult. There were precedents for this, although not on a nationwide scale.[2]

Far more troubling was the absence of any such stable system. This was the case in the event of civil conflicts, such as those of 1139–53, 1215–17, 1264–5, 1321–2, 1381, 1387, 1403, 1405, 1408, 1450, 1455–61, 1470–1, 1483–5, 1487, 1536, 1549, 1553, 1570, 1642–6, and 1648, in England (a list that is not exhaustive), but also when there was no united state for Britain. As late as 1745, the destruction of bridges was ordered for Derbyshire in the face of Jacobite advance to Derby under Bonnie Prince Charlie, and Warrington Bridge was deliberately breached, being rebuilt in 1747.

And so also for Scotland, Wales, and Ireland, each of which had plentiful internal conflict. Separately, there was no unified state in control of all of the British Isles until 1603 saw both the end of a major rebellion in Ireland (Tyrone's Rebellion, there were other rebellions later) and the union of the crowns of England and Scotland when James VI of Scotland became James I of England (and Wales and Ireland). Before that, there were the problems of crossing boundaries and of contested frontier areas.

The impact of internal order for transport is such that the Roman conquest of what became England, Wales and (more precariously) part of southern Scotland was a key episode, itself the product of the cross-Channel transport of an invasion force in 43 CE under Emperor Claudius, and of subsequent reinforcements. Accomplished by 83 CE, this was the first period of unification, and one that lasted until the early fifth century.

Prior to that, there was no such unity at all, either in the form of a unitary state or in terms of federal cohesion. This lack of unity matched the diversity of a very varied natural environment. The British Isles came into separate island existence in about 6500 BCE when changes in the sea level separated them from Continental Europe. The British Isles contain a very varied geology, topography, soils, drainage, climate and natural vegetation. There is longstanding human intervention, especially with the vegetation cover, notably in the form of deforestation, but the ability to affect geology, topography and climate, or to lessen their impact, have been far more limited. In simple terms, the bulk of the west and north, whether you are considering England, Scotland, Wales, Ireland, Britain, or the British Isles, is higher and wetter, its soils poorer, and its agriculture pastoral, rather than arable: centred on animals, not crops. As a result, the density of population is lower in these areas and so there are fewer demands on passenger and freight transport.

Alongside this fundamental divide, there were complications: notably, fertile lowlands in the north and west, such as the Central Lowlands of Scotland, the Vale of Eden in Cumbria, and the Vale of York. Correspondingly, the south and east include areas of poor fertility, such as the sandy wastes of the Breckland in Suffolk or the hilly greensand of the Weald in Kent. These also tend to have the dispersed settlement of upland areas, and that situation provided less support for transport development than the wealthy lowlands.[3] This situation only altered when British government in the late nineteenth and, even more, twentieth century became more redistributive in taxation (for example with financial transfers to support Scotland and Wales) and interventionist in policy, including transport links. This situation has persisted to the present and is likely to continue into the future, not least due to the recent weakness of the SNP which has made a second independence referendum currently unlikely.

Geographical variety helps ensure the mistake in assuming the existence of one optimal transport system. Instead, the focus was on fitness-for-purpose, which indeed is a classic feature of all transport systems. When in the spring of 1322 the Exchequer travelled from Westminster to York, part of the journey was along the Trent from Torksey, where the Foss Dyke joined the Trent, nine miles north-west of Lincoln, towards York. In January 1325, Robert de Nottingham, an Exchequer official, also used the Trent, in his case from Burton on Stather to Howden.[4]

Judging the systems, alternatively, whether in historical terms or presently, in terms of some supposed optimal situation of cutting-edge technology and massive investment, is unrealistic and sets up false parameters. There is no necessary agreement as to purpose nor indeed definition of fitness.

Fitness-for-purpose was exemplified by the practice of droving: 'driving' animals to market by foot. This was a major, and often-long-range, form of transport. At the national level, droving remained important into the twentieth century, despite a move to rail and then road. Yet, at the very local level, while no longer linking distant areas sheep and cattle today are still walked not only within farms, for example for milking, but also along country roads. Sheepdogs play a major role in this ancient form of transport. It can lead to cars being blocked or delayed, setting up an instructive tension over transport between insiders and outsiders.

The nature of transport is unclear during the Neanderthal period, as well as that in which anatomically modern humans came to the fore, the Upper Palaeolithic (*c*.40,000-*c*.10,000 years ago). Stone-blade technology made deforestation easier, while there was an interest in useful objects which encouraged not only accumulation but also trade. Trade meant transport and vice versa. During the Mesolithic period (*c*.8300 BCE to *c*.4500 BCE), settlements spread considerably and evidence for tool manufacture increased. The distribution and contents of archaeologists' findspots indicate that rivers served as Mesolithic travel routes.[5] Tree trunks could be hollowed out to provide boats.

Subsequently, as agriculture developed, so there was the clearing of forest, leading to a drop in surviving tree pollen. This clearing facilitated transport, as accessibility (and visibility) improved. The spread of domestic animals, the most significant change in transport history, was followed by wheeled vehicles, the former making possible the use of the latter and the latter multiplying the potential of the former. Trade increased as the flint necessary for agricultural tools and axes was mined and then exchanged for other goods.

The transport of blue stones from the Preseli Hills in Pembrokeshire 150 miles to Stonehenge in about 3000 BCE in the Neolithic period reflected an ability to transport objects long distance, in part overland, albeit at great expense in terms of resources and in taking considerable time. Again, this may not look so bad from the perspective of HS2 and the oft-delayed, and now cancelled, Stonehenge A303 bypass. There is also important recent evidence for the droving of pigs to Stonehenge and other sites over very long distances (in part probably moving them by water),[6] in order to support major feasts in *c*.2800–*c*.2400 BCE which were associated with the emergence of rulership. Participants also came from long distances.

Commerce along the coasts and across seas was part of the transport process and fed the increase in the material culture, including richer grave goods. For the Bronze Age (*c*.2200-*c*.800 BCE), numerous and large surviving burial mounds or barrows have been associated with areas likely to have benefited from trade. Trading routes, such as the middle Thames, were linked to permanent settlements and commercial networks. The situation was different in northern England, Wales, Scotland and Ireland with their relatively low population levels (although population estimates for Iron Age Scotland belie this to a degree) and a poorly-developed agricultural base ensuring a smaller surplus of wealth. Most of late Iron Age Wales, for example, has left no trace of pottery, although some fine metalwork has been found and Anglesey, a copper-working region, was a major centre of trade. There were numerous hillforts and their gateways had a transport purpose as well as defensive focus.[7]

Transport in Ireland is more obscure than in England and Wales as there was no Roman conquest and no Roman roads. Migration into Ireland in about 10000–8000 BCE had happened via various land bridges, with the Isle of Man perhaps a crossing point. The significance of sea travel in early Irish history was seen with the Broighter boat of the first century BCE, the golden model of an ocean-going rowed-boat, evidence both of the wealth that sea trade accumulated and of its dependency upon the gods of nature, in this case the Celtic sea god Manannán.

It was in southern England that trade was probably most highly developed, as definitely was the coinage. The latter reduced the role of barter. Discoveries in the London area include rich finds of Iron Age coins and objects from the Thames foreshore at Putney, Barnes, and further to the west near Runnymede. The Thames was clearly an important route, while the Fenlands were probably thick with waterways and boats.[8] Transport was the means by which new products and technologies were introduced: this was a key element of development in prehistoric times, as also more subsequently.

The routes of the period were trackways as well as rivers. The former are commonly discussed in terms of the Icknield Way, although the extent to which this had a prehistoric origin has been debated.[9] This trackway stretched from Norfolk to Wiltshire following the naturally well-drained chalk escarpment from Norfolk to Berkshire, and crossing the River Thames at Cholsey. It is likely that there was similar use of other escarpments not least because they were well-drained and generally unforested. The South Downs Way from Winchester to Eastbourne is an example.

In contrast, the Romans had the wherewithal to build new roads and, while they used topography acutely, strategic network requirements were to the fore in the roadbuilding, notably the ability to move large numbers of troops and their supplies across the country including across the topographical boundaries. This was made more necessary and possible because Roman Britain absorbed a relatively high percentage of Roman military expenditure and had a comparatively large number of troops who, indeed, were responsible for the road construction. Reflecting the general quality of Roman engineering, roads were built to a high standard, with stone foundations and gravel surfaces providing an impermeable structure. However, this description makes the situation look more regular than may have been the case given a variety of technique and approach. Roman roads were appropriate for troops marching in a predictable, regular, and speedy fashion, with comparable benefits for carts and couriers. Roads enabled the use of wheeled vehicles which were far more efficient than pack animals in terms of the volume carried per horse. Using conscripted local labour as well as military expertise, the Roman roads were built deliberately straight to facilitate faster journey times for moving troops and supplies, the two combining in the rations and equipment (weapons, armour, cooking gear, bedrolls) carried by soldiers, and to make it easier to handle wagons. Cuttings, embankments and bridges helped counter the impact of terrain. Moreover, Rome's strong government, with its ability to deploy military resources, was better able to repair roads than any regime until the twentieth century. In Wales, where an extensive network of about 35 fortresses was constructed, they were linked by roads to legionary bases at Chester and Caerleon.

The Vindolanda Tablets provide information from about 100 CE on the Roman forces in northern Britain. Each legion had a commissariat responsible for supplies. This had to interact with urban and provincial governments as well as with estate owners and merchants. These were the sources of the wagons and mules that were employed to move supplies, as the armies lacked sufficient numbers of either. Moreover, taxpayers moved food and other goods provided as taxes into warehouses. However, movement by sea and river was cheaper, easier and quicker for moving bulk goods. Supply zones encouraged legionary forts to be as self-sufficient as possible, drawing on staples grown or acquired locally, although some supplies, such as olive oil from Spain, had to be acquired from a distance.[10]

The road system fitted in with the expansion of the Roman province, the early roads primarily for military purposes, such as the Via Devana from Colchester to Chester being built of lighter materials, while, later, the emphasis on commerce ensured roads with thicker road surfaces as well as fitting in with the layout of town plans. The roads linked and structured an urban system that acted as the means of Roman governance, culture and consumption, and this, in turn, increased reliance on the roads. The greater quantity of archaeological material surviving from the Roman period suggests a society producing and trading far more goods than its Iron Age predecessors. Links between towns were significant, but it was also important to provide routes to supply and draw on the countryside where the bulk of the population lived and where there was considerable economic activity indeed a measure of prosperity. The extent of 'auto-production' within and between farms, neighbouring estates, villages and local communities reduced the need for more extensive trade, a process that remained the case until relatively recently. At the same time there was the flow of food and other rural products, such as leather for shoes, wool, and wood for construction, heating and industrial production to the cities. Moreover, there was production of goods, notably minerals, but also grain, hides, hounds, salt, slaves and wool, for export, goods that had to be moved to the ports, principally London, Richborough (near Sandwich), and Dover, the latter two the starting points for Watling Street. These exports ensured the value of Britain to the Roman empire.

The details of individual cities reflect the importance of transport links. *Londinium* (London) was rapidly established at a strategic location on the north bank of the Thames, which, in accordance with the natural state, was much wider than today, as it remained until the embankments were built from the mid-nineteenth century. Moreover, and with resultant tidal marshes, the river was tidal to beyond where the Romans built London. The port was a key opportunity for London, but one that had to respond to changes in the level of the Thames, which fell until the mid-third century as the sea-level lowered, such that the wharves had to be altered and moved forward. By the late Roman period, vessels of up to 200 tons were common at London. The low gravel banks of the north bank provided well-drained firmness for construction and a good site for the first bridge across the Thames, and London remained the lowest bridging point. This transport node, therefore, linked a maritime route to the remainder of the Roman Empire with roads within Britain, notably, but not only, Ermine Street to York and Watling Street to Chester.

As an illustration of the potential longevity of routes, these two Roman roads form the basis for modern routes, respectively the A10 and A5: the first stage of the latter is the Edgware Road, and the A5 ran straight to Brockley Hill from which it was realigned on another straight axis to Verulamium (St Albans). It went on to Towcester and Deva (Chester). Other roads, however, did not develop in this lasting way, including Stane Street (the name derived from Stone Street) that ran from London to Chichester, and is now in part a pleasant footpath, although, earlier, Kennington Park Road/Clapham Road/Balham High Road follow the route of Stane Street.[11] Portway went to Silchester (and on to Dorchester). The Fosse Way from Lincoln to Exeter is now in part only accessible by foot, which in 2023 were often generously puddled, although most of it is reachable by perfectly good roads: the A46 follows the route between Lincoln and Leicester and the B414, B4455 and A429, A433, A367 and A37, B3151 and A303 all play a role thence.

As goods and money were moved regularly across greater distances, inter-regional contact increased within Roman Britain, and London was the central point in this system. Proximity to the English Channel ensured this position for a city that was far from geographically central. The Roman system had about 2,000 miles of paved roads, but that underestimates a network of roads that may have covered about 6,000 miles.

There were also bridges, some with stone foundations, notably at Rochester to carry the road across the wide, tidal River Medway, at London, at Middleton St George to cross the Tees, and at Newcastle where the length would have been about 234 metres (768 feet).[12] Roman bridges had wooden beams and a wooden carriageway atop stone piers, rather than stone arches. The configuration of Roman roads helps in the location and significance of probable bridges, as across the Mersey at Warrington.

The Antonine Itinerary, a third-century listing (it was compiled after the division of Britain into two provinces in 197) of places and distances on various roads, the places being stage posts and possibly miliary supply storehouses, includes Roman Britain.[13] In practice, there were changes in the Roman road system, both during the period of conquest and subsequently as other defence tasks emerged. There were also roads that may primarily have served economic purposes, such as the Peddars Way from in Norfolk, the Pye Road from Colchester to near Norwich, and the Fen Causeway from Ermine Street near Peterborough east into Norfolk. So also with the roads in South-West England beyond Exeter that are currently being remapped in accordance with recent research, notably a LIDAR (Light Detecting and Ranging, remote sensing) survey carried out in 2019–22 alongside a GIS spatial analysis to calculate the most probable position of roads, with a model of human movement based on terrain and slope but adding the intricate river network which would have caused seasonal flooding.[14]

Some of these roads were linked to the minerals mined in the region, especially tin, copper and lead. From Roman Britain as a whole, the minerals mined included silver, copper, gold, iron, lead and tin, all minerals that were exported. The production of smelted metal declined, however, in the late fourth century, reducing the value of the goods that could be moved by road.[15]

The exact route of roads can be hypothetical, as with the idea of two linked roads from the ferry port of Brough to York and then from York via Chester-le-Street to Newcastle. Findspots of coins and other remains can help in the assessment of routes. So also with the analysis of aerial photography, as in 1992 when a Roman road west of Carmarthen was discerned.

The Romans devoted far less attention to canals, but appear to have been responsible for the eleven-mile-long Foss Dyke or Fossdyke from the River Witham at Lincoln, a major town for the Romans, to the River Trent at Torksey, possibly constructed around 120 CE. This may have been linked to the 85-mile Car Dyke along the western edge of the Fens, and possibly in part a canal but also a drain.[16] The Romans built roads to link with river systems they used, such as those in Somerset, where the River Parrett and its tributary the Yeo had ports, notably at Ilchester, Combwich and Crandon Bridge, linked to roads.[17]

The end of Roman Britain in the fifth century, although, like the following topics, subject to much debate, was more gradual than the customary focus on the years 409–10 might suggest. It broke up into a number of kingdoms and faced invasion, gradual conquest of most of it by Anglo-Saxon invaders, and widespread destruction and decay. Nevertheless, Romanised town and villa life did not cease abruptly, and there was continuity of site use in many towns, as well as of much of the human landscape. However, the need for transport, especially, but not only, governmental, military and commercial, declined in the fifth and sixth centuries, with relatively few ceramics or coins showing up in the archaeological record, and a concentration on largely self-sufficient agriculture. This reliance on subsistence ensured that trade was of limited importance, although subsistence agriculture did not exclude transhumance and the supply of meat from a distance, leading to impressive drove roads in north-east Kent into the Wealden Forest.[18]

Some Roman roads became overgrown, or, at least, grassed over. It is probable that in the earlier Anglo-Saxon period, with many towns abandoned so that roads between them were redundant, much of the Watling Street route in Kent was not used, with changes to the route when it was revived in the late Anglo-Saxon period.[19] Under the Anglo-Saxons, there was a reversion to fords in place of Roman bridges, and these fords were subsequently used as the site for new bridges, as at Nottingham in 923 after it had been captured from the Vikings.

At the same time, archaeological remains from seventh-century England suggest a high-status material culture whose demands required trade. More generally, across the Anglo-Saxon period, material culture reveals considerable transport of goods.[20] From the seventh century, trading settlements grew up along the south and east coasts. The remarkable new longships (that at Sutton Hoo is the best early example) then traded, originally peacefully, all over the greater North Sea area, with in England initially, only local roads going into the hinterland. Furthermore, trade links by sea were significant to the Celtic-dominated Irish Sea system. These links served passengers, including Christian figures, merchants and goods. There was a thriving trade across the Bristol Channel and between South Wales and places as far distant as Sicily, and also trade with Ireland. Subsequently, the Vikings made much use of the Irish Sea, bringing Ireland further into European sea lanes in a very significant way. Indeed, as a result, Dublin became one of the main ports for slave trading in Europe.[21]

Long-distance bulk transport was only economic by water. Initially, the two major water systems centred on the Wash/Humber and Severn/Avon, but the latter declined from the late sixth century as the related trade from the Mediterranean via Atlantic Spain and France to Cornwall lessened. Instead, the Thames system centred on London grew in both absolute terms and relative significance. However, rivers were affected by freezing, drought, silting and weirs, while sea travel was at the mercy of wind, waves and tides. In 1069, William I's advance northwards was delayed when heavy rain caused the swollen Aire to break the bridge at Pontefract.

Water routes were also significant for the new Anglo-Saxon kingdoms that came to control England. Near Charing Cross in London, there was a reinforced embankment upon which ships were beached so that they could be unloaded. In the 730s, Bede described London as 'a mart of many peoples', and wool or woollen cloth from the Cotswolds was probably transported via the Thames Valley to London and then exported. The linkage of transport to export was significant. Of the single coin finds in England and Wales dating to 924–1135, London's mints produced the largest, the majority lying 50–80 miles from London, of which 64 per cent were found in eastern Kent, Norfolk, Suffolk, Cambridgeshire and along the Sussex coast. This suggests that London was a key purchaser of goods from a south-eastern hinterland, using, to this end, silver obtained by exports to the Continent. The chance nature of many archaeological discoveries is significant but needs always to be kept in mind. Things like coins are probably always more likely to be unearthed in London where development is more or less continuous. Elsewhere the situation involves more chance, as with the discovery of what is now known as the Staffordshire Hoard.

In addition to London, other ports would also have been nodes of transport systems, internal, coastal and overseas. In the seventh century, Ipswich, Sandwich, Southampton and York all also became important as ports,[22] and the significant routes between them were by sea, as was probably the major route from east Kent to London. However, by the tenth century, as a result of new towns, an extensive urban network was in place in England, with numerous *burhs*: some were re-foundations of Roman towns or re-uses of their walls, as with Canterbury and Rochester, others newly-created, for example Wareham. *Burhs* had a military purpose. They did not all develop into successful towns in a modern sense. The *burhs* were linked by roads known as *herepaths* (army paths) enabling rapid troop movements as well as routes for the rural population to reach shelter.[23] These links provided a major rationale for the re-use of Roman roads, such as Watling Street, and this was to encourage bridge-building and, under the Normans, castle-building. Communications by the later Anglo-Saxon period made much of former Roman routes, and the Anglo-Saxons gave their current names to some of the Roman roads, notably the Fosse Way, Ermine Street and Watling Street, the last derived in the ninth century from Waeclingas Strate, the Waeclingas being the Saxon settlers who lived near Verulamium. The sources available are more limited than for following centuries, with documentary sources notably limited.[24] As a result, archaeology has to fill the gap.

On land, ridge routes, many used ever since the Iron Age, were important, as valleys were prone to flooding, while their soil was often heavy and difficult to traverse.[25] At the same time, the nature of the roads across England is obscure, and even more so in Ireland, Scotland and Wales. Once settled, notably from the seventh century, for example in South Oxfordshire, the Angles and Saxons built some roads from new, and this process became more prominent from the ninth century. Bridging and ferry points that could be reached by ridge-routes were the central nodes in the communication system, linking in with the key water-routes. These appear to have been more significant than in the Roman period, possibly in part as a reaction to the growing deficiencies of the road system as it declined from that period. Control over water-routes was also militarily useful.

The greater role of bridges is suggested by the extent to which, from the 740s, labour services for bridge-building and repair became an important provision in charters, with the emergence of powerful kings able to impose such services. There was bridge-building between the mid-eighth and mid-ninth centuries, while bridges became even more significant from the tenth century owing to a greater use of carts as well as faster run-off affecting fords. Large bridges were built or rebuilt at Chester, London, Rochester and York. The recreation in timber of bridges on the remains of the old Roman stone piers was hampered by the rising iso- and eustatic sea level changes of a foot a century in South-East England.[26]

The political context changed greatly with the eventual replacement, under Viking attack in the late ninth century, of a number of Anglo-Saxon kingdoms in England by an expanding English state based on Wessex.[27] Edward the Elder (r. 899–924) was probably responsible for the bridges at Nottingham and Huntingdon as part of his gaining and consolidating control over the East Midlands. Similarly, the Viking invasions of Scotland played a part in the growing power of the kingdom of the Scots.

In England, under the rulers of the House of Wessex, a county or shire system was consolidated and extended, the shires in turn being divided into hundreds. This provided the governmental basis for public policies judged necessary. The transformation of communications was not centrally one of these. Aside from place names, there is little definitive evidence for the situation under the English state of the tenth and eleventh centuries, but occasionally roads were mentioned alongside bridges as part of the so-called 'trinoda necessitas': the obligation, imposed on grantees of land, to help build and maintain bridges, to do likewise with fortifications, and to serve (or send other men to serve) in the levy. The military value of bridges is suggested by the fact that, alongside army-service and fortress (ie borough/burh) work, the third of the common burdens was bridge works. Although they are mentioned very rarely, there was a sense of roads being a public good and there being a shared responsibility to maintain them. The obligation was probably on every landholder and therefore on their tenants: landholders had to see to it that someone maintained the section of road close to their holdings.[28]

This was the legacy of the Normans after their conquest of England in 1066, the legacy they assessed in Domesday Book of 1086. Monetarisation, in the sense of the use of coin, varied in the tenth to twelfth centuries, being stronger in the south and east, and especially in East Anglia, whereas the north and west presumably had a greater use of barter for trade. The distribution of coin finds reflects in part population but also commercial forces, although the reasons for these finds can be unclear. Thus, the find spread from Chester's mint may reflect coastal trade from there, a trade indicated by the *Domesday* Book toll on each shipload leaving the city. The concentration of mints producing the most coins on and near the east coast reflected the importance of trade with the Continent.[29]

Although Robert D'Oyly, probably Sheriff of Warwickshire and possibly Oxfordshire and Berkshire for William I (r.1066–1087) was possibly responsible for Grandpont, a stone causeway over the Thames, he may only have rebuilt it. More generally, William did not build roads, but used the existing system to move his troops to suppress rebellions. Given the number of rebellions, that he could do this points to an adequate road system. The Norman governmental structure, however, was demonstrated by the construction of numerous castles, which, again, as with Roman roads, showed what could be done, a construction that involved a need to import stone. The general maintenance of highways and bridges was a duty of manorial tenants, that of the major bridges a duty of the hundred, a subdivision of the shire, and of the smaller bridges of the tithings. In much of Southern and Midland England, tithings were groups of ten, but in some cases whole vills, the smallest administrative unit. If just one vill, it would have been better able to look after a bridge, although that depends on the size of the vill and of the bridge. By the thirteenth century vills were often responsible for the maintenance of bridges, alone or with other vills. Chartered towns were responsible for their roads and bridges. Bridge-tolls, compulsory or as at Huntingdon voluntary, could be a recompense or a source of financing the structure.

The legacy of the Roman roads remained important to communications. Thus, Matthew Paris's 1250s map of the itinerary from London to the Holy Land depicts a linear route via Rochester and Canterbury to Dover. This was appropriate for Paris to be able to fit it into the space available, but the map also encapsulated the extensive use of Roman roads. The main roads of the twelfth century were Ermine Street, the Fosse Way, the Icknield Way, and Watling Street, the four highways mentioned in a mid-twelfth century compilation purporting to consist of the laws of Edward the Confessor (r. 1042–66). The slightly earlier (c.1115) *Leges Henri Primi* does not make mention of these roads, but does make some reference to royal jurisdiction over roads.[30] At the same time, there could be changes to the routes, with Watling Street for example affected in Kent by the rise in the mean sea-level from the late Roman period, which affected crossing places and encouraged the movement of routes to higher ground.[31]

Other earlier roads were also important. Thus, the Roman Dere Street ran from York to Corbridge and on to the Antonine Wall in Scotland. Edward I of England had used the road for his campaigning in 1298 when moving his forces into Scotland. Part of the route was known as the Royal Way in later medieval Scotland, linking Edinburgh and the Border abbeys, notably Jedburgh.

Edward supplied his invasion forces in Scotland by compulsory purchase of food in eastern England and then dispatch of the provisions northward by sea, notably to Berwick. This was necessary in order both to supply the invading forces which largely had to stick close to the coast and to counter Scottish scorched-earth policy which in 1385 obliged Richard II to retreat. Water and most forage were obtained on campaign, but grain was usually taken with the troops. It was relatively easily transportable, had a long life, and good nutritional value, but had to be kept dry. Meat was provided by taking animals and slaughtering them en route.

There was more to be transported in the twelfth and thirteenth centuries, with possibly a doubling of the English population between 1180 and 1330 to perhaps six million, and changes in crops and power sources increasing productivity. Thus, the spread of water-powered mills helped the fulling that was important to the textile industry. This was an aspect of the use and local transport of water that was vital to industry, agriculture, and transport, as with the weirs that were used to produce ponds and channels for sheep washes. There were also significant increases in the founding of towns, monetary transactions, the volume of the currency, economic diversification, trade, (both domestic and foreign), and specialisation in occupations. All these processes were encouraged by the use of credit and debt and by the extent to which towns were largely a matter of the interaction of royal government and urban authorities, unlike the French role for feudal control.[32] The spread of industry into some rural areas meant more transport of finished products. Roads and tracks could bear heavy carts, at least in the summer months.

In a society with many serfs who were dependent on their lords, 'freedom of movement' did not really exist for the majority of the population as either concept or reality; although, conversely, local migration, permanent or temporary, would have benefited from roads and tracks. Moreover, pilgrimage was very important, while monasteries and hospitals were generally sited on major roads.

A road described a right of way with both legal and customary status, which led from one place to another. It was regular use that turned such a route into a highway or road in the modern sense. Some roads were very small in width and poorly surfaced, but others pretty big with a better surface. In *c.*1115, Henry I laid down that two carts should be able to pass each other on the king's highway. There was no comparable standardisation for surfaces which would usually have been based on the soil of the area. Separately, on a longstanding basis, transhumance reflected both physical and commercial environments, with the creation and sharing of profit a key element.[33]

Moreover, horses slowly took over from oxen from the twelfth century onwards, particularly in areas of light soils where light ploughing was possible, notably to take goods to market, but also for agricultural tasks. They were faster than oxen, both in moving goods to market and in agricultural jobs such as harrowing and light hauling. Unlike oxen, horses could be ridden.[34] Other changes included, in the ninth century, the introduction of the shoulder rather than neck harness, and three centuries later the pivoting front axle and moveable whippletree. Together these made carts more effective, underlining the reliance on animals for transport on land and thus on muscle-power. Alongside rowing, the wind in the sails was the additional motive power on rivers and at sea.

Across the British Isles, although varying from one region to another, the economic infrastructure became denser, albeit in a context of rivalry, not least with foreign merchants. As a result, the Crown's approval of fairs and markets was in part a means of pursuing market control and profit.[35] By the thirteenth century, there were few places in Lincolnshire which were further than five miles from a market: seven markets in the county were mentioned in 1086, while 55 were licensed between 1250 and 1299.[36] By 1350, England had over 1,500 weekly markets.[37] The relationship between markets and transport routes was significant, although there can be uncertainty over the routes followed. River crossings were clearly an issue. Thus, for example, with reference to the 1201 grant to the Abbot of Crowland of a market at Wellingborough:

'… the market may be an indication of the use made of the river crossing there, although servants of the abbey, according to an entry in the fourteenth century manorial accounts, seem to have started their journey on the west bank of the Nene, paid toll at Thrapston bridge and then, possibly, used the Roman road on the east bank before going to Yaxley, where produce (in this case peas) was transferred to boats for the last part of the journey to the abbey.'[38]

About 140 rivers were navigable, with a total length of over 2,400 miles, such that most places were within 15 miles of the coast or a navigable river, and notably so for the rivers of eastern England. In contrast, there was no comparable system in much of upland Britain, including for example Devon and Cornwall. Rivers fed by heavy rainfall on upland areas also tended to be harder to work upriver than lowland equivalents in lower rainfall areas.

Areas that today are drained, such as the Fens and the Somerset Levels, were navigable. For freight, waterways predominated for inter-regional transport. Thus, pottery produced in kilns at Torksey in Lincolnshire was moved downriver on the Trent to the Humber and upriver into Derbyshire. In the 1110s, stone from near Stamford was moved by means of the Nene, Ouse and Lark to Bury-St-Edmunds and the first two rivers were also used for Stamford ware. Local journeys, in contrast, followed roads, essentially Roman ones.[39] Patterns of purveyance-account loads, coin finds and place names provide evidence for inland water transport. Evidence suggests a number of significant rivers including the Severn and Thames, as well as the linkage of major river systems by minor routes, whether river, canal or road,[40] along the line of coin distribution.

There was also an intensive phase of canal-building from *c.*1000 to *c.*1200. Combined with the roads, this led to a well-integrated transport system.[41] The markets linked the localities into wider commercial networks, transmitting goods, demands, information and innovation. River crossings continued to be important for town-foundation, and the latter, in turn, emphasised the significance of the crossing.[42] Thus, Maidstone's position on the Medway was important to its significance as a trading centre, and by the early fourteenth century it had a population of about 2,000.[43] Haverfordwest in Pembrokeshire enjoyed considerable growth in the thirteenth century, with a tidal quay providing important access to the Bristol Channel and Ireland. The town had a defensive site at the lowest fordable point of the Western Cleddau river, which was also the highest navigable point on the river.

Funded by tolls, bridges replaced fords, although both they and ferries remained significant, and indeed expanded. For example, in the thirteenth century Evesham Abbey established the Hampton Ferry across the Avon as a route to a new vineyard on Clark's Hill. Bridges increasingly rested on stone arches, not the more vulnerable wooden supports, and were able to accommodate carts. Stone piers were more resistant than wooden ones to the scouring of river beds and storm waters. Durham, where there were spate waters on the River Wear, saw a stone bridge constructed by Bishop Ranulf Flambard in about 1120, and a second bridge there, Elvet or New Bridge, later in the century, both leading directly into the market place. The city was not a key centre of trade, as the Wear was not navigable, but the river was a major obstacle, the city a significant market, and the bishop able to organise and spend to effect, which ensured that bridges were built.[44] Similarly, the bridge across the Ouse at St Ives led directly to the market place and probably was important to the establishment of the famous St Ives fair. In 1391, an 11-arch stone bridge replaced the decayed timber eighth-century Rochester bridge which, long challenged by tidal pressure and river silting, had been destroyed in 1381 by floodwater after a major freeze.[45]

At Warrington, the lowest crossing place over the Mersey until replaced by Runcorn in the nineteenth century, a right of ferry was granted to the Earl of Chester in 1195, but a bridge was mentioned in 1305. There was competition for a century between the Lords of the Manor who owned respectively bridge and ferry as this provided toll revenue, competition that could include violence but was mostly legal. The bridge had to be rebuilt in the 1360s and repaired in 1420 and 1453, and a new bridge was built in 1495.

There were also earth causeways interspersed with arches, as at Gloucester. Causeways were a response to the flooding of river plains. The Causeway, the road from Egham to Staines, is of medieval origin. Maud Heath's Causeway on each side of the River Avon in Wiltshire, at Kellaways near Bremhill, was of fifteenth-century origin and apparently paid for by a bequest in 1474 by Maud Heath, a widow who allegedly had used the path to take eggs to the market at Chippenham. Nearby 'Causeway' survives as a road name west of Malmesbury near a branch of the Avon.

Alongside new construction, bridges and causeways were kept in repair. They fulfilled what were in effect national purposes. From the late eleventh century, a large stone bridge and causeway at Oxford crossed both the Thames and its flood-plain, this route helping move goods, notably wool and later cloth, to the port at Southampton with wool, alum, and dyes all being important return cargoes. The replacement of London Bridge by a near 926-foot-long stone structure with 19 arches and high gateways in the late twelfth and early thirteenth centuries, completed in 1209, was important to government as well as the economy. However, maintenance was frequent and expensive as the tides washed away at the structure. Tolls as well as rents on the buildings on the bridge financed the repairs which required a significant workforce under bridge wardens.[46] Under a charter of 1393, Richard II granted York the right to acquire property worth up to £100 yearly to pay for the upkeep of the city's two principal bridges, those over the Ouse and the Foss.[47]

Bridges were impressive instances of place-specific design and engineering. They had to cope with often difficult circumstances as river flow was little controlled, which led to broad flood plains as well as floods. The general benefit derived from roads as well as their more specific value for pilgrimages encouraged the Church to support their maintenance, which was presented as a pious undertaking meriting indulgences. Major efforts accordingly were made to maintain bridges, not least bridge trusts, with large charitable bequests, most notably at Bideford, London, and Rochester. There was understandable continuity in bridging sites and also a variety in funding. In North Devon, the long bridge at Bideford over the Torridge and that at Barnstaple over the Taw were both built on the sites of Roman crossings. The former dated to Bishop Stapledon's will of 1326 and was repaired thanks to a papal indulgence of 1459, being later rebuilt in 1795, 1810, 1869 and 1925. The Taw Bridge, in contrast, was a municipal construction. Ecclesiastical indulgences helped fund repairs, but the bridge was regarded as the town's responsibility. Six of the 27 bridges that span the Tamar today have medieval origins, with ecclesiastical indulgences also an important source of funds for repairs.[48] Pilgrims travelling to shrines were often the beneficiaries of indulgences which secured remission of penances for the living and of purgatory for the dead, in return for good works, of which the repair or maintenance of roads and bridges was one. Analysis of indulgences, for example in Herefordshire and concerning the Augustinian priory of Christchurch (Hampshire), frequently show a relationship to bridge repair, in the latter case a bridge over the Avon.[49]

Founded in 1392, the Guild of the Holy Cross in Birmingham maintained not only almshouses but also roads and a bridge at Deritend. Being found effective, the Guild survived the chantry commissioners in 1545, but was suppressed in 1547. This was an instance of the challenge posed by the Reformation to the transport system. Wills frequently contained bequests to roads and bridges.[50]

The highest point of navigation of many rivers diminished, but the expansion in the network of bridges ensured more reliable crossing points, as with the bridge across the Trent at Newark in the second half of the twelfth century, and across the Nene at Wansford by 1221. A network of bridges, in the sense of bridges linked to a road network, was in place from the thirteenth century, and in some areas earlier, and able to serve economy, state and society, a network that lasted until eighteenth-century develoments. As already noted, the transition to the use of horses rather than oxen increased flexibility and was enhanced by innovations in horseshoes, harnesses, horse breeding, and carts. Innovation is the key term, not revolution.

In turn, water routes, both sea and river, such as the Thames, were particularly important for the movement of bulky goods, grain moving downriver from the busy entrepot of Henley to London, which also received food from East Anglia via the River Lea.[51] Water transport was especially useful for stone because of its weight.[52] Indeed, whereas robberies on roads were frequently recorded, this was not the case on rivers, partly because the bulky nature of most goods sent by water made them of scant ease and therefore difficult for thieves to carry away.[53] At the same time, the construction accounts of brick-built Caister Castle in Norfolk has suggested that land transport for heavy loads may have been more common than often supposed, not least due to obstructions on many waterways as well as problems in loading and unloading barges.[54]

Although some areas could not be reached by inland waterways,[55] most benefited from at least some access, benefiting from the far less expensive carriage by water, often about a halfpenny per ton/mile. Yet, the navigability of rivers was hit by watermills, weirs, and a lack of maintenance. Thus, the Foss Dyke became blocked in the fourteenth century and did not fully reopen until 1672. The use of rivers could compete with the construction of bridges and (very differently) weirs, as they affected the ease of usage. As a result, towns sought control over waterways. Restrictions on weirs were frequent, including in the 1190s, in Acts of 1351, 1371, 1399 and 1402, and by instructions to JPs (Justices of the Peace) in 1398. Magna Carta c.33 was directed against fish-traps which could be substantial. Repetition reflected a failure of enforcement, and in 1423, for example, there were complaints about ineffective execution in Essex, Kent and Surrey. Weirs were the focus of complaint on particular rivers, for example in 1314 that weirs on the Wye were blocking trade to Hereford.

By the early fourteenth century, possibly a fifth of the English population may have depended on trade and services. People probably mostly travelled on foot, but, although riding and travelling by vehicles was for the wealthier, there was also extensive use of carts. All travelling took time. This time required, at a minimum, enough agricultural surplus or trade-generated wealth for the travellers to have the time to travel and to support themselves while travelling. Travelling on foot limited most travel to the locality of the traveller: the village, the market town, the church. Most travelling today is still within the travellers' locality, but with road and public transport that locality is much larger.

Travelling further afield was a significant commitment, driven by trade, pilgrimage, war, migration, or legal or political in the shape of attendance at courts. The impact of the costs and risks of transport limited trading and affected society. Subsequently, there was to be an intertwining of the development of means of transport and of agriculture, industry and trade, with the wool, later also cloth, trades a key element of economic transport. For these and other trades, transport routes followed local and longer-distance needs – to markets and ports, and greatly changed over time on an *ad hoc* demand-led basis. Riverine and maritime transport were defined by geography, with the construction of ports a combination of need and possibility.

In Wales, the situation was more difficult than in England because of its more mountainous terrain, many rivers and estuaries, and poor road repair. Bandits and wolves each posed difficulties. Yet, there were also new routes, both military and civilian. Thus, the 24-mile-long Monks Trod was a road across the Cambrian Mountains from the Teifi Basin to the Upper Wye Valley, linking the Cistercian abbeys of Cwmhir and Strata Florida, both thirteenth-century foundations. The slope was transformed by a cut-and-fill technique into a pathway. A low-tide path was used by the monks of Quarr Abbey founded in 1332 on the Isle of Wight in order to get to the mainland.

The use of written itineraries suggests that there was already a significant choice of routes prior to the Gough Map of the late fourteenth century, these routes being used for example by Edward I (r. 1272–1307) for campaigning, pilgrimages and hunting. The choice could be maintained by particular action, as in 1277 when Edward cleared a route from Chester to Snowdonia, but also by more general instructions to maintain highways. Their diversion to the profit of others was regarded as particularly unacceptable.[56] In 1281, Edward I ordered the bishops to allow royal collectors to address 'pious exhortations' to the people for the repair of London Bridge.

However, complaints about the ruinous state of bridges were frequent in the Rolls of Parliament. Conflicting jurisdictions affected the liability to make repairs. In such cases, the Court of Chancery issued commissions for inquiry. Upon default being proved, information lay in the King's Bench. The way-wardens in the courts of manors and the sheriffs in the counties were both bound to hold inquests on roads and bridges.[57] Prior to this situation that began in the early fourteenth century, justices itinerant in the later thirteenth century, including under Edward I, received presentments 'concerning bridges and causeways' giving details of decay and saying who was responsible for upkeep, while for roads there were presentments 'concerning encroachments' often referring to building or cultivating roads or digging holes on them, as at the 1293/4 Yorkshire eyre when the abbots of Holy Trinity York and Pontefract were presented by a jury for digging pits in the road and providing hiding places for thieves between Castleford and Aberford (in the outskirts of Leeds), making it very difficult for carts to pass and providing opportunities for thieves. The provision 'concerning bridges and causeways' was new at the beginning of Edward's reign, probably in response to the damage done to bridges in the civil war of 1264–6 under Henry III; for instance, the bridges over the Severn were broken by the royalists as part of the campaign leading up to the battle of Evesham in 1265. Earlier, the oversight of the care of bridges was probably left to sheriffs and other agents of local government, as with the Huntingdon example already given. The articles of the tourn, a twice-yearly circuit made by sheriffs, with many parallels in the eyre, in 1260 included one of 'paths obstructed to the detriment of the countryside,' which could have been extended to cover damage to bridges.[58]

There is evidence for more investment in roads, especially from the reign of Edward I onwards. The peripatetic nature of government, and of justice and tax-collection in particular, both lay and ecclesiastical, ensured a need to be able readily to get around the country. Under Edward I, Edward II and in the early years of Edward III's reign, the monarch frequently travelled to the North, whereas Richard II seldom went further north than Nottingham, although he went twice as far north as York and in 1385 invaded Scotland. Thus, the transport of the Court adapted to the needs and pleasures of the Crown, the latter focused on hunting. The display of majesty was a key element and it required mobility.

A snapshot is offered by the 'Gough Map' of Britain, a copy, made in about 1400, of a map, now lost, that was drawn in the mid-fourteenth century, which provided a guide to routes and the resulting transport networks. Nearly 3,000 miles of red lines, many of which followed Roman routes, are provided. In his *British Topography* (1780), Richard Gough, who bought the map in 1774 and bequeathed it to the Bodleian Library in Oxford in 1809, stated that it could 'justly boast itself the first amongst us wherein the roads and distances are laid down.'[59] From slightly before, one of the marginalia in the Luttrell Psalter of *c.*1340 provided a drawing of the Luttrells in transit with some rather grumpy passengers looking out from the back of a carriage or covered wagon. This showed how the well-to-do travelled as they visited their estates, a slow and bumpy process. The paved state of The Strand connecting London with Westminster was unusual. Furthermore, in 1353, it was ordered that property-holders along it should make a footpath seven feet wide on each side, thus differentiating mounted from foot transport.

In practice, the Black Death of the mid fourteenth century hit the population (and therefore workforce) and economy hard, reducing the volume of goods in circulation and rejigging the market system, with many towns losing their markets. The resulting demand for transport declined, and the Thames route was adversely affected by economic difficulties. This disaster was followed by a period in which domestic division and an expensive and ultimately unsuccessful war with France hit government and also liquidity. There was a general decay of highways and bridges, although a huge amount of transport took place in the later Middle Ages, including for export purposes. Certain kinds of source, for example manorial accounts and assize rolls, become more or less prolific with time, which can distort our impression. There was an apparent switch from river to road, or, more particularly, from a complex network of big and small waterways to a combination of roads with major rivers. Parliaments were adjourned in 1331, 1339 and 1380 because the state of the roads prevented sufficient attendance. In both 1344 and 1353 Edward III ordered the repair of roads near London, and the collection of tolls from horses and carts. Other provincial towns established turnpikes at their approaches for this purpose. Edward's successor, Richard II (r. 1377–99), commonly ordered instructions for road maintenance, but did not personally give money for such projects, nor for bridge building or repair. Paying for road and bridge maintenance was still generally left to local communities, local lords, and, in the case of bridges, local trusts, with, also, many bequests in wills. In 1406, a complaint was made to Parliament that the sheriffs of various counties were enforcing unreasonable fines upon the religious houses and the secular clergy for the repair of highways. The pressure of conflict on transport was felt elsewhere in the British Isles. Thus, in Ireland, where English control was resisted, Athlone's bridge was broken down in an attack of about 1272.

Yet, at the same time, there was a degree of transport integration within England, with a developing network of regular carriers' routes, certainly from the mid-fifteenth century, instrumental in creating a national transport system, with markets and fairs providing key intermediary points. By the late fourteenth century, road transport, by the horse-drawn two-wheel carts built in many villages, and therefore readily available generally cost 1d to 1½d per ten miles, travelling 15–20 miles daily. River transport was 0.7d per mile and sea transport 0.2d per mile.[60] Costs were far from constant, with land transport becoming less expensive in the fourteenth century before rising in the fifteenth. At the same time, the cost of road transport depended largely on fodder prices which fluctuated. The context was that of different forms of transport serving different needs, often very effectively.

Mercantile credit was crucial to getting the system to work, covering the gap between the purchase and sale of goods.[61] Kendal, in distant (for Londoners) Cumbria, was served by regular packhorse trains (organised groups of packhorses) moving goods as far as London. This stronger emphasis on land routes supplemented London's position as England's most important port. In London itself, improved road surfaces eased the use of wheeled transport, both wagons and coaches.[62]

Improvements in land transport reduced its cost and unpredictability, which encouraged use. The road system was far from static.[63] Thus, in place of the Gloucester-Oxford road which had been significant in the late fourteenth century, the construction of a bridge and causeway in and near Abingdon in 1416–22 meant that goods from Gloucester to London moved to a more southern route. The bridge and causeway still survive. The range of suppliers of Winchester College (founded in 1382) included not only local retailers but also producers and suppliers in the Forest of Dean (nails), the West Midlands (nails, especially from Dudley), London and Salisbury, as well as material shipped in through Southampton, including iron and wax.[64]

In contrast to the Gough Map, there was not the same depiction of roads in John Hardyng's *Map of Scotland* of the 1440s, although admittedly that map was intended to facilitate the English conquest of Scotland, not the movement of goods. Scotland lacked exports on the scale of England, but benefited from a similar expansion of wool and cloth sales. By 1500, Edinburgh was responsible for about 60 per cent of Scotland's exports.

Alongside roads, which benefited greatly from the integration offered by the building of bridges, water routes remained crucial, although there was stagnation in terms of canalisation, as well as a silting up of minor waterways. The head (limit) of Thames navigation retreated from Radcot to Henley. More bridges meant more silting, which would have increased the deterioration of the minor natural and artificial waterways which needed regular maintenance to keep them open.[65] Particular goods, such as stone, benefited greatly from water transport. Thus, wood's bulk involved transportation costs which were eased by water transport. The largest market for wood was London, and access to water transport defined its supply zone. Wood traders and wharves, such as Woodwharf in London, reflected the supply system. Wood was traded only domestically, but other products also had export demand.

The growth in wool and cloth exports brought activity and wealth to cloth centres and ports, for example Lavenham and Great Yarmouth respectively. The transport of wool and then cloth was a matter not only of routes but also of markets. Thus, Banbury acted as a focus for Cotswold production en route to London, with packhorses collected there.[66] At the same time, routes change. By 1500, 70 per cent of England's exports of cloth were shipped through London, with the earlier role of Boston in Lincolnshire relatively declining around 1300, as had the other 'fair towns,' merchants having come to prefer dealing at fixed points like London. However, London's significance as an internal cloth market included the dispatch of much cloth to Southampton for export from there.[67] Road links to ports ensured that some places became entrepots, and not just for cloth: Faversham, for example, for the movement of Kent grain to London. The significance of coastal trade is also apparent for Exeter.[68]

Coastal trade was also very important in Scotland as was seafaring to the Low Countries, Norway, Ireland and the Isle of Man. It was not really faster to reach London from Leith by land than to reach Bergen in Norway by sea until the late eighteenth century.

Ships and sailors, however, were vulnerable. The number of ships that were lost is a ready testimony to a range of problems that included inadequate pumps, weak anchors, vulnerable rudders, and difficulties with seams and caulking, the last ensuring that ships were not reliably watertight. 'The Canon's Yeoman's Tale' in Chaucer's *Canterbury Tales* observes that merchants 'don't maintain a fixed prosperity.... Sometimes their goods are swallowed by the sea, and sometimes they come safely back to port.'There were also problems with pirates.

At the same time, the nature of some ships improved. Late-fourteenth and fifteenth-century improvements in ship construction and navigation included the fusion of Atlantic and Mediterranean techniques of hull construction and lateen- and square-rigging, the spread of the sternpost rudder and advances in location-finding at sea. The number of masts on large English ships rose from one to three in the fifteenth century, increasing the range of choices for rigging and providing a crucial margin of safety in the event of damage to one mast, while development in rigging, including an increase in the number of sails per mast and the variety of sail shapes, permitted greater speed, a better ability to sail close to the wind and improved manoeuvrability, although the latter was limited by difficulty in tacking close to the wind.[69] Navigational expertise also increased, thanks to the use of the magnetic compass, astrolabes, cross-staffs and quadrants.

The fishing industry, while exceptional in its range – for it included fishing in Icelandic waters and in the North Atlantic as well as the import of dried fish from Norway – was nevertheless typical in having particular transport requirements as well as being part of a more general network. In the case of fishing, a key element in the latter was the focus on supplying major urban markets, especially London, but, as far as particular requirements were concerned, issues of spoiling and the cost of alternatives such as smoking. Over the long sweep closing in the fifteenth century, there was an increased consumption and transport of sea as opposed to river fish.[70] A very different set of particular requirements arose from the transport of alcohol, due to issues of preservation.

Ending this chapter on a note of growth is a reasonable response to the economic recovery that was gathering pace by the end of the fifteenth century, and also captures the overall expansion over the last half-millennium. Both counter any focus solely on the crisis period centred on the Black Death in the mid fourteenth century.[71] This was the case for economic, social, cultural and political links. Thus, communications were important for the development of inter-urban political networks.[72]

At the same time, irrespective of scale, it is necessary to understand the constraints of transport. Space and distance are not simply measurements, suggesting as they do that the past is but a prelude to the present. There were also different experiences of space, and contrasting meanings of travel. Attitudes of mind were created by the nature of travel and these in turn shaped perceptions and experiences. It is necessary to appreciate the impact of lengthy journeys that were made unpredictable and hazardous by a multitude of circumstances. These included theft and violence, breakdowns in equipment – axles snapping and horses bolting – and accidents caused by poor road surfaces.

In addition, road surfaces were unreliable. They were greatly affected by rain, especially on clay soils, and routes as well as settlements and land use are reflected in historical mapping.[73] Travel through the greensand of the 'Weald Clay' posed particular problems as did heavy clays, for example in southern Essex and the Vale of Berkeley (Gloucestershire), the latter an instance of the more general problem with valleys. The extensive clays of the English and Irish Midlands were particularly difficult after rainfall. The road from London to York avoided the marshy Fens.

Furthermore, standards of road maintenance were low. Upkeep became largely the responsibility of the local parish, and the resources for a speedy and effective response to deficiencies were lacking. Indeed, it is not surprising that medieval merchants, among the main sufferers from dreadful roads, left money for their repairs in their wills.

At the same time, although road conditions were variable and often bad, there is plenty of evidence of road users overcoming the obstacles and making extensive use of the roads. The entire road transport sector was geared to low-quality roads.

Yet, the slowness of much land travel, and, even more, the difficulty of moving bulk goods by land, and Britain's island character ensured an emphasis on waterborne travel. At the same time, the two types of transport could be complementary, with land travel relatively expensive but, where roads were adequate, often faster compared to less expensive water transport. Much local traffic must always have been by road, but much was also by water, and longer distance trade would have been adapted to where water routes were available. By weight, water transport was more significant than by value, which tended to favour land transport.

However, at sea, there were the difficulties of shipwreck, storm-tossed seas, and contrary winds. Furthermore, coastal charts were absent or, at best, imperfect, and there were few lighthouses, although the Normans built a famous one at Hook Head, Wexford in the early thirteenth century, and it is one of the oldest surviving lighthouse sites in the world.

The pervading sense was one of uncertainty, and notably so for travel at night and in the winter. Yet, problems were more widespread. Spring thaws and autumn floods could bring difficulties, especially by sending rivers into spate, making them impossible to ford, and flooding low-lying areas. Boats were more important than bridges in crossing most rivers and also the numerous and extensive estuaries on the country's indented coastline, such as the Humber, Severn and Thames. They were affected by tides and, in some cases, such as the Neath in Wales, the Dee at Chester, the Wash and Morecambe Bay, quicksands. Guides and carts to get people safely across Morecambe Bay were maintained by Conishead and Cartmel Priories.[74]

There was also the unfamiliarity created by distance. In the preface to his *Eneydos* (1490), William Caxton recounted a tale of London boatmen who stopped in Kent and could not make themselves understood because the Kentish dialect was so strong. One farmer's wife thought they were French because their language was so strong. The frictions affecting transport were not solely those of technology, or, separately, different governments.

The experience of transport is most distant for this period, partly because of the expanse of time, but also due to the illiteracy of most of the population, and the limited scope and stylised nature of the written sources that survive. Nevertheless, they, notably the legal records, provide much information on the range of travails from storms to brigands.

Chapter 2

Sixteenth-Century Days

T he century, one of major political and religious change, most notably the Protestant Reformation, did not see any comparable transformation in transport. In this respect, as in so many others, the sixteenth century and much of the seventeenth were a continuation of what were later to be called the Middle Ages rather than an era of modernity, however defined. There were, nevertheless, significant developments, notably with transoceanic shipping from England. Indeed, two English expeditions sailed round the world. However, transoceanic trade remained small-scale in the sixteenth century, although the seventeenth saw important organizational developments, especially in the form of the activity launched by the new East India Company, founded in 1600.

There were attempts to improve the roads prior to the statute of 1555 which enforced on parishes the obligation to maintain the local highway. In 1523, Parliament passed an Act to encourage landowners in the Weald of Kent to make new roads, and this Act was extended to Sussex two years later. This was an area of particular difficulty due to the soil, as well as of importance due to the regional iron industry that rested on charcoal from the Wealden forest, providing the major national supply of iron in what was still an Iron Age.

In 1530, a general Act was passed dealing with bridges, empowering JPs (Justices of the Peace), in cases where the liability to repair was doubtful, to rate the inhabitants of counties and of corporate towns for their repair and that of the highways within 300 feet of either end of them. JPs were entrusted with the responsibility for their maintenance. An Act of 1545 provided for a permanent highway overseer for 2½ miles of road leading to Chester. Acts were passed for paving the streets of London and Westminster and the neighbourhood in 1533, 1534, 1540 and 1543.

The 1555 Act, passed under Queen Mary, was modelled on the 1530 Bridges Act. As the highways were 'now both very noisome and tedious to travel in and dangerous to all passengers and carriages', every parish was bound to elect two road surveyors at Easter and the parishioners to give four days, free labour before Midsummer for their maintenance and repair; which was later changed to six days. The wealthier were to provide horses and carts. Surveyors were to summon carts and workers from among the inhabitants to labour with shovels, spades, pikes, mattocks and other tools to mend the roads leading to the nearest market town. This measure was rendered urgent by the dissolution of the monasteries, of which the wealthier had maintained the roads as a pious work and which had been the focus of endowments. It was now as if there was, to a degree, a secularization of roads and bridges. The dissolution of individual monasteries such as Bruton and Glastonbury greatly affected local transport needs and patterns, and the funds available for repairs, while at the same time altering patterns of poor relief.

In practice, the Act of 1555 and the extension of its scope in 1563 under Elizabeth I (r. 1558–1603) for another twenty years and for six rather than four days' labour, had an impact that is difficult to evaluate. The legislation, made permanent in the 1580s was repealed by the Statute Law Revision Act of 1863. Probably, the situation of travel difficulties described by John Leland in 1534–43[1] did not change greatly, although road-repair accidents increased, with carts laden with stones either running over drivers and bystanders or falling onto those who were repairing roads. The availability of stone for repairs varied across the country. Visiting St Albans in the 1710s, William Stukeley found local people removing cartloads of Roman bricks and stones to mend the roads.

It is of course conventional to criticize the parochial system. Thus, recently, Pat Rogers has referred to 'the chaotic highways found in the age of unpaid statute labour supplied by unwilling rural parishes.'[2] This approach, however, needs to be advanced with care, not least as in part at least it is a matter of attitude rather than analysis. First, it is classically the case that those praising a certain innovation or innovatory period, in Rogers' case turnpikes, are apt to denigrate or at least disparage what came before, as with so-called 'revolutions in government.' Thus, advocates for canals were critical of rivers, those for rail of turnpikes and canals, and those for road transport of rail. So also more specifically supporters of rail nationalization criticized the earlier private companies, and advocates of privatization subsequently attacked British Rail. When a woman was delivered of a baby on a train in the 1980s, my dour Head of Department, W.R. Ward, told me that the woman was not even pregnant when the train set off. This oft-repeated joke was extrapolated onto all ages of rail. In turn, the new private companies that replaced British Rail were criticized.

Separately, there is the question of the analysis of Tudor local government. There is a tendency to characterize it by reference to the farcical depictions by Shakespeare, as in *Much Ado About Nothing* (*c*.1598–9), but these scarcely equate with proof.

It is more pertinent to note the extent to which public government, in the shape of action, co-operation and consent by public bodies, such as the parish and the vestry, was a characteristic of English government, and contrasted with systems centred on aristocratic power. Consent provided an essential strength in flexibility and flexibility in strength. Part of this rested on an ability to accept and work with variations, and this was typical of government in this period. There is a parallel with the poor relief system which equally empowered local authorities at parish level to take measures suitable to local needs and resources. There was a contrast between what may be seen as the authoritarianism of legislation and other measures, and the need to adapt.

Variations lessened the consistency that might appear appropriate at the national level, but most transport is local and that is the nature of transport for most, one that tends to be underplayed by commentators. So also recently with the debate over HS2, a project pushed hard without sufficient consideration of the transport needs of much of the country, not least the North.

The impression of transport was set in part by the context and perspective. Thus, in marshy regions there were no real roads. In the Somerset Levels, peddlers carried packs of goods to villages that were inaccessible to wagons or even packhorses. The Fens were permanently flooded and its people made a living of sorts by catching eels or harvesting reeds. Some coastal communities such as Whitehaven in Cumbria were open to the sea but comparatively isolated by land.

There was much need for movement,[3] and fairs and markets registered seasonal rhythms, although most roads were passable even in winter. Communities sought reasonably safe and efficient local roads, if only to get into and out of the nearest market town with agricultural produce and firewood. Many went back to the Romans. Mileage per day varied, and horse riders could do more than 20 miles per day, as even in the seventeenth century could wagons and pack horses. However, poor weather and terrain caused delays, and encouraged the frequency of inns and taverns which could cluster every 20 miles.

In addition, varied needs and opportunities created a diverse supply system as the relevant goods and services came from across a broad area. This helped to structure the hierarchies and profits of supplies and transport. Local areas were the usual source of food, but other goods came from further afield. For Cambridge, this meant wood from Essex and Suffolk, luxury goods from London, and coal from Newcastle, brought via King's Lynn, the pivot between coastal shipping and an extensive internal waterway system. Regional specialization was mediated through credit networks and market systems.[4]

Industrial production is frequently misrepresented if shown in terms of static plant and processes, for most manufacturing involved a degree of out-work and assembly, or, at least, of the movement of raw materials. Rural manufacturing, a crucial source of social change,[5] was dependent on transport. The distribution of wool among spinners and weavers in industrial cloth-making villages was the most important example.

In addition, transhumance – the movement of animals to summer and winter pastures – linked upland and lowland areas, while, more generally, there was a close interdependence between areas of difference. This was true both of the economy as a whole, and of regional and local economies. For example, the moorlands of Dartmoor and Exmoor had important commercial relationships with nearby parishes, with animals summering on moorland pastures. Droving also joined areas of difference, as food that could make its own way to market, for eating or processing (notably turning cattle hides into leather). Droving, which was mostly cattle, but included sheep, geese and turkeys, solved many problems in food distribution. Somewhat differently, but as another food system, fishing continued to provide a means of transport linked to work as well as a product that then had to be moved inland in order to maximise sales.[6]

The importance of rivers focused attention on those bridges and ferries that existed. The seven-arched medieval stone bridge over the

Tyne at Newcastle was a crucial feature of that city's local, regional and national position. The same was true for Barnstaple, Bideford, Exeter, Gloucester, Oxford and York. London Bridge remained the lowest crossing point on the Thames, and there was no road crossing of the Tamar downriver of Gunnislake, a situation that continued until 1961 and that long encouraged a dependence on coastal shipping in order to travel to Cornwall. The crossing of the River Chelmer was crucial at Chelmsford. However, bridges continued to be under pressure from decay, the weather and storms. Thus, Rochester bridge was a ruin for part of the century and had to be rebuilt from the 1560s.

Shakespeare was one of the Stratford-upon-Avon citizens who subscribed to the cost of promoting an act of Parliament for road repairs. It is understandable that details of the movements of letters and couriers, and of their all-too-frequent mishaps and related uncertainties, crop up regularly in his plays and in the correspondence and diaries of the period. Frequent references to the flow of rivers assumed that the listeners of his plays were very familiar with the experience of being on the water, as in *Two Gentlemen of Verona* (c.1589–93) in which Julia compares true love to a stream flowing naturally:

'The current that with gentle murmur glides,
Thou know'st, being stopp'd, impatiently doth rage' (II,vii).

Many settlements and country houses, for example Antony House in Cornwall and Hampton Court on the Thames, were best reached by water, and the grand London houses on the Thames had watergates through which visitors and goods moved. The Tower of London was frequently approached from the Thames, most famously by Traitors' Gate. More generally, water – both the sea and inland waterways – had far more of an impact on people's lives than is the case today. Many towns that now lack quays and wharves were then ports.

Although they did not link most of the country to London except by means also of coastal transport, rivers combined to form trading systems that covered much of the country. In the West Midlands, the Severn was navigable as far as Bewdley, near Kidderminster, the Stratford Avon almost up to Warwick, and the Lugg to Leominster. All these waterways combined to enhance the importance of the Severn system and thus of the nearby major seaport, Bristol. Nearby, but not tributaries, the Wye, which was navigable to Hereford, and the Parrett extended the significance of the riverborne network flowing into the Bristol Channel. Inland ports included Bridgwater, Gloucester, Langport, Lincoln, Norwich, Stratford, Tewkesbury, and York. In contrast, in this period, Scotland and, separately, Wales were far worse served by inland waterways than lowland England, although both were well served by coastal trade.

A corollary to the role of rivers was provided by a high water table across much of lowland England and the difficulties of 'the wet' for road transport. These were exacerbated in areas of clay soil, such as much of Cheshire.

A larger number of ports handled foreign trade than was to be the case from the nineteenth century when the greater size of merchantmen led to the concentration of long-distance trade on the fewer harbours that had the necessary draught, as well as facilities for handling large ships. Shakespeare frequently presented or mentioned storms and shipwrecks, as in *The Tempest, The Merchant of Venice, Twelfth Night, A Winter's Tale, Pericles, The Comedy of Errors, Measure for Measure* and *Richard III*. In *Othello*, Montano asks

'What ribs of oak, when mountains [mountainous seas] melt on them,
   Can hold the mortise?' (II,i).

In *Richard III*, shortly before being drowned in a butt of wine, George, Duke of Clarence, dreams of drowning in the sea, seeing

'A thousand men that fishes gnaw'd upon' (I,iv).

At Dunster Castle in Somerset, close to the Bristol Channel, there is an allegorical painting by the London-based Hans Eworth, dated 1550, of Sir John Luttrell, the owner, depicting him emerging half naked from a storm-tossed sea, while in the background sailors abandon a sinking ship. Commentators have related this to Luttrell's career as a military commander, but, even if so, the example and image are still striking. Lundy's reefs claimed many ships in the Bristol Channel, and the construction there of a major lighthouse, completed in 1820, was long overdue. The route itself was important to the trade with Ireland which developed not least because of a major increase in English settlement, one that encouraged imports from Bristol, Chester and other ports.[7] The improvement of navigation by means of lighthouses was linked to the 1514 foundation of Trinity House and 1566 powers for it to build lighthouses.

There was scant major improvement to the transport system. Instead, the great wealth produced by the despoliation of the monasteries, economic growth and parliamentary taxation, was largely spent on wars with France, Scotland and Spain. The routes of roads in the 1675 Ogilby atlas are the same as those in the Gough Map, indicating both consistency and a lack of new investment.

Rivers were seen as crucial, but there was little change to the situation, and Harry Hotspur's fictional proposal of a 'new channel' for the Trent in Shakespeare's *Henry IV, Part I* (1597, III,i) was treated in the play as fantastical. Instead, a sense of stability was presented in his *Survey of London* (1598) by John Stow who proudly compared London to the prospects offered elsewhere by other rivers:

'This realm has only three principal rivers on which a royal city may be situated: Trent in the north, Severn in the southwest, and Thames in the southeast; of which the Thames, both for the straight course in length reaches furthest into the belly of the land, and for the breadth and stillness of the water, is most navigable up and down the stream: by reason whereof London, standing almost in the middle of that course, is more commodiously served with provision of necessaries than any town standing upon the other two rivers can be, and doth also more easily communicate to the rest of the realm the commodities of her own production and trade.'

On a longstanding pattern, water transport was hindered by the need to use water power for manufacturing, as reflected in mills and weirs. As a result, there were longstanding disputes on many rivers. The Earl of Devon's weir over the Exe downstream of Exeter was a major point of disagreement from the thirteenth to the sixteenth centuries because it stopped ships from reaching Exeter and benefited the rival port of

Topsham. The river channel was reopened after the execution in 1538 of Henry, 1st Marquess of Exeter, who had fallen foul of his former friend Henry VIII, but the river channel had by then become silted up and was circumvented only in 1564–7 by the construction of a channel, the Exeter Ship Canal, which remains in use to the present, albeit no longer for freight.

The Trent was a similar cause of controversy, with Newark's mills a major issue and the millowners opposed to plans, for example in about 1540, to divert the river. There was a particular controversy about a mill weir over the Trent near Shelford Priory, which, as a result of the despoliation of the monasteries, had been acquired by the Stanhope family. They clashed over the weir with another powerful local landowner, Gilbert, Earl of Shrewsbury. In the event, a long diversion channel was dug in 1593 to bypass the mill. The importance of the cloth industry encouraged the authorization of weirs for mills, as in an Act for the Wye in 1555.

However, the Statute of Sewers of 1531 pressed for action to stop flooding and improve navigation. This entailed the pulling down of weirs and mills, for which legislation had for long been ineffective, a failure that had contributed to the decline of navigation. A Commission of Sewers was established in 1535 to pull down all weirs and mills obstructing river navigation.

There were also improvements in some harbours. At Dover, Henry VII (r. 1485–1509) gave money to encourage the building of a new harbour. *Holinshed's Chronicles* (1577) noted the construction of a round tower about 1500:

'which served somewhat to defend the ships from the rage of south-west winds, but especially to moor ships that were tied thereto. Many great rings were fastened to the tower for that purpose. Nevertheless, this was thought very insufficient for the number of ships which usually lay for harbour in the Road.'

Henry VIII (r. 1509–47) began the construction of a long stone mole at the port of Dover to provide protection. However, cost as well as the difficulty of the task led to the abandonment of the unfinished plan at the end of the reign. For all harbours, sea and river, the rotting impact of water on wooden quays and the pressure of tides on stone structures were major causes of expenditure.[8]

More generally, Kent displayed both possibility and problem. Grain was moved thence to London both overland and by sea from ports including Sandwich, one of the Cinque Ports, which enjoyed a degree of self-government. This transport capability, however, posed social problems. In the harsh harvests of the 1590s, the pressure to serve London led to food shortages elsewhere, which are often a silent adjunct to transport history on the local, regional or national levels. Effective transport thus could move social turmoil, and grain riots were often aimed against shipping grain out of other localities to feed London. In contrast with Kent, the difficulties of transportation across the Weald ensured there was no comparable effect in Sussex.

Coal was shipped from Newcastle in increasing quantities: 15,000 tons annually in the fifteenth century, 400,000 by 1625, a trade that was the most important form of coastal transport. Yet, much transport was more traditional in form, notably droving. In Scotland, the scale of cattle droving, which was a major source of wealth interchange between the Highlands and the Lowlands, rose greatly, while an increasing number of animals were to find their way to England. Change in the scale of transport therefore did not necessarily equate with transformation in method or system. The possibilities for droving were linked to the animal in question. Cattle were best moved on the hoof, but with sheep their wool tended to be transported after they were sheared, rather than the sheep themselves.

As ever, the emphasis can vary. Compared to the situation by 1880, fewer people travelled far, apart from the very rich, and long-distance goods transport was mostly limited to high-value and low-bulk goods. Coach travel, if sharing a coach, was very expensive. Going by horseback could be even more expensive, although it depended on who owned the horse, as many servants and labourers were riding about on their masters' (cheaper) horses in order to get things done faster. Winter travel was particularly difficult. Poor communications magnified the effects of distance and imposed high costs on economic exchange. This encouraged activities based on local resources, as in Cumbria, where salt was extracted from clay sand by using inexpensive sea-coal to evaporate the brine into salt. At the same time, famine largely ended in England long before most parts of Europe because long rivers and long coasts made it easier to get grain even to places like the Lake District by the early seventeenth century.

Land communications were generally slow, expensive and unreliable to an extent that it is difficult for modern readers to appreciate, accustomed as they are to tarmacked roads and mechanized transport. Indeed, we must be careful in using the term 'road' in a modern sense, since many were little more than bridle paths. There were no roads suitable for wheeled traffic apart from the town and trunk or major roads. These were not suitable in the sense we would expect, as they were unpaved outside towns. Outside southern England, non-trunk roads were mostly narrow paths on which packhorses often could not pass each other. Horses could readily follow paths and tracks, albeit finding difficulties, but carriages had to be used on roads. More generally, the quality of the roads reflected the local terrain, in particular drainage and soil type. Thus, travelling into Cornwall in August 1702, John Evelyn found 'dirty or stony lanes', dirty meaning muddy, for which the description was often deep. Such circumstances were a particular challenge for the major expeditions of royal progresses.

Yet, these occurred and coaches aplenty were used with success, notably in London. Coaches were similar to medieval carriages albeit with a use of suspension with leather straps, followed from about 1600 by a pavilion roof rising to a central point supported on four corner posts. The use of coaches in England began from the 1550s and Elizabeth I (1558–1603) spent heavily on them.[9] Subsequently, their use spread socially to a considerable degree and in particular from women to men as well. Coach etiquette developed. In the mid-seventeenth century, both glass windows and steel springs were developed.[10]

Hilly and, even more, mountainous terrain increased the need for draught animals and limited the speed of transport. The need to travel up or down even small hills added greatly to distance, and thus increased the time and cost of travel. As a result, for example, it was easier to sail to Wales and Cornwall than go overland. Yet that should not be treated as an indication of failure but rather of the adaptability inherent in the system as well as the possibilities offered by Britain's coastline, both its presence and the extent to which it was indented and then supplemented by navigable rivers. There were few equivalents to the sandbar of Chesil Beach in Dorset blocking access to coast and rivers.

Poor roads contributed to long and unpredictable journeys that strained individuals, damaged goods and tied up scarce capital in transit. Large four-wheeled road wagons, replacing carts, were introduced in the Elizabethan period, although they only became widespread in the 1610s. Poorly-constructed roads, however, led often to a reliance on light carts with only two horses for shorter-distance goods movements. This increased the number of carts necessary to move a given load, with resulting costs in manpower and forage. Indeed, carters and porters were crucial for life to function. Still, more often, although there are few reliable figures for the century, burdens were probably limited to 240lbs (125kg) or so, which could be carried in panniers on a horse or mule, against the heavier load which could be drawn by a single horse over good level roads. A wagon horse could draw about six cwt (304kg) in this period. However, packhorses, which were faster than four-horse wagons, could be more efficient than carts. They were also more flexible and reliable than wheeled vehicles, and hawkers using packhorses were important across the country. There was no single form of road transport which met all the needs, but it was scarcely surprising, however, that coastal travel offered attractions.

So also in Ireland, where English armies were always frustrated by poor road systems. Their heavy weaponry kept sinking in the bogs they repeatedly complained about, as in the Nine Years' War of 1593–1603, which was waged particularly in northern Ireland. The English found themselves dependent on pack animals.

The most significant travels in the imagination of the period remained spiritual and emotional ones: toward love, spiritual and human, and the former leading to redemption. That remained significant even when the means of such an end had been changed by the ending of shrines and pilgrimages. At the same time, there was a continued belief in the interaction of human and superhuman agencies. The rise in concern about witchcraft seen after the Reformation led to greater interest in diabolical means of transport that were not bound by human temporalities. Witches who could fly were a particular terror. On the other hand, angels were credited with the ability to fly for beneficent purposes.

Witches' flight was a major topic, not least in drama, as in Thomas Middleton's *The Witch* (c. 1613–16). Theatrical representations were often far more elaborate (drawing on Continental demonologies and Classical literature) than anything found in witch trials. Witches could be described as using broomsticks to fly, but because they did not, by and large, meet in collective gatherings in England, so they did not need a standard means of transporting themselves, and the issue usually arose only if they were accused of doing *maleficium* in some way which involved flight.[11] Such flight was a reminder of the grounded nature of transport, but with two English circumnavigations of the world by the end of the century, there were also indications of new possibilities.

Chapter 3

Seventeenth-Century Delays?

Celia Fiennes (1662–1741), the unmarried daughter of a politician and granddaughter of a Viscount, was unusual in travelling extensively for pleasure, which she did on horseback, although accompanied by servants, from about 1684 until about 1712, but particularly in 1697–8. Her travel memoir, not published in full until 1888, provided a clear account of the deficiencies of the road system. These were deficiencies by her standards, not later ones.[1] Thus, en route to Wales, Fiennes 'crossed over the marshes, which is hazardous to strangers,' and on her return she:

> 'forded over the [estuary of the River] Dee when the tide was out … the sands are here so loose that the tides do move them … many persons that have known the fords well, that have come a year or half a year after, if they venture on their former knowledge have been overwhelmed in the ditches made by the sands, which are deep enough to swallow up a coach or wagon.'[2]

In 1698, she encountered a pair of highwaymen. As a reminder, however, of the very varied character of transport, Fiennes also provided an account of coal mining in North-East Wales which included vertical transport:

> 'they have also engines that draw up their coal in sort of baskets like hand barrows which they wind up like a bucket in a well, for their mines are dug down through a sort of well and sometimes its pretty low before they come to the coals.'

Droving meanwhile remained significant, and as part, as in Cumbria, of a widespread and profitable economy of transhumance, animal fairs and the supply of meat and hides.[3]

The standard stress on a transport revolution in the eighteenth century, variously the counterpart, precursor, cause and effect of industrial, agricultural and financial revolutions, inevitably implies a lack of 'impressive' development in the pre-revolutionary period, in other words more continuity in the latter in order to emphasise the revolutionary character of what follows. This, moreover, appears fully understandable given the extent to which civil war affected the British Isles, although, in turn, that involved major requirements for transport, from logistics, notably artillery trains, to itinerant preachers. In May 1643, Charles I (1625–49) had 122 carts in his artillery train, which was essential to the capture of fortified positions but also a major transport problem. In the Civil Wars of 1642–8 in England, poor communications emphasized the importance of fortified towns or strongpoints at key locations, notably crossing points. The Ribble Bridge was crucial to the battles at Preston in 1648 and 1715, in the latter case a defeat for a Jacobite force. So also in Ireland, Scotland and Wales, for example Athlone in 1691. Two of the bridges over the Tamar were damaged in the Civil War and not repaired for over a century.

Naval action, privateering and sieges made coastal shipping dangerous during the Civil Wars and that was also an issue with Britain's international conflicts. The greater strength of the navy from the 1690s made the situation less serious, but it continued to be important in wartime. More significant, for the North Sea coastal shipping was peace with the Dutch from 1674 to 1780.

When London was partly destroyed in the Great Fire of 1666, there were plans for its rebuilding that included major changes in its road system, not least a regular grid. In the event, there was no such transformation, in part due to a lack of will and resources, as well as the existing property rights of individuals. The sole new street was King Street – and from that Queen Street, which created a new route from Guildhall to the Thames. There was also, again, no new bridge across the Thames during the century which increased reliance on the watermen whose reputation was poor.

Meanwhile, the Statute for the Mending of Highways of 1555 remained in force, with each parish responsible for road upkeep. As the resistance of the surface, usually loose and rough, to bad weather or heavy use was limited, there was a need for frequent repair. Expensive in both materials and labour, because it could not be mechanized, this duty was generally not adequately carried out. Only the largest of holes were usually filled, although from the perspective of extensive potholes in 2023–4, it is possible that criticism of seventeenth-century roads should be reined in. Indeed, present-day conditions and discontents throw instructive light on earlier situations. Just as modern lorries damage road surfaces, so heavy wagons did in the past, not least those of the iron workers of the Weald who, accordingly, were pressed to contribute to their upkeep. Pressure on the road surface was increased by the use of four-wheeled wagons rather than the earlier two-wheeled wain (cart). Laden ploughs, which had a box attachment for transport, were also a problem. The lack of local stone for repairs could be a major issue, one that encouraged the denuding of monastic ruins as well as substitutes such as loose stones, pebbles and clay. Cart ruts were often not properly levelled, but, rather, beaten down and sprinkled with gravel or stones. No attempt was made to bind the surface. Once repaired, the roads still suffered from the problems of traffic, leading in 1614 and 1622 to the prohibition of laden ploughs in Somerset on specific newly-repaired roads. Heavier wagons, those with four (not two) wheels and more horses and oxen, continued to be a particular difficulty.[4] Alongside repairs to road surfaces, there was the need for those to bridges, as at Warrington in 1621. Indeed, alongside the emphasis on new developments, it is necessary to stress the lasting burdens of maintenance and repair.

The problem of the road surface led to attention to loads and wheels. This was frequently reflected in legislation, but that also represented a range of opinions. Thus, the 1741 Highways Act, repealed the recent legislation that 'obliges persons not travelling for hire, to make use of wagons with wheels bound with streaks, or tyre, of a certain breadth, or the said streaks to be fastened with nails'. In addition, ditching was frequently neglected, and this made the run-off of rainfall more difficult, which encouraged flooding. The poor nature of the roads encouraged going off-road and crossing private property.

Deficiencies in the road surface so affected carriages that more social engagements were held once the moon was in its brighter waxing phase, because it meant the road surface could be seen more readily at night. This affected the timing of meetings. Founded in 1727, those of the Faversham

Farmers' Club was always held at full moon so that the horses could find the way home. So later with Birmingham's Lunar Society.

Carriages were also affected by springs snapping and by horses bolting. Going up and down steep hills could be particularly difficult and dangerous, and being on the roof of a coach was especially risky. Overturning could be fatal. Problems with roads encouraged an emphasis on taking the major ones which tended to be the ones in best repair. Again, there are comparisons with the current situation.

Packhorses carried iron ore up the River Angidy from the tidal dock constructed on the River Wye at Abbey Mill in 1693 to the Abbey Tintern Furnace up the valley built in 1672–3. They were present elsewhere across the country for similar purposes. This contributed greatly to a ubiquity of horses that is all too easy to forget, one that helped ensure that blacksmiths were key figures in local communities and their forges ubiquitous industrial sites as well as sources of expertise. Horses needed shoes as well as food and water. The horse trade was another form of transport, one focused on horse fairs, such as that at Banbury, which also held a major cattle market until 1998.

Packhorses represented a decision not to rely on wheels. Indeed, wheeled vehicles were not widely used in many areas. Thus, Fiennes did not find the route between Exeter and Plymouth, the two main towns in Devon, acceptable in 1698:

'the lanes are exceeding narrow ... the ways now become so difficult that one could scarcely pass by each other, even the single horses, and so dirty in many places and just a track for one horse's feet.'5

In turn, there was an effort for improvement in the 1660s, with the first turnpike road on part of the Great North Road from London to York: a 1663 Act of Parliament authorized Justices of the Peace in Hertfordshire, Cambridgeshire and Huntingdonshire to take a toll in order to improve the road. The earliest turnpike was between Wadesmill and Royston, while the first trust, set up in 1706, improved a section of Watling Street. Long-distance coach and wagon services had particular need of such reliability. However, the second such Act was not passed until 1695. As part of the 'privatization' of government functions, or, rather, of the public-private 'partnership' necessary to add liquidity, the collection of turnpike tolls was let out to the highest bidder by the trustees although only some trusts let out their tolls.

There can be a marked tendency to underplay change before turnpikes, but in practice it was considerable. Thus, in Wiltshire, the licensing of premises able to provide accommodation increased between 1620 and 1740. Accommodation could relate to individuals, horses and stagecoaches. There was a complex road network. Indeed, the extent of road links qualifies the idea that drainage basins were the key basis for cultural provinces within England.[6] Moreover, it is clear from constables' accounts, for example those of Upton, Nottinghamshire, that there were many travellers in English villages even in places such as Upton that were not on an important road.[7] The Settlement Act of 1662 was predicated on the idea that everyone had a 'home' parish to which they could and would return for poor relief. Although there is scant evidence of roads being better than in the fifteenth century, very regular and reliable carrying and coach services were provided, in both winter and summer, and road transport was often faster and more reliable than water transport.

There was an attempt to help predictability in the shape of publishing maps, as with the *Description of all the Postroads in England* (1668) by Captain Richard Carr, who made the map from a draft by James Hicks, the Chief Clerk to the Post Office. The map was organized by and for the purpose of postage; it covered all the postroads, their stages and distances, and advertised that it was possible to travel seven miles an hour in the summer and five in the winter. So also with *Britannia* (1675), the first volume of what was intended to be a multi-volume road atlas based on surveys sponsored by Charles II for whom Ogilby was Cosmographer and Geographic Printer. Ogilby (1600–76) was a Scot whose career indicated the often eclectic nature of those of the period. Having run a dancing school until lamed in a fall, when he became a tutor, Ogilby founded Ireland's first theatre and then had his career derailed by the Irish rising of 1641, whereupon he turned to making money by translating the Classics. Under Charles II (r. 1660–85), Ogilby established a printing press in London, which published atlases among other works. He hoped his road atlas would cover over 22,000 miles of road, but died before he could do so. The volume published had a standard scale of one inch to a mile, and a standard mile of 1,760 yards in place of the frequent use of local measures. Ogilby emphasized his Wheel Dimensurator, a measuring wheel that showed the distance travelled on a dial. About 7,500 miles of road were surveyed and the maps were supported by 200 pages of text which included helpful information, notably a summary of the state of the road, distances and turnings to be avoided. The maps included landmarks, the building material of the bridge, the direction of slope, inns, fords, and whether roads were enclosed or not. Woods, a haunt of highwaymen, were shown.

Reflecting both need and entrepreneurship, other route maps included William Berry's *Grand Roads of England* (1679) and John Seller's *A New Map of the Roads of England* (c.1690). Such maps created a stronger mental image of a country joined by roads and with particular roads of significance.

There was a comparable engagement with the charting of the coast. In 1681, Charles II appointed a naval officer, Captain Greenville Collins, 'to make a survey of the sea coasts of the kingdom by measuring all the sea coasts with a chain and taking all the bearings of all the headlands with their exact latitudes.' The survey, which took seven years, had many limitations due to the speed with which it was accomplished, the limited manpower available, and the lack of an available comprehensive land survey of the coastline as the basis for a marine survey, the last a common problem. The results, published in 1693 in *Great Britain's Coasting Pilot*, were frequently reprinted.

Meanwhile, coastal transport was increasing and with significant economic consequences. The first shipload of Cheshire cheese reached London in 1650, by 1664 more than 14 cheese ships were sailing from the Northwest, and by the 1680s over 50. This was an aspect of the transition of Cheshire from an inward-looking, partly subsistence economy to one integrated into that of the country as a whole. Coastal trading was risky but could be rewarding.[8] Cheese, a food not dependent on immediate consumption, also came to London from Somerset by sea via Bristol, which, in turn, was supplied from South Wales with butter and milk. Return cargoes from London helped to transform the regional economy in the Northwest and elsewhere, and encouraged shipbuilding, Coastal transport indeed aided development in many distant areas, as with grain exports from Cardiganshire from the late seventeenth century.

The possibilities for coastal transport were enhanced by the number of ports able to take part in foreign trade. Indeed, there was a considerable overlap, with these ports operating rather as hubs for broader regional and local networks, coast, river and on land.[9] Thus, Bristol's twice-yearly fairs were important to a network defined by coastal and river trade. The potential of ports, in turn, was lessened by silting up. This hit Chester on the Dee to the benefit of Liverpool on the Mersey where the depth of water was good for large vessels even if the tide was out. Silting also hit Barnstaple, as the Taw was silting up, to the benefit of Bideford, which was closer to the estuary.

In his *A Journal of the Plague Year* (1722), about the plague of 1665, Daniel Defoe commented on the coastal trade for grain and coal:

'The first of these was particularly carried on by small vessels from the port of Hull and other places on the Humber, by which great quantities of corn were brought in from Yorkshire and Lincolnshire. The other part of this corn-trade was from Lynn, in Norfolk, from Wells and Burnham, and from [Great] Yarmouth, all in the same county [Norfolk]; and the third branch was from the river Medway, and from Milton, Feversham, Margate, and Sandwich, and all the other little places and ports round the coast of Kent and Essex. There was also a very good trade from the coast of Suffolk with corn, butter, and cheese...'

Comparisons are difficult. While better than divided Germany, Britain did not have a transport system comparable to China. Nor was there anything to match the road building in Mughal India, nor the road and canal building in France. This, however, was not inherently a sign of failure as there was scant point investing considerable sums just to insert infrastructure for which there might be only limited economic purpose. Indeed, government-driven provision tended to reflect aspirations for economic improvement that in part were unrealistic, as in France where attempts to use transport to create a national market overriding a series of regional economies were unsuccessful. There were also military-strategic intentions behind roadbuilding, as in Mughal India and France, and as in what was to come in Highland Scotland in the eighteenth century.

In comparison, seventeenth-century British developments in river improvement, canals and roads were modest, and certainly relatively so compared with what was to come. The stretch of the Thames below Oxford became navigable again for barges in 1635 following the construction of pound locks. The 15.5 mile Wey navigation between the Thames and Guildford in 1653, the first major river navigation involving extensive new cutoffs, was predicated on the booming and profitable trade in grain and timber from west Surrey to London. Such improvement, however, was uncommon. In 1623, John Taylor, a pamphleteer who visited Salisbury, pressed for an improvement in the navigation of the Avon, but nothing happened. Soon after, in 1626, Henry Briggs, a prominent mathematician interested in economic development, made a survey of the rivers Avon and Thames and proposed a canal to link them, but the plan was not pursued, and the same was true of plans to this end after the Civil War,[10] a period in which Parliament considered eleven bills for river improvement in 1662–5, eight of which were passed. In 1665, it was argued that the pressure of wagons with excessive burdens on the highways merited such legislation.

Despite earlier legislation, this situation was only really transformed after the 'Glorious Revolution' in 1688–9 as the subsequent establishment of regular parliamentary sessions helped underline fiscal stability and provided the opportunity to pass private legislation to give effect to schemes for improvement. This, indeed, was the key background to what has been called the 'transport revolution', for the issue in the eighteenth century was not technological transformation. Instead, it was the governmental context, including the stabilization of public finances by means of the establishment of the Bank of England and a publicly-guaranteed national debt. Improvement for the goal of a stronger public economy was a key objective, one noted by a publicist for change, Daniel Defoe, when writing in the *Review* on 9 July 1709: 'The roads are the arteries that convey, and the manufactures, provisions and produce of the whole flow through them, to the general supply of every part.'

The new governmental practice reached across the country. Carriers' maximum rates were controlled by Quarter Sessions from the end of the seventeenth to the early nineteenth century[11] and Quarter Sessions also became responsible for county bridges, such that records for the latter appear in those of the Quarter Sessions.[12] In Devon, the carriers' rate was 8d per hundredweight, initially for up to ten miles. Rates to London varied between horseback and wagon carriage.[13]

Separate to government develoments, but also benefiting from it, carrier services improved, in part benefiting from the change from carts to wagons. The Whitmarsh family of Taunton began in 1685 with a once-weekly wagon service from Taunton to London that took six or seven days to cover the 148 miles, largely carrying Somerset cloth; but they built up a Somerset carrying quasi-monopoly with routes added to Bath, Barnstaple, Exeter and Bristol, as well as passengers and faster travel. More generally, carriers provided and drew on an infrastructure including warehouses, inns, packhorse routes and wagoning.[14]

There was already change prior to the major construction of canals from the mid-eighteenth century. In particular, there was a series of improvements to river navigation, the Aire and Calder navigation to Leeds and Halifax in 1699–1700 proving an important step, easing links to Wakefield and Hull and thus the movement of coal and woollen goods. Parliament held hearings over the merits of the navigation scheme in 1698, petitions were printed, and *Reasons* published on both sides. More generally, partisan rivalries within urban politics did not stop in the case of transport.[15] Nevertheless, 81 Turnpike Acts were passed between 1695 and 1729. Britain's first dry-dock was constructed on the Thames in the 1690s.

The political institutions and culture of Britain were more conducive for the local (albeit local élite) initiatives and control required for the creation of new transport links such as canals and turnpikes; whereas in France control was more in the hands of a small bureaucracy that was less responsive to local needs. The situation in Britain was eased by the possibility of establishing trusts by private Acts of Parliament, while in France the insistence on central government control precluded necessary private investment and led to a concentration on a small number of prestigious projects.[16]

Henry Pratt's *Map of the Kingdom of Ireland* (1708) included numerous roads, but, as with England, their quality was highly variable. Across the British Isles, the depiction of roads not only provided no guidance to usage, but also no evidence of the continued salience of droving. Far from receding this became more significant, as with increased numbers of Welsh cattle and sheep driven to English markets, especially London. This could involve ferries across the Bristol Channel: from Sully, near Cardiff, to Uphill in Somerset, and from Beachley to Aust. Droving and packhorses also brought Welsh goods to English markets in Chester, Oswestry, Shrewsbury and Ludlow. Droving within Scotland and from there to England, for example to the major East Anglian cattle fairs at St Faith's and Sprowston, also increased, and with the Scottish addition added as part of an English pattern of droving that for example moved cattle from the Lake District. Droving, however, blocked roads. A letter in the *London Evening Post* of 16 February 1762 referred 'to an old grievance … the driving cattle about the streets of this metropolis, at a time when they are full of people.'

Communications were crucial for commercial activity, and notably so at the regional or national level. Thus, the relatively slow growth of many Cheshire towns in the seventeenth and early eighteenth centuries in part was due to their relatively poor links with the more dynamic centres of Lancashire. What stimulated growth was not necessarily intrinsic to particular towns but to do with external relationships in the shape of their linkages with town and country across at least a regional range.[17] Much transport continued to be between market towns and their surrounding villages,[18] but was also between both and more distant places.

Established in 1680, the Penny Post benefited from the road system and from the stagecoach system that had begun in the early seventeenth century and became more developed by mid-century. Stagecoaches stopped at inns at each stage of the journey, obtained fresh horses, and thereby travelled faster. The press, which expanded greatly from the lapsing of the Licensing Act (of newspapers) in 1695, which ended pre-publication censorship, also benefited, not least the tri-weeklies which circulated from London into the countryside. The net effect was that of an intensification of linkages.

The imagination of transport was very much fixed on the present as there was no experience of different means. Indeed, the sense of the future was somewhat constrained as a result. At the same time, governments and commentators proposed change in the sense of a more directive rise of the state in order to bring about social and economic improvement. The causes and contexts of these ideas varied but Baconian notions of improvement and, later, the advocacy of 'Political Economy' were significant ones. From the perspective of transport, what is striking is that this was not a central area for policy prescription or speculation. Yet, by the end of the century, there was a clear sense of purposed improvement in government regulation of the economy as well as in the pursuit of local improvements.

The balance in the treatment of the seventeenth century might have been different if, like the following three centuries, it was divided into two chapters at mid-century. For the seventeenth century, this would provide a very different account, with the first half of the century essentially a continuation of the previous period, but a change from mid-century. This is different from the situation for the sixteenth century in that there was less of a change then, although such a suggestion may lead to an underestimation of the disruption linked to the Dissolution of the Monasteries and the remedy attempted with mid-century legislation; legislation, however, that was less persistent than the Poor Laws made necessary by fears of vagrancy and disorder. Such comparisons remind us of the difficulty of dealing with transport without offering a comparative context. The same is seen today with the vastly greater governmental concern for the health service compared to transport, at the same time that most public commentary on the latter does not address the issue of relative calls on the public purse.

The absence of parliamentary sessions for most of the period 1610–40 ensured that Parliament could not then be a consistently significant sphere for the discussion of transport issues. So also with the complaints about royal government expressed in 1640–2 as the country moved toward civil war. In part, that serves as a reminder that leaving transport essentially to local authorities was uncontentious. The situation would have been different, and probably far worse, if transport had been handed to the monopolists and chartered companies favoured by James I (1603–25) and Charles I. To a degree, turnpike trusts might be seen in that light, but, although unpopular with some, notably the poor, they were made more acceptable by parliamentary approval as well as the extent to which the key players were all locals. Indeed, this underlined the political value of the mid-sixteenth century governmental solution to transport. The privilege of access to the Crown did not serve to direct and tax local transport unlike, for example, some of the monopoly trading companies, such as the East India, Hudson Bay, Levant and Russia. There was no similar restriction for coastal shipping. Here the key organising bodies were urban authorities.

The fundamental continuity suggested by this discussion could have worked out very differently if the republican Rump or monarchical Protectorate governments of the Interregnum (1649–60) had taken a more pro-active and sustained stance in transport. They certainly did so with foreign trade, advancing a series of significant protectionist measures. There were no domestic equivalents to the Navigation Acts, but then there appeared no need. In particular, the challenge posed by Dutch shipping and trade was not matched as far as internal transport was concerned. Indeed, there were no domestic transport assets that could be taken over by foreign interests. That is an aspect of the 'silences' of British transport history. With both shipping services and rail investment, Britain was to be important as an external player, for example for Argentina. There was concern about French and Spanish political and cultural challenge and Dutch economic interests and political models during the seventeenth century, but they did not relate essentially to transport with the significant exception of coastal shipping. There was to be significant Dutch investment in the national debt, but not in transport assets which were not really organized in a way to attract such investment. Indeed, that was a major reason for the limited change of the seventeenth century.

Looked at differently, it is conceptually questionable to focus on why changes did not occur as though they should have done with the future anticipated. That application of Whig history is unhelpful as a whole and more particularly to seventeenth-century transport for either half of the century.

Chapter 4

Toward Take-Off, 1700–50

'I have heard some talk of a project to join the Avon in Somersetshire, to the Thames; and the Severn with the Trent ... as opening a way to circulate a share of commerce, and the advantages that attend it, from one extreme of the kingdom to the other.' The *Champion*, 14 August 1740.

'I set forward towards Cork ... but I met with contrary wind and was driven into Wales and so after four days came home again and stayed about a week at home and so set sail again and met with contrary winds again and was driven upon the coasts of Ireland near the mountains of Newry ... but after six days at sea got safe and well to Dublin.' Jonathan Wilson, 1726.

If, in July 1726, Jonathan Wilson, a Cumbrian malt dealer, faced difficulties; so also, earlier that year, did George I, who was driven ashore near Rye on his return from Hanover, in a journey by land and sea that the Saxon envoy referred to as nearly impracticable and very dangerous, indeed one in which he had nearly lost his life more than once.[1] In 1740, ice stranded ships in the Humber estuary.[2] Winds cut off maritime links, affecting everything from trade and diplomacy to travel and newspapers. The *St James's Post* of 13 September 1717 observed: 'The contrary winds continuing to deprive us of the Dutch mails.' This theme was frequently reiterated,[3] which was a testimony to its significance.

These problems, and, increasing the sources cited simply adds to the list, underline the turmoil that travel could cause, and therefore the unpredictability and risk involved. So also with war. In 1745, the Merchant Adventurers of Bristol successfully encouraged the city MPs to press for a more powerful warship to provide nearby protection against French privateers, not least because the insurers did not think the current one adequate.[4]

These and other factors stand as a reproach to any focus solely on improvement, steady or otherwise. Moreover, this point underlines the need for repetition when approaching new periods of time, because repetition was a continuing factor in many respects. Linked to this, it is all-too-easy to present an *ancien régime* of travel, one in which past conditions exist to be overcome and can be neglected in discussion because what is of interest is the causes, course and consequences of change. The last will attract attention, and the change indeed was impressive. Thus, Liverpool's Old Dock, built in 1705–15, was the world's first enclosed dock and could accommodate up to 100 ships. This very much meant that Chester would be in the shadows.

First, however, it is appropriate to draw attention to caveats and context, both of which owed more to continuity. This point is underlined if, as in this book, the eighteenth century is divided between two chapters because, rather than the century as a whole being one of transformation, this was more truly the case with the second half. Systemic constraints emerged clearly in 1745–6 in the eventually successful attempt to destroy the Jacobite army. On 17 March, William, 2nd Earl of Albemarle, an experienced commander, wrote from Aberdeen:

'You happy Londoners may be surprised at our long stay here, but the deep snow, bad weather, and consequently bad roads, and, above all these difficulties, contrary winds keeping our provisions and necessaries coming from Leith [by sea] had obliged His Royal Highness [William, Duke of Cumberland], against his will, to it.'[5]

Coal supplies were also an issue, coal being shipped to Montrose 'and so along the coast to Aberdeen.'[6] By April, with the rivers dropping, it proved possible to ford the Spey.

Water routes, both coastal and internal, remained particularly favourable for the movement of heavy or bulky goods, for which road transport was inadequate and/or expensive. Thus, the Severn was the major north-south route for freight in the West Midlands, and was particularly important for the movement downriver of coal from the East Shropshire coalfield. Goods carried upstream included products from outside Britain, such as wine, Baltic timber, and, from further afield, tea, sugar, spices, tobacco and citrus fruit, most of which had been transhipped at Bristol (although Gloucester was also a transhipment point), including from elsewhere in Britain. Tributaries, such as the Warwickshire Avon for the Severn, further extended river systems, while also ensuring the need for bridges, ferries, or fords.

The river system, however, had many deficiencies. Rivers did not always supply the necessary links, for example between Somerset and both Devon and Dorset, while many were not navigable, transport was often only easy downstream, and many rivers were obstructed by mills and weirs. Moreover, the un- or poorly-controlled flow of water ensured that spring thaws and autumn floods could bring problems, by sending rivers into spate, while, in the summer, due to lower rainfall, they could be too shallow to use; this was a particular problem in the upper parts of rivers. Thus, in the North Riding of Yorkshire, the navigable rivers – the Tees, Ouse and Derwent – were all on its boundaries, while the Swale, Esk and Rye were too swift, shallow or liable to flood for navigation. As a result, lead from the western dales had to be moved overland to the Tees ports, an expensive process.

Wales provides clear instances of limitations. In the 1720s, the Bishop of Bangor could only visit his diocese in north Wales on horseback and not in a carriage. In 1735, John Campbell of Calder (Cawdor), MP for Pembrokeshire and possessor of estates there and in Scotland, wrote to his son:

'On Sunday there came here … two Highlanders in Highland clothes without breeches, with long swords and each a pistol stuck in his girdle, they brought your uncle Philipps eight dogs…. The Highlanders came by Shrewsbury, through Montgomeryshire and Cardiganshire. The people in England were very civil to them and pleased with their dress, but when they came some miles into Wales the people were afraid of them and the folks of the inns would not have given them lodging. They were forced when they came into an inn to say that they would pay for what they had and to behave themselves civilly and, so doing, they would not be turned out of a public house, saying this with their pistols in their hands frightened the folks into compliance, or else they have lain under the hedges, and maybe got no victuals.'[7]

Land communications were faster and more reliable than the alternatives, even in snow, but, by later standards, were generally slow, variable and unreliable to an extent that it is difficult for modern readers, accustomed to carefully-modelled and maintained roads and bridges, and mechanised transportation, to appreciate. The series of legislation passed in the shape of Highways Acts was instructive, including Acts in 1695, 1696, 1707, 1710, 1714, 1715, 1718, 1733, 1741, 1742, 1747 and 1753. This legislation included provisions against heavy wagons, thus fixing a limit of 'six horses, or other beasts, except up hills,' or 'to refrain all waggoners, carriers, and others, for drawing any carriage with more than five horses in length. The 1753 Act was 'for the preventing of the inconveniences and dangers that may arise from the present methods of digging gravel, sandy stone, chalk, and other materials, on the several commons and waste grounds within this kingdom, for the repair of the highways, and for other purposes.'

The theme was picked up in fiction. Arriving in Henry Fielding's play *The Intriguing Chambermaid* (1733), Goodall complains: 'This cursed stage-coach from Portsmouth hath fatigued me more than my voyage from the Cape of Good Hope.' In Fielding's *Miss Lucy in Town* (1742), Mrs Midnight is told by a servant 'a gentleman and lady to enquire for lodgings; they seem to be just come out of the country, for the coach and horses are in a terrible dirty pickle.' They would have been spattered with mud. In *Tom Jones* (1749), Mrs Western 'had lately remitted the trespass of a stage-coachman, who had overturned her post-chaise into a ditch' and she had been robbed by a highwayman.[8] As so often, Fielding is blunter in *Amelia* (1751): 'by the overturning of a chaise ... her lovely nose was beat all to pieces',[9] which was a major event for the protagonist, rather than being an aside for a minor character.

Problems of a different type were highlighted in the *Leeds Mercury* of 12 April 1743: 'Jacob Newton, a hawker of the *Leeds Mercury* was attacked about a mile from Nantwich ... and robbed ... and almost killed ... for selling and distributing the said newspapers.'

Nevertheless, there were claims that the press exaggerated the hazards of travel: 'your domestic fables of assaults upon stage-coaches and skirmishes of highwaymen.'[10] Moreover, it would be mistaken to ignore the extent and use of the pre-turnpike road system, nor the degree to which, as long as there had not been heavy rainfall, most roads were passable, even in winter,[11] although in December 1725 snows meant that there was no mail in Leeds and therefore no news for the newspaper.

Although sometimes reluctant to travel to Westminster to attend to Parliamentary duties,[12] the gentry travelled widely for social purposes, not least attending races[13] and the assizes, and for hunting. Sir Roger Newdigate of Arbury wrote to his wife in December 1745 about a journey in the difficult Weald and Midlands, indicating that in the harshest season of the year roads were still in the last resort passable:

'At five this morning we set out and bated at Grinstead and Uckfield, the roads very bad but much worse from thence, about twice as deep as the deepest slough to Coton Church, but no ways dangerous.'[14]

So also the previous month with the march of an army from Newcastle westward to Hexham en route toward Carlisle, a route affected by very heavy snow on 'miserable roads.'[15] The army got to Hexham and stopped in part due to transport problems but largely because Carlisle had fallen to the Jacobites. Subsequently, that army having marched south advanced back north, its commander writing from near Wetherby: 'We are going forward to Newcastle, as fast as the bad roads and this rigorous season will admit of.'[16]

The Highways Act of 1715 clarified the powers of the parochial Surveyors of the Highways. However, there was to be no technological or engineering innovation to transform the road surface in the early eighteenth century.

Furthermore, where bridges already existed, they were often poorly maintained. Alongside lists that suggest steady improvement contributing to a Transport Revolution and toward the Industrial Revolution, it is worth noting episodes that lead towards a different conclusion. Thus, the group of bridges over the watercourses of the River Otter at Fenny Bridges on the major route east of Exeter toward London, a route used by the Romans, were reported as in a poor state of repair to the Quarter Sessions in 1704. The parishioners of Gittisham were able to show that the parish was too poor to carry out the necessary repairs, and when the Sessions provided £15, requests from other parishes for help with their bridges led the Sessions to withdraw the grant. A report was ordered, but none was made until 1711 when the court was told that a local landowner, Lady Kirkham, had conveyed nearby land in trust to provide funds for bridge repairs. However, the trustees declared that the profits from the land were insufficient and claimed to be responsible for the bridges in Feniton parish and not also in Gittisham, an interpretation that was challenged.

The court took the charity into its hands, but it was not until 1723 that the trustees provided the accounts ordered in 1714. Deciding that they had money in hand that should have been used for bridge repairs, the magistrates ordered the trustees to pay it into court, but the trustees refused and the administration of the trust was not settled by the High Court of Chancery until 1750, the year in which Dr. Richard Pococke recorded being delayed several hours by the road flooding. A new brick arch bridge was built at Fenny in 1769, but it had to be rebuilt in 1809 after complaints in 1797 and an indictment of the county in 1806 for not keeping the bridge in repair.[17]

This story could be repeated elsewhere for bridges, roads and other transport improvements; as well as more generally for industrialization and agriculture. Transport played a repeated role in local disputes, as in 1737 when Thomas Hill of Tern, a prominent Shropshire landowner, lost his temper with Joseph Gee, who had a lease from him to operate a forge and mills on a river near his house. The carters who used the road in front of Tern Hill to reach these, finding the road surface spoilt by wet weather, sought a better surface across Hill's land which led him to close the gate. Gee objected that he had been cut 'off from a road which had been a way time out of mind,' and Hill reopened it. The responsibility of the parish to repair the road to Hill's house proved part of the dispute, while the issue of the line of the road in front of the house was still a matter for discussion in 1758.[18] Such problems have to be recalled rather than the uncomplicated account of progress that is too often offered. The focus on action after 1750 in the cases above is also instructive.

Until the 1750s, when a period of canal construction began, the improvement of rivers took precedence over canals, with peaks of activity in the late 1690s and in 1719–21. In *Reasons for making the River Avon Navigable from Bristol to Bath*, an undated flysheet, the case was made for an improvement that was to be by 1727:

'Bristol and Bath are situate in a rich soil, but surrounded by a mountainous country; so that land carriage is very chargeable and difficult, and therefore not only weighty, but light and bulky things are there carried on horseback, or on men's shoulders ... the neighbouring counties of Gloucester, Wiltshire etc find it more easy to bring goods fourscore miles from London, than twenty from Bristol. Whereas if this river be made navigable, it will open such a prospect for trade in all the adjacent counties ... silence those who take advantage from their being locked in, and enclosed by rocks and mountains, for enhancing the prices of all necessaries.'[19]

The improvement owed a lot to Ralph Allen (1693–1764), who made money from his contracts with the Post Office before purchasing quarries of Bath stone at Combe Down and Bathampton. The river improvement ensured that the stone could be transported to Bristol and beyond. In about 1730, Allen had a wooden railway constructed on the Tyneside model using it to bring stone from his quarries on Combe Down to an Avon wharf at Widcombe. This stone in part served to support the expansion of Bath. The carriages were powered by horses and controlled by brakemen with the spoked wheels early examples of the use of iron for this purpose. Allen also built a country house at Prior Park, Bath.[20]

The Yare was made more navigable between Great Yarmouth and Norwich, helping Norfolk's grain exports and the movement of coal from north east England via Great Yarmouth to Norwich. The funds had been made available by a 1698 Act providing for tolls for coal traffic using the Yare with the money for river improvements and for harbour works at Great Yarmouth where goods were transhipped onto smaller ships for the journey upriver.

A Wear Improvement Bill failed in 1706 but a successful one was passed in 1717, establishing the River Wear Commissioners who improved the habour.[21] Work on the Mersey to improve navigation to Manchester began in 1724, the Douglas between Wigan and the sea was opened to navigation in 1742, and improvements in the Weaver helped Cheshire's economy. The river was a substitute for the movement by packhorse of coal from Lancashire and North Staffordshire to the mid-Cheshire salt industry. The Weaver was unreliable for navigation, and four bills were brought before Parliament between 1711 and 1720 with improvement in mind, only for the first three to be thwarted by the overland carriers as well as the concerns of riverside farmers over fishing rights and possible flooding. The 1720 Bill, in contrast, succeeded the following year and provided for the construction of twelve locks on the Weaver, which was to be funded by tolls. The 22.5 mile navigation was opened in 1731, with the boats hauled by men until a tow path was opened in 1792, permitting the use of horses. Other Acts of 1721 and 1734 opened the way for extension of the system on the Weaver to Nantwich and on the Dane tributary to Middlewich, but neither was done.[22]

Thirty-four Acts for river improvement were passed between 1689 and 1727, and the mileage of navigable rivers in England rose from 685 in 1660 to 1,160 in 1725. The general theme was one of improvement, not least as a way to escape the cyclical pattern of history, the *Honest True Briton* of 22 May 1724 declaring

'Empires and kingdoms, how flourishing and powerful soever, are not immortal. All lesser states have the same uncertain fate attending them: and as nothing but numbers of people industriously employed in trade and manufactories in husbandry and navigation can build up a mighty empire; so nothing can preserve and prolong it, but the continuance of the same methods by which it was raised.'

The Fossdyke between Lincoln and the Trent, built by the Romans, was restored in 1740–4. The improvement of the Witham to Lincoln was largely complete by 1770. In 1731, Alexander Pope referred to rolling 'obedient rivers through the land.' In practice, the possibilities for improving rivers were very much determined by the courses of the latter, although still involving rival economic and political interests, as with the River Dee in Cheshire in 1732–4[23] or Great Yarmouth taking most of the money that could have been spent on the Yare until an Act specifying that the port should only have 40 per cent.

There were also setbacks, with projects taking longer than anticipated or proving more difficult. Thus, in April 1719 an Act was passed 'for enlarging the time' granted by legislation of the late 1690s 'for cleansing and making navigable the channel from The Hythe at Colchester to Wivenhoe; and for making the said Act more effectual.' The Hampshire Avon, not a major river, was improved from 1675 to enable commercial navigation from Salisbury to the sea at Christchurch, but the link was not possible after 1715 and by 1744 two unsuccessful attempts had been made to re-establish the route.[24] Aside from such work on, for example dredging, towing paths were constructed along rivers to permit the replacement of human bow haulers by horses.

Whatever the level of improvement, river transport could be hazardous. Appointed Bishop of St Asaph, Thomas Tanner, the Dean of Norwich, travelled to Wales by sea to London, up the Thames to Oxford and then overland to North Wales. His goods included huge quantities of his manuscripts and books, but the barges ran aground in Abingdon, probably having been swamped by a storm. Once dried, they were taken, probably by packhorse, to Wales. The Thames remained significant as a river system, as for the wheat sold at Reading market in 1734 mostly en route to export from London.[25]

There was also an incremental process on the roads. Early turnpike trusts dealt largely with repairs, highly significant as they were, rather than the construction of new roads. Many trusts, such as the Bath Trust, which was established in 1707, had considerable success in improving the situation. At the same time, early turnpikes did not necessarily make a change to the speed or cost of road services, while non-turnpike roads remained important, and crucially so in local economies. In the British Isles as a whole, although Arthur Young's works suggest that even local roads were improving from the 1770s, much of the dense network of local routes changed little during the century, in quality, direction or use. Many roads essentially remained bridleways, although these could have been fit-for-purpose however much that assessment might involve value judgments. When new roads were constructed, they usually followed existing routes.

Although parliamentary legislation, such as the Westmorland Roads Act, Bedford and Buckingham Roads Act, Warminster Roads Act,

Yorkshire Roads Act, and Wiltshire Roads Act, all passed in March 1742, provided the enabling framework, most transport schemes were not state-planned or directed. Whereas today a large number of parliamentary Acts would be seen as evidence of central government activity, in the eighteenth century, and certainly as far as transport was concerned, they were largely a product of local or private initiatives. With no equivalent to the role of Continental governments and, until 1919 no ministry of transport, the investment capital and planning decisions were largely private. Thus, there was no need to fight other calls on the public purse and yet it was possible to tap national wealth. Turnpikes also transferred the cost of roads from local inhabitants to road users. Reliance on private capital was also to make it easier to transfer from canal to rail, as canals, like turnpikes, were a state public/private enterprise, with the financing private and the authorisation public.

Initially, trusts were given powers and responsibilities for twenty-one years, but this was subsequently extended, in order to keep an effective system going and also to encourage investment by offering a longer term for revenue. The decision to establish trusts reflected confidence in the financial return and the security of the property and capital invested, and thus in the economic prospects, of transport links. The availability of investment capital was crucial. In many respects, therefore, turnpike trusts were a consequence of economic health and a testimony to a confidence in the future that came from local communities, and a good example, to use modern language, of public/private enterprise. As later with canals and railways, not all turnpike schemes were implemented, while some were not effective. Moreover, early trusts sometimes lacked the capital for investment. Nevertheless, turnpiked roads benefited from more expenditure than their counterparts, and were therefore generally better, and often far better.

However, with both canals and rail, the absence of central planning contributed to mixed-gauge development which lessened the possibility of effective integration. So also did competition between companies. To a degree, the lack of effective integration combined with competition helped lessen profitability and thus the possibility of fresh investment.

The co-operation between parliamentary authorisation and local charge-levying bodies, reflected the absence of a national road policy, let alone a transport ministry. Unlike elsewhere in Europe, for example France, Prussia, Russia and Spain, the government played only a small direct role in road construction. This role was particular to the Scottish Highlands, where the army built about 250 miles of road between 1726 and 1738 to aid a rapid response to any Jacobite rising. As with the enclosure of agricultural land, the possibility of creating turnpike trusts was thus a permissive national policy, not a prescriptive one. Rather than following some master plan, the road system came in large part to reflect the degree of dynamism of individual trusts, and the ability of particular routes to produce revenue. The last was essentially a consequence of the strength of the regional economy and the role of the route in intra-regional communications. Although trusts reflected local initiatives, a national turnpike system was created, but this was due to commercial opportunity in defining necessary and profitable links, not national planning.

Economic trends helped. From the mid-1740s, sustained population growth led to a rapid rise in the price of food, as well as to demand increasing the need for, and profitability of, more predictable and rapid transport. High yields could be combined with high prices, unlike earlier when more limited population growth had helped keep prices down causing serious problems in the agrarian economy in the 1720s and 1730s. As agricultural wages in the 1740s or, indeed more generally, did not rise greatly, demand for food increased the prosperity of farmers as well as rental income. This situation provided more money for agricultural improvement and encouraged investment in it. That in transport was in part an aspect of this more general situation.

By 1750, a sizeable network of new turnpikes, radiating from London, had been created. London and north-west England were well linked, with the road to Chester and both roads to Manchester turnpiked for most of their length. A spur from the Chester road had been turnpiked to Shrewsbury in 1725. By 1750, three routes from Yorkshire to Manchester were also turnpiked, as were the routes from London to Bath, Canterbury and Portsmouth. In Lincolnshire, the Great North Road was turnpiked from Grantham northwards in 1726 and from Grantham to Stamford in 1739; the year in which a trust was also authorised for the road from Lincoln to Baumber.[26] That relatively minor Lincolnshire village benefited from this and is still on the A158, the major route from Lincoln to eastern

Lincolnshire. At the same time, the use of the term network or system has to take note of tensions and rivalries between trusts. Complaints by neighbouring trusts about stretches of the same road were frequent.

Newspaper distribution networks developed rapidly in this period, both for London newspapers circulating across England and for provincial newspapers, a form that began in the early 1700s. These networks made use of turnpikes but also indicated the value of the broader road system. In 1737, the *Weekly Courant*, a newspaper published in Nottingham, advertised an extensive regional network, being sold in Ashbourne, Burton-upon-Trent, Chesterfield, Derby, Doncaster, Gainsborough, Mansfield, Melton Mowbray, Newark, Sheffield, Southwell and Uttoxeter. For the *York Courant* agents were named in Scarborough, Malton, Wakefield, Hull, Beverley and Doncaster.[27] And so also for books, with the *Newcastle Journal* of 19 July 1740 advertising the selling of *A New History of Jamaica* by named agents in Newcastle, Stockton, Durham, Penrith, Carlisle, Richmond, Alnwick and Berwick and by unnamed counterparts in Edinburgh, Glasgow and Dumfries.

In Ireland, turnpike trusts constructed a number of new arterial routes in the 1730s and 1750s, and they affected the relative position of towns. When the road from Naas to Maryborough was turnpiked in 1731, Kildare found itself on the new main route between Dublin and the south-west and benefited accordingly. Many turnpikes improved road maintenance and widened roads so they could take wheeled vehicles moving at speed, which led to the spread of such traffic. In contrast, walkers turned to 'turnpike tracks' in order to bypass the tolls, but that was essentially the recourse of the poor.

Nevertheless, as in agriculture and industry, although with significant differences, compared with what was to come, the 1730s and 1740s were decades of limited progress. For example, at that point, the already bad communication system in Wales arising from the limited nature of inland waterways looked as though it would receive no improvement by road; while improvements in England, although far greater in scale and impact, were still limited. Thus, no trusts covering any of Devon were authorised until 1753.[28] The Exeter Trust set up that year was to have oversight of the later Countess Wear Bridge Trust responsible for building a bridge near Exeter. More generally, at this stage, the surface of turnpikes scarcely matched those associated with John McAdam.

Non-turnpike roads remained important, crucially so in local economies, and much of the dense network of local routes changed little during the century, in quality, direction or use. For example, North Devon had poor land links and was largely dependent on shipping. In Henry Fielding's play *An Old Man taught Wisdom* (1734), the lawyer Wornwood reaches Goodwill's rural house through roads that 'are very dirty,' a reference to the mud. In *Tom Jones*, in Squire Western's Somerset neighbourhood, the bad roads deter visiting by coach.[29] Many roads essentially remained bridleways.

The weather very much affected both the roads and travellers. Thus, in *Tom Jones*, Mrs Waters and Ensign Northerton set off from Worcester 'on foot; for which purpose the hardness of the frost was very seasonable.'[30] As with the two lawyers who sought shelter in the novel *Joseph Andrews* (1742), 'a violent shower of rain' could lead horsemen to seek shelter.[31] The multiplicity of factors that could affect travellers was seen when Dowling pressed Tom Jones:

'to go no further that night; and backed his solicitations with many unanswerable arguments, such as, that it was almost dark, that the roads were very dirty, and that he would be able to travel much better by day-light'.[32]

Jones insists on setting out for Coventry by night, only for the guide to get lost and rain to come on. If not walking, riding horseback rather than in a carriage was still normal, as at the end of *Joseph Andrews*:

'The company were ranged in this manner: the two old people, with their two daughters, rode in the coach; the Squire, Mr Wilson, Joseph, Parson Adams, and the pedlar proceeded on horseback'.[33]

There was also the continued impact of social distinctions. Thus, in *Joseph Andrews*, there is a dispute over who can gain entry into a stagecoach:

'Mrs Graveairs insisting, against the remonstrance of all the rest, that she would not admit a footman into the coach, for poor Joseph was too lame to mount a horse. A young lady who was, as it seems, an Earl's grand-daughter, begged it, with almost tears in her eyes … but all to no purpose. She [Miss Graveairs] said she would not demean herself to ride with a footman: that there were waggons on the road; that if the master of the coach desired it, she would pay for two places, but would suffer no such fellow to come in. 'Madam,' says Slipslop, 'I am sure no-one can refuse another coming into a stage-coach.' 'I don't know, madam,' says the lady; 'I am not much used to stage-coaches; I seldom travel in them.' 'That may be madam,' replied Slipslop; 'very good people do; and some people's betters for aught I know'.[34]

Those who could not afford to travel by carriage and who did not find wagons available, had to resort to a variety of means that focused on walking.[35] Fielding described one at length, possibly because some of his readers did not know of it, but also so as to make a moral point:

'to ride and tie – a method of travelling much used by persons who have but one horse between them, and is thus performed. The two travellers set out together, one on horseback, the other on foot: now as it generally happens that he on horseback outgoes him on foot, the custom is that when he arrives at the distance agreed on, he is to dismount, tie the horse to some gate, tree, post, or other thing, and then proceed on foot; when the other comes up to the horse, he unties him, mounts, and gallops on till, having passed by his fellow-traveller, he likewise arrives at the place of tying. And this is that method of travelling so much in use among our prudent ancestors, who knew that horses had mouths as well as legs, and that they could not use the latter without being at the expense of suffering the beasts themselves to use the former. This was the method in use in those days when, instead of a coach and six, a Member of Parliament's lady used to mount a pillion behind her husband, and a grave sergeant-at-law condescended to amble to Westminster on an easy pad with his clerk kicking his heels behind him.'[36]

Tom Jones is not alone in being happy to walk:

'Mrs Waters was not of that delicate race of women who are obliged
to the invention of vehicles for the capacity of removing themselves
from one place to another, and with whom consequently a coach is
reckoned among the necessaries of life. Her limbs were indeed full
of strength and agility, and as her mind was no less animated with
spirit, she was perfectly able to keep pace with her nimble lover'.[37]

From the mid-eighteenth century, the road system was further enhanced
by a marked increase in the number of bridges, the most marked for several
centuries. Stone bridges replaced wooden ones and ferries, improving the
load-bearing capacity and reliability of the system. Existing bridges were
widened, and new and wider bridges erected with large spans, which thus
made navigation easier for boats and also reduced the water, storm and
accident damage to bridges.

The importance of London and the availability of resources was shown
with the building of bridges there and nearby. Several replaced ferries.
Across the Thames, bridges were built in Fielding's lifetime at Putney
(1729), Westminster (1738–50), Walton (1750), and Hampton Court
(1753). Bridge building was not restricted to the London area, although
the second half of the century was far more important than the first, and
no new bridges were built across the Severn between 1540 and 1772.
In 1754, Cambridge's Great Bridge was rebuilt in stone, as was the Old
Bath Bridge. The significance of bridges contributed to the prominence
of nodal points in the transport system, for example Upton on Severn
in *Tom Jones*; a novel in which alternative routes for the protagonists
played a major role.

Old inns were rebuilt or extended, and new inns were built. Travel-
narratives offered much of a role for inns and innkeepers, and therefore
for contrasts between them, inns providing both the causes of actions
and the setting for action, and Fielding ran a full range in both, from
brawls to conversation. Inns were particularly significant in his stories as
providing opportunities to bring together people of different backgrounds
and beliefs and thus for his mastery of a narrative of contingencies. The
whole was policed by innkeepers some of whom were presented as rogues,
or, at least, far from being considerate hosts. In *Tom Jones*, the landlady
in Upton on Severn is shown as very concerned with her reputation:

'at a house of exceedingly good repute, whither Irish ladies of strict virtue, and many northern lasses of the same predicament, were accustomed to resort in their way to Bath. The landlady therefore would by no means have admitted any conversation of a disreputable kind to pass under her roof. Indeed so foul and contagious are all such proceedings, that they contaminate the very innocent scenes where they are committed, and give the name of a bad house, or of a house of ill repute, to all those where they are suffered to be carried on'.[38]

Explaining her harsh treatment of Mrs Waters, the landlady remarks:

'where gentry come and spend their money, I am not willing that they should be scandalized by a set of poor shabby vermin, that wherever they go, leave more lice than money behind them; such folks never raise my compassion: for to be certain, it is foolish to have any for them, and if our justices did as they ought, they would be all whipt out of the kingdom.'[39]

Inns provided horses for travellers, but, as Tom Jones discovered at Upton, these could be taken up by those who came first, obliging the others to wait or walk,[40] and thus providing more space for the narrative. Separately, in *Jonathan Wild* (1749), Fielding refers to travelling near Bath, at length arriving at: 'some vile inn, where he finds no kind of entertainment nor conveniency for repose'.[41] Inns were also important for highwaymen and other criminals, two of the former being seized while in bed at the Bear in Burwash, Sussex in 1749.[42]

Meanwhile, like the perpetually rising middle class, the sense of a national economy grew stronger. Writing in the *Newcastle Journal* of 19 July 1740, 'Philalethes' portrayed the grain market as nationally linked: 'London (which place governs the value of all grain in England) ... all the markets in England have a natural dependence on each other, and expect a mutual assistance.' Yet, such transport improvements posed problems, with food shortages and prices reflecting the subordination of local markets to the exigencies of national ones. There were riots near Poole against grain exports in 1737. In 1740, prices rose after rain at harvest-time in 1739, the severe 1739 winter, and then three months of drought. The poor in the North-East suffered and broke into granaries in Newcastle before taking over much of the town until intimidated by troops.[43] At Stockton, the shipping of grain was blocked until the local MPs arranged for the grain to be purchased for sale to the poor at prices they could afford.

Power, local as well as national, as well as boosterism, were involved in plans to a degree not captured by reference simply to the scale of activity. In 1749, William Wood noted 'The Duke of Bedford has had a contest with Lord Halifax and others upon a road-bill in the House of Commons,' contesting it through their allies there; while a decade later the editor of the *Union Journal or Halifax Advertiser* suggested that a road be built from Halifax via Sheffield to Mansfield in order to make travel from Halifax to London easier, and thereby attract routes thither to go via Halifax.[44] Potential was the key point. Tolls helped explain opposition, as in 1740 when the inhabitants of Hedworth and Monkwearmouth petitioned for exemption from the tolls for a proposed turnpike from Durham to Tyne Bridge.[45] Four years later, the proposed Newcastle-Alnwick turnpike, part of any route to Edinburgh, faced 'many difficulties' as a result of private interests.[46]

Greater national integration as a result of improved communications can be seen in the rise, at a time of low inflation, of Post Office revenues from £116,000 in 1698 to £210,000 in 1755 as new routes were founded – for example Exeter to Chester via Bristol from 1700 – or became more frequent, as the London to Bristol and Birmingham services were in the 1740s. The improved postal services enabled learned societies such as the Spaulding Gentlemen's Society to play a major role in corresponding with others, as that Society did, especially in the 1730s and 1740s.[47]

Looking to the future, coal and iron, or at least coalmining and ironworking, led the way with the technology and practice of rail traffic. Indeed, without steam locomotion, wagonways had existed for many years, with horses drawing wagons along wooden, later, from 1767, cast iron rails, especially from the collieries to the coal-loading staithes on the Rivers Tyne and Wear in North-East England, but also elsewhere. Other products, such as stone, were also carried.

It was no surprise that the North-East of England was the forcing-house in the creation of rail use. In 1700 the North-East had nearly half the national output of coal of about 3 million tons. It was also the crucial source of coal for London and intermediate ports, such as King's Lynn and Great Yarmouth, with the coal shipped from the Tyne and, to a lesser extent, the Wear. The average annual amount of coal shipped from the Tyne rose from just over 400,000 tons in the 1660s to well over 600,000 by 1730–1, and to nearly 800,000 tons in the 1750s.

The movement of this coal was the key basis for railway developments, which initially did not involve locomotive steam engines, although stationary steam engines were used to pump water out of pits. Wagonways were developed to link coalfields to riverside wharves. The horse-drawn wagons ran on wooden wheels, which were later flanged (ribbed for strength and guiding). Horses were also used to provide the pull on canals. Indeed, they linked rails, roads and canals. In 1725, Thomas Coryat, who was in the party of Edward, 2nd Earl of Oxford, an inveterate traveller, observed from the mines near Chester-le-Street, County Durham:

'towards Newcastle we pass over two way leaves [rights of way] which cross the great road. These way leaves are an artificial road made for the conveyance of coal from the pit to the staithes on the riverside; whereby one horse shall carry a greater burden than a whole team on a common way… the loaded cart goes upon one, and the empty one returns upon the other. The whole length of these two way leaves from the coal pits to the place from whence the coals are loaded into the lighters or keels at Sunderland [on the River Wear], is five miles.'

In 1725–6, the first railway bridge in the world, Causey Arch, was built for the movement of Durham coal across the Causey Burn towards the wharves on the River Tyne. It had the largest span of any bridge built in Britain since Roman times, and the architect had to work from Roman models. After the formation of the Grand Alliance of leading coal-mining families in the North-East in 1726, a process of sharing and rationalising existing wagonways and of improving the system led to an increase in the length of wagonways and thus in their efficiency. This was to be more generally the case subsequently with railways. In 1720, the first railway in Scotland was opened. It went from the Tranent coal mines east of Edinburgh to the Firth of Forth, from where the coal could be shipped, in particular southwards towards English markets. Yet, the line was only 2.5 miles long and (as in England) relied on wooden rails, gravity and horses.[48]

It was not until the application of steam power that such railways could develop into anything other than feeders to existing water links and, in particular, become a long-distance network of their own. Steam power helped not only on level terrain but also to confront slopes, and the latter was a key advantage over waterways.

The imagination of transport in this period was affected by an engagement with the new, one celebrated in Richard Wilson's depiction on canvas of the building of Westminster Bridge, the second in the London area. The new vistas that were possible from or including the bridge were a potent reminder of the possibilities for change. So also with discussion of new river improvements or turnpikes. Many schemes did not result in action, or at least at this stage, but they all contributed to a novel degree of an awareness that transport could change and across the country. At the same time, turnpike tolls were a potent reminder of the social cost of improvement.

The extent to which trade was important to politics and policy contributed to the emphasis on transport.[49] This was related to a stress on a commercial, market solution to socio-economic issues including food supply. Demand for transport had in this sense an important political component, and was an aspect of a broader public accountability. So also with the enforced integration of the British Isles (though Dublin retained a separate parliament) as a result of the 'Glorious Revolution' and the defeat of Jacobitism. Scotland benefited from Union and its sheltered position within the British imperial state with the rising fortunes of the cattle, tobacco and linen trades of particular significance.[50] Cattle droving to England increased with the Union of 1707, from about 30,000 yearly to perhaps 80,000 yearly in the 1750s. The profit spread the benefit of the Union widely.

The transport of information was an aspect not just of profitability, with business letters conveying news on prices and markets, and more generally, notably with newspapers and books. There was also a more widespread flow of information as part of an increase not only in its supply but also in innovations in the methods of handling it as part of information systems. Statistics were an aspect and form of this transport of information, and they contributed to its use in what was defined as orderly, rational decision-making.[51] The transport of information was crucial to the interconnectedness of experience that was important for society,[52] while production for exchange, a commodity-based capitalist economy, depended on transport, as did the related unlocking of opportunity through credit.

Chapter 5

Turnpikes and Canals, 1750–1800

'A letter from Cirencester, Gloucestershire, says: "A navigable work of a most arduous and extensive nature is now carrying on in this neighbourhood, which is nothing less than a junction between the Thames and Severn. In this undertaking a prodigious mountain, of more than two miles and a half in length, will be cut through so that barges of 50 or 70 tons' burthen may pass. Near two miles of this subterraneous work are nearly finished, and the whole navigation, which is nearly thirty miles long, is expected to be finished in a year and a half. When completed, London will have a grand inland navigation with almost all parts of England and Wales, so that the trade thereupon must be immense. The people near the part of it that is already finished feel its good effects by a considerable reduction in the price of coals".' *Newcastle Chronicle*, 6 January 1787.

There was large-scale expansion in the transport infrastructure in this half-century, indeed to an unprecedented extent. While the novelty of new routes in a short period had been seen with the first half century of Roman rule, the latter did not cover the entire British Isles. Moreover, the coverage of the turnpike system by 1800 was greater than that of Roman roads. So also, by a far greater extent, with bridges, canals, river improvements and harbour facilities. If the Romans are taken out of the equation, then there was nothing even to suggest as a prefiguring comparison with the situation in the half-century from 1750.

The standard government emphasis was on the significance of trade, as in 1753 when Thomas, Duke of Newcastle, one of the two Secretaries of State, observed: 'The power and influence of this country depends upon the extent of our trade.'[1] This focus was on international trade but there was a corollary in the shape of support for domestic trade.

In contrast to the situation with turnpikes earlier in the century, there was substantial expansion in the 1750s and 1760s, so that, by 1770, when there were 15,000 miles of turnpiked roads in England, most of it was within 12.5 miles of one. After 1751, it became easier to obtain Turnpike Acts which was important in ensuring further improvement and maintenance, turnpike trusts developed better ways of raising capital, and, by 1770, a network of turnpikes radiated from major provincial centres.[2] The first turnpike from Chichester was begun in 1749, and, by 1779, the city was the junction of four turnpikes, which led to an increase in overland trade from West Sussex to London, and a relative decline in the longer sea route. The first Devon trust, the Exeter Trust, was established in 1753, and was rapidly followed by many others, notably the Tiverton Trust in 1758, the Totnes and Bridgetown Pomeroy Trust in 1759, and the Barnstaple one in 1763, leading to major improvements. The first trust in Cornwall, to turnpike the Falmouth-Truro road, was established in 1754. Birmingham benefited from the convergence of improved routes: the Bromsgrove (1726), Hagley (1753) and Dudley (1760) turnpikes. At this point, canal alternatives were absent.

Aside from towns as destinations, others, such as High Wycombe, benefited from being on the junction of turnpikes that were heading for major destinations. This helped ensure the infrastructure, including inns and blacksmiths, that encouraged travellers to stop. The individual consequences of turnpiked roads were different but significant, much depending on particular geographical circumstances and other transport availability.

In 1756–65, thirteen new turnpike trusts were formed for Lincolnshire and two others were enlarged. The first road in north Lincolnshire to be turnpiked was that from Lincoln to Barton on Humber in 1765, part of a system for north Lincolnshire laid out that year, that also saw the turnpiking of side-roads to Caistor and Melton Ross, as well as of a road from Louth to Gainsborough and then into Nottinghamshire, that crossed the Lincoln-Barton road. However, in December 1782, Jeremy Lister wrote from Gainsborough, an area where the roads are still poor: 'The roads are exceeding bad, the road towards Lincoln being the only one that is anything tolerable, and that in general is through very deep sand.'[3]

Turnpiking was both patchwork and yet also contributing to a system. For example, following an Act of 1764, two turnpikes improved the links to the Shropshire coalfield, while most roads between Norwich and rural Norfolk were turnpiked between 1760 and 1800.

Turnpikes could also compensate for the deficiencies in river links and the absence of canal ones. Thus, river traffic to Shrewsbury on the Severn suffered because of navigational issues and the problems caused by the use of larger vessels requiring a deeper draft. However, Shrewsbury benefited by the building of turnpikes.

The growth of London in population, activity and size made travel more difficult, encouraging the search for improvement. To make access to the City easier, while bypassing the congestion of Holborn, the 'New Road' and City Road were built from 1756 to 1761 to link Paddington and Shoreditch. The New Road, now the Marylebone, Euston and Pentonville Roads, was paid for by tolls. Urban improvement was seen more generally, with transport within towns eased by the paving, repairing, widening, cleansing, lighting and policing of the streets.[4]

Improved roads were not restricted to England. Important routes in Wales included Hereford to Brecon (1757), and on to Haverfordwest (1787), and Cardiff to Neath, and on to Carmarthen. In Montgomeryshire, a turnpike trust was authorised in 1769, as part of a route from Newtown to Aberystwyth across mountainous terrain, and the first turnpike was in use from the early 1770s. Earlier, the situation was poor, as Richard Gough noted in 1761 when crossing the Severn to Chepstow:

'We leapt the horses into a high boat: both mine took it very well both in and out: but Mr Howel's tumbled about very much, and his brother's having been hurt at a former passage, made much worse work of it…. The tides come in here exceeding strong … they [boats] could not now come within 6 yards of the shore, and the horses were up to their bellies in water … [from Pembroke] in Wales the roads steep, narrow and stony … the inns bad…. [from Caernarvon] the badness of the roads prevent travelling very fast…. [from Ruthin] as we get nearer England the roads are kept up by turnpikes and there are some new ones making.'[5]

In Ireland, an Act of 1729 established turnpike trusts, while local landlords sponsored a widespread turnpike system in the linen region of Ulster. Aside from turnpikes, there were important legislative initiatives that created the possibility for better roads in Ireland, although the travel writing of Lord Chief Baron Edward Willes leaves few illusions about problems.[6] Replacing the requirement on every landholding to supply six days of free labour to mend roads in the parish, a Road Act of 1765 allowed county grand juries to levy a charge per acre on all farming households for the repair of roads and bridges, or the construction of new ones, which had to be at least 21 feet wide. This helped lead to a major expansion and improvement of the rural road network and a welcome measure of standardisation. Further Acts in 1771–2 enabled parishes to raise an extra tax for roads and grand juries to raise funds to construct roads through unimproved regions.

These changes helped a spread of the market economy in which there was increasing diversification and commercialisation of agriculture, as with the spread of cereal cultivation and flour mills in County Tipperary from the 1760s, and in County Wexford. Manufacturing areas, such as east Ulster, provided growing markets, in this case for the barley and oatmeal of nearby counties such as Monaghan and for the young stock reared in nearby uplands. Beef, butter and salted pork were moved to Cork for use by the navy and for export. There were relatively few new markets in the first half of the century, but in the second half 200 market centres were granted patents so that little of Ireland was more than twenty kilometres from a market. Hitherto remote areas, such as West Mayo, were, for the first time, provided with markets and roads.

The Irish road system, however, was worse than that in Britain, with less extensive turnpiking than in England, while roads in Scotland and Wales were not as good as the English system. The development of turnpikes across Scotland as a whole was slower than in England and Wales. Thus, the first turnpike trust in north-east Scotland was not formed until 1795.

Turnpiking was not necessarily a solution but always at least a new context for activity. A letter in the *Reading Mercury and Oxford Gazette* of 26 October 1767 claimed the road at Henley, scarcely a town remote from London, was much worse than reported, and one in the issue of 3 February 1773 provided a letter from a Commissioner for the Reading to Newbury road to his fellow trustees urging the sacking of the surveyor for failing to keep the road in repair. Turnpike trustees were able to call upon parishes to employ part of the labour stipulated by the statues of 1555 and 1563 for road repairs (refusal could lead to action at Quarter Sessions), but most of this labour was used on parish roads.

Separately, road repair methods were often limited, for example that of ploughing up the surface in order to offer a fresh one. The Chard Trust specified this method in 1753 and 1754.[7] Problems with rainfall and drainage were such that it was joked at Taunton that it would be less expensive to make the roads navigable for boats rather than passable for coaches. To this day, there are major inundations nearby notably on Sedgemoor after heavy rain and they can affect both roads and railways. Very differently, a local report in the *Leeds Mercury* of 18 October 1794 urged new surveyors to have sledge hammers available in every parish to break up the larger stones that were lying in nearly every road and also pointed out that direction posts at crossroads were mandatory by law and therefore should be seen to. Aside from maintenance, care was an issue. On 19 January 1795, *Aris's Birmingham Gazette* reported a horse breaking it's leg in Redditch when it slipped on the ice adding: 'Persons who are so careless as to suffer the water to run from their houses into the streets in frosty weather, or who will not strew ashes over ice before their doors are certainly guilty of the most culpable negligence.

Furthermore, throughout the British Isles, many roads that were not turnpiked, for example those on the Isle of Man, remained inadequate. There were deficiencies in many parts of England. For example, North Devon had poor land links and was largely dependent on shipping. By 1800, there were still no turnpikes between Bideford and Launceston and from Ilfracombe to Lynton, while, in South Devon the district of the South Hams was poorly served. More generally, drove roads remained crucial for animals, the turkeys being tar-shod. In his play *She Stoops to Conquer* (1773), Oliver Goldsmith wrote of a rural journey 'it is a damned long, dark, boggy, dirty, dangerous way'. This was somewhat different from the preference for travelling in pursuit of the 'picturesque' character of many hilly or mountainous regions, such as the Lake District, the Peak District, the Wye Valley, and, eventually, the Scottish Highlands, as well as the literary tourism that was to take travellers to Shakespeare County and then its Scott counterpart.[8]

A sense of new possibilities was captured by Joseph Spence visiting Scotland in 1760:

> 'they laid a map of the whole country before them; first marked lines of communication from the most considerable towns to the capital, and to one another, for the benefit of commerce and travelling; made a fund of £30,000 by a subscription; and began at once with nine roads from Edinburgh, which are already branched out into above thirty. I went no farther than Glasgow … all [the roads] very good, and mostly made so within these eight years.'

In the Highlands, in contrast, roadbuilding owed much to the governmental determination to ensure a quick military response to any Jacobite rising. In 1771, Richard Gough wrote to his mother about travelling in the Highlands to Inverness and then on to Aberdeen:

> 'The roads here were made by Marshall Wade's soldiers after the last rebellion and are kept up by the country people without turnpikes: for all the materials lie so near that they have nothing to do but throw them on as fast as the winter rains wash them off … ferried across two rivers, one of two miles broad, the other of eight. We crossed the first at noon: the other between one and two this morning. We were four hours on the water and then got into a smaller boat, which soon run aground, and after waiting half an hour we were carried to shore on mens backs. The great boat with the horses did not come up till noon.'[9]

John Ainslie's 'Travelling Map of Scotland showing the distances from one stage to another' (1783) reflected the impact of turnpiking. More generally, road guides were an increasingly important aspect of publication. In 1771, David Paterson, an army cartographer, published *A New and Accurate Description of all the Direct and Principal Cross Roads in Great Britain*, the 18th and final edition appearing in 1829, soon after his death, as *Paterson's Roads*. There was also a growth of travel writing about journies within the British Isles. This could note improvement. Thus, Smollett's *The Adventures of Launcelot Greaves* (1760) began:

'It was on the great northern road from York to London, about the beginning of the month of October, and the hour of eight in the evening, that four travellers were, by a violent shower of rain, driven for shelter into a little public-house on the side of the highway.'

Yet, far from a dingy pub, this had a kitchen paved in red bricks, Windsor chairs, pewter plates, copper saucepans, and 'a cheerful fire of sea-coal blazed in the chimney.' His novel *The Expedition of Humphry Clinker* (1771) was less positive. The Bramble party set off northwards from London, fighting off highwaymen near Hatfield, and pressing on to Harrogate, in June, which was usually a good month for travel. However,

'the roads having been broke up by the heavy rains in the spring, were so rough, that although we travelled very slowly, the jolting occasioned such pain to my uncle, that he was becoming exceedingly peevish… considering the tax we pay for turnpikes, the roads of this country constitute a most intolerable grievance. Between Newark and Wetherby, I have suffered more from jolting and swinging than ever I felt in the whole course of my life, although the carriage is remarkably commodious and well hung, and the postillions were very careful in driving.'

En route from Whitby to Stockton: 'Crossing a deep gutter, made by a torrent, the coach was so hard strained, that one of the irons, which connects the frame, snapped, and the leather sling on the same side… We were eight miles distant from any place where we could be supplied with carriages … we discovered a blacksmith's forge … about half a mile … and thither the postilions made shift to draw the carriage slowly, while the company walked afoot.'

Canals led to and reflected a major sense of new potential. Having viewed the Bridgewater Canal in 1767, Joseph Banks reflected: 'Trade is opened between two very large towns [Manchester and Liverpool] before labouring under great inconveniences.' They were the second and third largest in population respectively in England in the 1810 census.

The differences in scale from the situation in the first half was striking, and this was true not only of routes but also of services. Moreover, the movement both of passengers and of freight was transformed. Although freight could be moved on the turnpikes, this transformation was largely due to the combination of turnpikes and canals. As a result, there was a combination in improvement different from that shown in the case of rail in the nineteenth century and road in the twentieth. Yet, with regard to the turnpikes and canals of 1750–1800, these largely were separate rather than producing an interacting system, for goods and passengers did not generally move between the two. In part, this reflected the canal and river-linked location of much industrial activity.

Moreover, road links were important in helping influence locations, as with militia encampments designed against possible invasions. Thus those near Salisbury in 1757, 1778 and 1779 reflected the access to much of the south coast provided by the roads that converged on Salisbury. A similar pattern was seen in militia encampments elsewhere, for example Kent.

The expansion in the late eighteenth century in turnpikes and canals was the case more generally of the economy as a whole, as well as of the population. This helped produce greater demand, but also provided a larger labour force able to fulfil the extensive requirements of building and operating transport facilities. These extended to the work necessary in order to care for horses, carriages and wagons. Relatively cheap labour was important to expansion as it also had been for Roman roads and was to be for nineteenth-century railways. The availability of capital was also significant. Despite the development of banking, capital markets were poorly developed in contrast to the situation for rail the following century, and there was not the state financial support that was to be seen with motorways.

However, the support of wealthy individuals, both landowners and industrialists, categories which often overlapped, as with the Dudley family, proved crucial. It was also possible to raise necessary subscriptions, for both canals and turnpikes. These were commercial propositions and benefited from the extent to which investment opportunities were limited. Investment in turnpikes and canals was sometimes to further personal interests in getting products to market, sometimes an investment in itself, simply to gain a return on the capital from tolls, and sometimes the investment was for public benefit. Significant capital was found, but capital was also a limiting factor. The piecemeal improvement of roads and building of canals involved speculation and boosterism as much as being demand-driven, but both were limited by the supply of capital. To a large extent, the latter provided an efficient 'network' albeit an insufficient one because of a lack of capital.

The ratio between land and water transport varied greatly, and for coastal as well as inland counties. Thus, Essex was not a canal county nor one of improving rivers, its most significant river was the Thames, and none of its ports had a major role in international trade. Although there were key secondary road nodes at Chelmsford and Colchester, the biggest node for Essex was London, which was the destination of most Essex production.

For expanding cities, in the late eighteenth century, such as Manchester, there were no systems of rapid transit and/or public transport. Instead, walking was the norm, with carriages for the more affluent. As a result, distance was a far greater issue than in cities a century later.

Road transport to a degree was encouraged by canals. Thus, after the opening of Samuel Greg's cotton mill at Quarry Bank in Cheshire south of Manchester in the 1780s, wagons carried his raw cotton and spun yarn to and from his warehouse on the Bridgewater Canal.[10]

So also with the linkage between rivers and wagonways, not only the Tyne and Wear for the coal trade, but also the Severn for the Coalbrookdale works where large iron cylinders were made for steam engines, being hauled thence to the river by horses along a wooden wagonway.

Important bridgebuilding was not only the case in the London area where Westminster Bridge (1750) was followed by Blackfriars (1769). Designed in 1775 by Thomas Farnolls Pritchard, built by local ironmasters, notably Abraham Darby III, and opened in 1781, the iron bridge erected at Coalbrookdale in Shropshire showed progress in action. It had a 120-foot span and carried the road on arched ribs springing from the bases of two vertical iron uprights. The construction details were worked out by experienced iron-founders. In an area of economic transformation, the bridge both enabled an easy crossing of the Severn Gorge and was an abrupt demonstration of new consequences and symbols, of a growth in national wealth, and of a sense of just such a change, one that, variously, was potential, embryonic and actual.[11] A site for visitors, Coalbrookdale was one of the subjects of the heroic paintings produced in praise of scientific discovery and technological advance and to record the newly-prominent in the new age of enterprise.

Elsewhere there were other prominent bridges, such as the iron, single-span Wear Bridge built by Rowland Burdon and Thomas Wilson in 1796, providing both the new lowest crossing point on the river (replacing Chester-le-Street) and the first bridge in Sunderland where it was crucial to the town's development, replacing the ferry. When built it was the longest single-span bridge in the world, and high enough for large boats to pass underneath, and did not require replacing until 1929. Burdon, a County Durham MP and banker, provided important political and financial support. Much other improvement was less dramatic but still significant. Thus, Cheshire's bridges were improved in the 1770s, with repairs as well as a new bridge across the River Bollin.

As with turnpikes, so for bridgebuilding, the second half of the century was far more important than the first. In Cambridge, the Great Bridge was rebuilt in stone in 1754. In Bath, the Old Bath Bridge was rebuilt in 1754, and Pulteney Bridge added between 1769 and 1774. A wide three-arched bridge over the Avon was opened at Bristol in 1768, while a stone bridge built at Stockton between 1764 and 1768 replaced ferries and fording points and supplanted Yarm Bridge as the lowest bridging-point on the Tees. The seven-arch English Bridge across the Severn at Shrewsbury, built in 1769–74, replaced an older bridge thought dangerous. In 1774, a new crossing over the Exe provided a bridging point below Exeter. Yet as a reminder that such processes were not free from problems, the new bridge built in Exeter to replace the overly narrow medieval one was destroyed in 1775 as the arches could not resist the powerful current of a flood. It was replaced by another in 1778, the year in which Prebends Bridge in Durham, on which construction had begun in 1772 was finished, replacing a footbridge destroyed in a flood in 1771.

No new bridges had been built across the Severn between 1540 and 1772, but, thereafter, six more were built by 1850, including at Stourport (1775) and the Iron Bridge at Coalbrookdale (1779, opened for traffic

1781).[12] The New Bridge, the second across the Clyde in Glasgow, was built in Glasgow in the 1760s, and a new bridge at Worcester in 1780. In Carrickfergus in Ulster, the wooden bridge was replaced in stone in 1740. It took a while for many bridges to be built, for example the bridges over the Trent at Gainsborough (1790–1) and Dunham (1830–2), but the direction of improvement to the infrastructure was clear. There was the replacement of old bridges that had not been able to cope with floods such as that in 1771 that destroyed the seven-arch Old Tyne Bridge in Newcastle and others on that river. In response, the mathematician Charles Hutton, in his *Principles of Bridges* (1772), argued for improved construction, notably of the arches. However, the 1781 replacement to the Old Tyne Bridge was too low for shipping and was to be replaced in the nineteenth century by the Swing Bridge. There were also aesthetic considerations. Bridges were designed as monuments to learning, taste and setting.[13]

A revolution in transport was a major component of the Industrial Revolution. In particular, coal without transport was not sufficient. Indeed, South Wales before the railway demonstrated that clearly. However, coal with transport tended to create buoyant mixed-industrial regions with large pools of labour and demand, and specialist services. Infrastructure was crucial to agricultural and industrial development, and at its simplest to get goods to markets and raw materials to manufacturers. Without effective transport systems and viable financial structures, regions could not benefit from the diffusion of new methods or from new demands. Economic activities had different requirements, and the spread of competition brought by improvements in infrastructure did not benefit all, but most of the country was affected by changes in communications and by improvements in banking facilities.

It was not until the late 1760s that the first coach in Falmouth, the most important Cornish port, was recorded. Even when roads were improved, there were still major problems. In Smollett's novel *The Expedition of Humphry Clinker* (1771), Jeremy Melford, who was accompanying on horseback the hired coach and four [horses] taking his uncle, Matthew Bramble, and the rest of the party, recorded their arrival:

'on the edge of Marlborough Downs. There one of the four horses fell, in going down hill at a round trot; and the postilion behind, endeavouring to stop the carriage, pulled it on one side into a deep rut, where it was fairly overturned.'

Controlling horses was a serious problem, one requiring skill, especially going up and down slopes. Passengers were heavily dependent on this skill, and it underlined the dangers of travel and the need to hope that the coachman was not intoxicated. Road handling varied greatly due to the nature of the road. Thus, visiting Sheffield in 1781, Sylas Neville noted: 'Roads about this town made with hard stone not enough broken like some roads in the North.' Byng found a 'bad stony road' between Manchester and Stockport.[14] Existing sources of stone were cannibalised. Thus, building the New Road to the centre of Oxford in 1769, the Botley Turnpike used stone from the northern ramparts and walls of the castle.

Because narrow wheels dug ruts, commentators from the 1750s advocated broader wheels for carriages and wagons. In the 1770s, James Sharp pressed for rollers sixteen inches wide, rather than wheels, claiming that they would consolidate the road surface and that his rollers approached the efficiency of 'railed roads' as the road and the vehicle were in effect part of the same mechanism.[15] Despite parliamentary support, such rollers were impracticable as they were cumbersome and expensive. Aside from affecting the road surface, the wheels used were significant for the amount that could be covered. On 11 January 1768, the *Reading Mercury and Oxford Gazette* noted:

'By the present state of the tolls at two different gates ... a great farmer with his great wagon, whose wheels roll a surface of 16 inches, can bring to market with six horses in one day as much corn for three-pence through one gate, as a little farmer with narrow wheels and three horses can bring through the other in four days for five shillings.'

Wagons and carts often provided merchandise only inadequate shelter, and the methods of packing and of moving heavy goods on and off carts were primitive. The road transport of freight improved with the introduction by the 1720s of fly wagons. By changing teams of horses, these could travel day and night, covering 40 miles every 24 hours. This was probably why packhorse services from London disappeared.

Yet, much was on a very different scale. On 23 May 1761, the *Bristol Chronicle, Or, Universal Mercantile Register*, a weekly launched in 1760, added named agents in Haverfordwest and Pembroke, presumably conveyed by sea, and on 20 June 1761 others due to a man on horseback: 'this paper will, for the future, be constantly vended through … Chepstow, Newport, Raglan, Abergavenny, Pontypool and Caerleon, by John Powell … [who] will deliver any message or small parcel if properly directed and left at the printing-office.' The multilayered nature of distribution systems was captured on 5 October 1791 in the first number of the *Newark Herald and Nottinghamshire and Lincolnshire General Advertiser*, national range and local and local circulation both necessary to show that it was an intermediary between nation and locality:

'Being published early in the morning, it will be dispatched by the South Mail of that day, to London, and all the intermediate market towns; and by the North Mail, and by-posts, at two o'clock, it will be forwarded to a number of key cities, including Newcastle, Hull, Leeds, York, Liverpool, and Birmingham. In addition, in the following villages in the counties of Nottingham and Lincoln, it will be regularly published every Wednesday, free of expense, by distributors employed for that purpose; and any orders given to them will be punctually executed.'

River improvement continued. *Jackson's Oxford Journal* of 3 July 1790 included a notice of a committee meeting on the 'Thames Navigation' to consider proposals for erecting a lock near Godstow and 'ballasting the shallows' between there and Osney. However, although revived in 1754, a proposal to make the River Wear navigable from Sunderland to Durham was expensive, did not attract investors and was not started. Unlike canals which were narrow, and with still, not flowing, water, rivers were often the site of mills, many sites being long-established.

There were more canals than in the first half of the century. In 1765, Wedgwood turned to James Brindley, who had made his reputation planning this canal, to link the Trent and the Mersey. Brindley did this with the 'Grand Trunk Canal' completed in 1775. The building of the 46 mile long Staffordshire and Worcester Canal from the Trent and Mersey Canal between 1766 and 1772 added a link to the new Birmingham Canal and to the River Severn at the new port of Stourport, so that Staffordshire's coal, iron and pottery could be readily transported to the major English cities. The first coal barge arrived in Birmingham in 1772.

The system was amplified with additional links and spurs, for example the Dudley and Stourbridge canals opened in 1779 which improved links between the Severn and the Black Country.[16] Aside from the development of canal systems, there was also the digging of individual canals to create or improve particular links. For example, 1770 saw the opening of the Louth Canal, making Louth a port. Demand for coal helped to drive the growth of the canal system, and, more specifically, that of horse-drawn railways, Thomas Pennant writing of Newcastle in 1769: 'The great business of the place is the coal trade.... The coal is brought down in wagons along rail roads and discharged from covered buildings at the edge of the water into the keels of boats that are to convey it.' The absence of canals as a feeder to the rivers in this region or as a separate system helped explain the development of horse-drawn railways and later the railway in the North East.

Sir Roger Newdigate MP noted in 1767:

'A navigable canal from [the] Trent to Coventry is determin'd upon, & our surveyor is very positive it may be continued upon one level to within 6 miles of Banbury, & by locks thro' the Vale of Cherwell to the University. This is [a] great project, too great it seems for our gentry to comprehend at once, but as soon as the Coventry Canal is set about I dare say their eyes will be open'd. The advantages of it are so great it must force its way, if practicable, as we are told it is.'[17]

The Coventry Canal carried coal from the 1780s and the completion of the Oxford Canal in 1790 was followed by the advertising for sale at 'Coal Wharf' in Oxford of Warwickshire coal and Staffordshire coke, thus benefiting Newdigate interests. Horse-drawn railways were also elsewhere. The 25 mile-long Glamorganshire Canal along the Taff Valley from Merthyr Tydfil to the sea at Cardiff, constructed in 1790–4, was supplemented by 'tramroads' or feeder railways. So also from the East Shropshire coalfield to wharves on the River Severn.

The construction of horse-drawn railways for transporting led to parliamentary discussion as in the Leeds Coal Way Act of 1758. Developed by Charles Brandling who had a coal mine at Middleton, this wagon-way remained in use supplying Leeds, Ripon, and Knaresborough until 1807. This represented a transfer of North-Eastern technology, with Richard Humble, the colliery manager, coming from Northumbria. Reducing the cost of coal enabled Brandling to dominate the Leeds coal trade and by the close of the century the average annual output from Middleton was 78,500 tons. There were, however, human costs, the *Leeds Intelligencer* of 29 April 1760 reporting: 'Last Saturday, one of the coal-waggons, belonging to Charles Brandling, esq; coming down a hill, nigh Hunslet, overturned upon the driver, and crushed him so terribly, that he died a few hours later.'

And so also for other goods. The extension of the Shropshire Union Canal transported Montgomeryshire timber into the Midlands. From the 1790s, the Grand Junction Canal provided a link between the Thames at Brentford and the Midlands that eliminated the need for the long river journey to Oxford to join the earlier Oxford canal. Bath stone was moved east along the Kennet and Avon Canal, being used for churches as far as Hungerford. As with many canals, this was an instance of the linkage of rivers and canals, improvements to the two rivers in the 1720s being followed by a canal built between 1794 and 1810, with the completion of Caen Hill Locks at Devizes, a still impressive flight of 29 locks.

In 1788, George III visited the Sapperton Tunnel through which the Thames-Severn canal runs. Celebration of new links emphasised the liberating nature of transport for ordinary people. This celebration included engravings, poems and other works, including a skit on 'Come Holy Ghost, our souls inspire':

'Your Patriots I will straight inspire,
And touch them with commercial fire.'

John Watson, a Yorkshire curate, in his 1759 verses on the navigation of the River Calder, published in the *Union Journal: or Halifax Advertiser* of 27 February, had Neptune, the God of the Sea, address a Briton, then in the throes of war with France, in terms that clearly linked commercial activity to patriotism. J.F.'s 'Song on Obtaining the Birmingham and Worcester Canal Bill,' printed in *Swinney's Birmingham and Stafford Chronicle* of 4 August 1791, urged that the digging begin.

Not centred on London, canals were important in developing intra-regional links, especially between the West Midlands and Lancashire, and cutting transport costs. Thanks to the extent of British construction, the industries benefited from cheaper transport costs and more reliable links than French counterparts. The potential for regional specialisation increased, because regions that could produce goods cheaply were now better able to compete in areas with higher-cost local production. This was to be crucial to economic development, because division of labour was only effective with a high volume of production and this required a large market.

However, it would be foolish to neglect the limitations of the canal system in this period. Canals hit frequent problems in funding. In his novel *Humphry Clinker* (1771), Smollett observed 'the merchants of Glasgow have determined to make a navigable canal betwixt the two Firths, which will be of incredible advantage to their commerce, in transporting merchandise from one side of the island to the other.' Yet, although approved in 1768, the Forth and Clyde canal was left incomplete in 1775 due to a shortage of funds, and the 38-mile canal was only completed in 1790. The Glasgow, Paisley and Ardrossan canal was proposed in 1791, begun in 1807 and opened, albeit not as far as Ardrossan, in 1811. Such delays sit alongside the interest in canals seen in Thomas Conder's *The General History of Inland Navigation* (1795) which included a map surveyed by John Philips of canals, both completed and proposed.

The canal network was sparse, fragmented, and especially limited in Scotland, Wales and Ireland. Nevertheless, alongside the Swansea Canal in Wales in the 1790s, the Newry Navigation was built in Ireland in 1731–42. Linking Carlingford Lough with the River Banna at Portadown, and opening up maritime links between mid-Ulster and Dublin, it took coal to the capital from east Tyrone. This system was expanded when the

Newry ship canal was finished in 1769, making Newry an important port. The Tyrone navigation, finished in 1787, linked Coalisland to the River Blackwater, while the Lagan navigation from Belfast to Lough Neagh was completed in the 1780s. The Strabane Canal was completed in 1796.

In the 1750s a programme of works on the River Shannon included the cutting of a canal that bypassed the obstacles to navigation in the main channel at Athlone. Through traffic was therefore made possible for the first time. The Grand and Royal Canals were built between 1756 and 1805 and 1789 and 1817 respectively to link Dublin and the Irish Midlands.

In parts of England the network was sparse. In some regions, such as Cumbria, the terrain limited the development of waterways. Bar an abortive attempt by George Dixon to construct a canal on Cockfield Fell in the 1760s, the North East was scarcely affected. After the failure of the short canal near St. Austell in 1731, none was opened in the South West until 1794. These regions were better served by the development of the turnpike system. Such points, however, underrate interest in new links in the intervening period, and the sense of profitable change that this reflected or created. For example Beavis Wood, Town Clerk of Tiverton, recorded in 1768:

'A subscription is set on foot here to raise a sum of money to bring down Mr. Brindley to take a survey of the country in order to make a navigable canal through part of Somerset and down by way of Taunton and Tiverton or Cullompton to Exeter or Topsham. Subscriptions have also been opened for this purpose at Exeter, Cullompton and Uffculm and other parts of this neighbourbood … people in general, (gentlemen and others) seem in earnest and to believe such a scheme very practicable and advantageous.'[18]

The reliance on subscriptions for the survey reflected the voluntarist, rather than governmental, nature of local activism; although a canal craze, or 'mania' for opportunity, did not hit much of the country until the 1790s. The lack of governmental activism in part reflected the absence of an international example to follow, unlike the experience of other states after the industrialisation of Britain and, separately, the beginning of rail there. In Britain, most initiatives were local as well as voluntary.

Construction problems included the provision of an adequate water supply and preventing leaks. Steam engines helped in the development of canals as they filled their reservoirs and wound their inclined planes, which are devices for raising and lowering boats between different levels of a canal by hauling them up or down a ramp built for the purpose. These were used for the first time in England in 1788 on the Ketley Canal in Shropshire, being followed by the Shropshire Tub Boat Canals built in 1792.

As later with the railways, numerous canals that were planned were never completed and many other schemes were never even pursued. Others took much longer than had been intended or produced disappointing financial returns.

In his *Travels through France and Italy* (1766), Smollett offered reflections on his journey in Britain. Of the journey from London to Dover:

'he could not help being chagrined at the bad accommodation and impudent imposition to which I was exposed… The chambers are in general cold and comfortless, the beds paltry, the cookery execrable, the wine poison, the attendance bad, the publicans insolent, and the bills extortion; there is not a drop of tolerable malt liquor to be had from London to Dover… If it was a reproach upon the English nation, that an innkeeper should pillage strangers at that rate; it is a greater scandal, that the same fellow should be able to keep his house still open. I own, I think it would be for the honour of the kingdom to reform the abuses of this road.'

Yet, Smollett also made it clear that the attitude taken by travellers could be crucial:

'When I came last from Bath [to London] it rained so hard, that the postilion who drove the chaise was wet to the skin before we had gone a couple of miles. When we arrived at Devizes I gave him two shillings instead of one, out of pure compassion. The consequence of this liberality was that, in the next stage, we seemed rather to fly than to travel upon solid ground. I continued my bounty to the second driver, and indeed through the whole journey, and found myself accommodated in a very different manner from what I had experienced before. I had elegant chaises, with excellent horses; and the postilions of their own accord used such diligence that although the roads were broken by the rain I travelled at the rate of twelve miles an hour.'

Allowing for deficiencies, it is still appropriate to stress change. Within towns, access and routes were improved, although not with the purposefulness that was to characterise the Victorians. In order to improve access, Nottingham's last surviving medieval gate was pulled down in 1743, and the North Gate in Exeter in 1769. Three new openings were made in Exeter's city walls.

Better links were used to transport both people and goods, and it became easier to move between major centres.[19] By 1783 there were 25 departures a week from Norwich to London. Travel was made faster by the improved breeding of English horses and cross-breeding of fast Arab horses, while further improvements came from the replacement of leather straps by steel coach springs and the introduction of elliptical springs. The time of a journey from Manchester to London fell from three days in 1760 to 28 hours in 1788, while average speeds between London and Birmingham rose.[20] Even if slower, other services were established, the first stagecoach from London to Monmouth in 1763.

From 1784, there was a major development in postal services by coach, the extra cost helped by a Post Office subsidy. The *London Packet* of 5 January 1795 announced that those wanting the paper should send their address to the printer 'or to the Clerks of the respective Roads at the Post-Office,' while the *Oracle* that 29 January claimed that its Bath agent 'receives regularly by express … this paper on the first day of its publication.' Artists engaged with these new services, as in Paul Sandby's *The Bayswater Turnpike*, painted in about the 1770s and depicting a stagecoach. In turn, these speedy routes were coordinated through timetabling, and, in a process of differentiation, smaller branch services with fewer horses aided the depth of penetration.

In 1790, the 'Southampton Frigate,' the name a reference to a particularly nimble and speedy ship, began as a new thrice-weekly coach service each way between Oxford and Southampton. To attract customers, this service was advertised as part of a wider system, as at Southampton, the coach met the Brighton, Chichester, Lymington, Poole, Portsmouth, Ringwood and Salisbury post coaches. From Oxford there were also daily post coaches to London (at 7 am, 8 am and 12 am), Birmingham, Bristol and Worcester. The first coach service between Limerick and Dublin was established in the 1750s, although only as a summer service. Travel was also made easier by the improvement of facilities. Old inns were rebuilt or extended, and new inns were built. Innkeepers provided fresh horses.

With roads, as with canals, the development was not simply a matter of routes, but also of vehicles, related facilities and infrastructure, and the services offered, as well as the development of an effective national credit network. The infrastructure reflected profitability which thereby became a self-sustaining process. Aside from routes between major centres, it was also easier to move into rural areas, which was important for a host of activities, for example for the voluntary inspectors of the Foundling Hospital in London who identified and supervised rural wet-nurses and arranged for transport.[21]

There were very important improvements in carrying services, although there had already been two services weekly from Norwich to London in the 1680s. Turnpikes transformed the availability of fish as noted in a York letter in the *St James's Chronicle* of 16 March 1765:

> '…we see three or four times a week, fish machines passing through this city to Leeds, Sheffield, Doncaster, nay, as far as Derby and Worcester, of so great utility … are turnpike roads, to which place it was impossible before they were made to carry sea-fish either with proper expedition or security.'

By 1783, about 150 places within 30 miles were visited at least once weekly by a carrier from Norwich. More generally, wagons became larger as did teams and individual horses. The improved carrying system both served to link regional centres with each other (and with the metropolis), and also strengthened their position within the region.

The increased speed and frequency of deliveries also improved the integration of production and consumption, and furthered the development of the market; it became easier to dispatch salesmen, samples, catalogues, orders and replacements. Increased speed was reflected in prices of journey, for both passengers and freight. The development of the turnpikes was central to the creation of regular long-distance horse-drawn wagon services, which also benefited from the construction of bridges. Whereas Kendal in Cumbria had been served by regular packhorse trains moving goods as far as London from the fifteenth century, in the eighteenth horsedrawn wagon services with their greater capacity for moving goods took over long-distance and regional routes to and from Cumbria. Similarly, wagon access to Liverpool began in the 1730s and a direct coach service thence in 1760 to London; the alternatives provided by maritime links were lengthy, while no canal routes had yet been developed. At the same time, packhorses remained important. Visiting Leeds in 1763, Richard Gough commented on the large quantities of cloth sold in the Mixed Cloth Hall opened in 1758: 'from thence carried on packhorses to almost all the fairs and market-towns in England for wholesale sale.'[22] The greater uniformity of prices had less attractive consequences, Arthur Young claiming 'Make but a turnpike road and all the cheapness vanishes at once.'[23]

A wariness about the interaction of capitalism with the transport system was expressed in *Owen's Weekly Chronicle* on 22 April 1758, in a piece that testified to the continual significance of droving:

'it is thought the present high price of meat in London might be greatly lowered, if an Order of Council, or otherwise, were made, allowing a bounty on all cattle brought into Smithfield Market, and sold by the farmers, on proof that they bred and fed them on their own farms, and all those which should appear to be sold by graziers, forestallers etc to be taxed ... the present methods of buying and selling cattle several times before they come to market might be put a stop to.'

Improvements with roads did not prevent a major development in water transport. Indeed, a focus on canals and turnpikes can lead to a lack of attention to both coastal trade and unturnpiked roads. Coastal trade was important for a whole series of local and regional economies. It also grew with the developing economy, and notably with the transport of bulky goods. For example, Cornish, Irish and Anglesey copper was brought by sea to the works near Swansea, while Bristol received copper for smelting from Anglesey and Cornwall, China clay from Cornwall, and iron, coal and naval timber from the Forest of Dean. Ports were also developed for exporting raw materials. Slate was dispatched from Snowdonia via Bangor, Caerarvon, and Port Penrhyn, which was developed by Richard Pennant, 1st Lord Penrhyn, who was responsible for the systematic working of local slate deposits from 1765.

The east coast, where Captain James Cook acquired his nautical skills, was an important route, especially for the shipment of coal from Newcastle to London and intermediate ports such as King's Lynn and Great Yarmouth, the ports for East Anglia. The average annual amount of coal shipped from the Tyne rose from just over 400,000 tons in the 1660s to well over 600,000 by 1730–31, and to nearly 800,000 tons in the 1750s. Seventy per cent of this coal went to London in 1682, and King's Lynn and Great Yarmouth took half of the rest. Companies that originated in the coal trade were able to diversify into other aspects of shipping. Thus, Henleys of Wapping added the role of a military shipping contractor.[24]

From the introduction of powdered ice in 1788, large quantities of salmon were shipped direct from Berwick to London. This was as part of an east coast trade that involved far more than coal. Thus, the *Edinburgh Advertiser* of 17 June 1783 noted the arrival in Leith, the port for Edinburgh, of six ships from Alnmouth, London, Wells and Yarmouth with grain. London continued to receive grain shipments from the South-East, for example Margate, with Richard Gough noting in 1767 that 'The harbour is pleasant but not adapted for large ships, yet great quantities of grain are shipped here for London.[25] As throughout history, the Isle of Wight was linked by ships, not least for grain movements,[26] but, prior to the nineteenth century, many places on the coastline were in effect at least in part islands due to the greater convenience of ship movements and the difficulties of those overland.

The widespread improvement in docks and harbour facilities benefited domestic as well as international trade. For example, an Act of Parliament of 1717 established the River Wear Commissioners in order to develop harbour facilities on the lower Wear. In place of a hazardous anchorage made difficult and dangerous by rocks, sandbanks, the passage of a dangerous bar, and exposure to north-easterly gales, came buoying, dredging, lighting, pier-building and controls over the dumping of ballast. The result was a much-improved harbour entrance and navigable channel that permitted a major growth in trade with the Wear, and thus aided the development of Sunderland. This was an important example of what could be achieved, and also indicated the importance of a legislative framework. Another Act, of 1749, enabled the new Port Commission of Lancaster to develop St. George's Quay (1750–5), and this was followed by a Custom House in 1764 and the New Quay in 1767. The Port Commission, in which slave traders played an active role, also promoted Lancaster's representation in commercial issues of national importance.[27] Glasgow suffered from the sandbanks in the Clyde estuary, but port facilities were developed at Port Glasgow on the estuary and later Greenock and these ensured that larger vessels could be used.

Economic activity benefited greatly from such responsive institutionalism, but it operated within a competitive context, one in which rivalry and anxiety played a major role. Thus, the Hull Dock Act of 1774 survived opposition from Beverley, while in 1785 a committee was founded in Worcester to resist any parliamentary bill for tolls on the Severn.

Nevertheless, alongside improved facilities, there was scant improvement in the condition of marine transport, which still remained heavily dependent on the weather. The seasonal variation of insurance rates reflected the vulnerability of wind-powered wooden ships, which had not reached their mid-nineteenth century levels of design efficiency and seaworthiness. By modern standards, they lacked deep keels. There could also be problems arising from a lack of safe procedures, as discussed in the *Morning Post* of 17 March 1786 with a report of an American ship running aground in Pembrokeshire:

> 'having lost her course in foggy weather, owing to the negligence of the pilots who undertook to carry her to Milford Haven: for they were no sooner on board, but were invited by the Captain … to go down to the cabin, where they continued drinking, till the vessel was dashed against the rocks.'

'Wrecking', looting the cargoes of wrecked ships, and, in some cases, luring them to their destruction, were problems in parts of Cornwall, Wales and Scotland.

On the south and west coasts, strong south-westerly winds were a problem where shelter was absent or poor. This led to an emphasis on sea walls and local natural features. The Cobb, a sea wall at Lyme Regis dating from the early fourteenth century, was strengthened several times between 1742 and 1826 in response to heavy storms. Moreover, the distance between the Cobb and the town meant that goods had to be moved from the former by horse-borne panniers. However, coastal trade continued as a key activity there until the railway arrived.

Acting as a more general cost, and thus economic constraint, sea travel was very slow compared with what it was to become the following century. However, it was the cheapest method for the movement of goods. Maritime links brought together regions such as south-western Scotland and eastern Ireland, whose road links to their own hinterlands were poor. The Irish Sea also formed an economic zone held together by marine links based on major ports, such as Belfast, Bristol, Dublin, Lancaster, Liverpool,[28] Milford Haven, Wexford and Whitehaven, as well as now-forgotten or tiny ports, such as Parkgate in Wirral,[29] Aberaeron and Bangor. These links provided crucial supplies. For example, Ireland's fuel shortage was met by coal from Cumbria and, to a lesser extent, Ayrshire and Lancashire. Lancashire iron ore was shipped to the blast furnaces of South Wales, while from Penarth, the harbour for nearby Cardiff, South Wales products as well as grain were exported. This was part of the Bristol Channel trade which included ports at Swansea, Minehead, Bristol, Watchet and other centres. These could benefit from related river links, as did Carmarthen, which exported wool and leather down the River Towy. Harbour improvements were seen including in Swansea in the 1760s. Coastal shipping, however, lacked the profitability of foreign commerce.

More generally, inland towns might be most accessible via their nearest ports rather than by long-distance overland routes. Thus, economic zones existed and/or were developing in a way that created greater potential once locomotive steam engines became widespread in the nineteenth century.

The dangers of transport continued, perhaps increased as more people were travelling. Quarter Session Records almost casually noted deaths, for example from those of Sussex: 'Young child killed falling from a carriage at Chailey [15 September 1771]. Mary Weller killed by a cart at Clayton [5 October 1771]'.[30]

For each neighbourhood to which a turnpike was extended, the impact of improved transport was rapidly felt in the possibilities of novelty. The slow plod of the pedlar's packhorse was replaced by coach services advertised and sold on their rapidity. Indeed, speed became a more apparent part of experience, one encouraged by the spread of timepieces. The experience and perception of change became more striking, as in Gloucestershire, where at Alveston, a new turnpike road was being built, providing the main road to Gloucester, and the Ship Inn, which dates back to 1589, fitted up for travellers, while the 19 mile long Thames and Severn Canal was built in 1783–7 through Gloucestershire across the Cotswolds: this involved 44 locks. Conversely, the move of the Severn ferry to Beachley adversely affected the village of Alvington.[31]

Unlike in the Low Countries and northern Italy, internal waterways were not greatly significant for the transport of passengers, with rare exceptions such as across the Thames in London. Yet, for freight the already strong importance of waterways was greatly enhanced by the significant development of canals which were able to fulfil local, regional, and national purposes. Moreover, their value was enhanced as the issues, problems and specifications of particular stretches attracted attention, and as towpaths were established in order to enhance canal horsepower. This was a significant aid to industrialisation.

There were also initiatives that did not have significant consequences. Ballooning, which was criticized as 'but a servile imitation of France, building *airy* castles', was a fashionable new risk from the mid-1780s, notably at Exeter, Oxford and Taunton, but not a way to travel. Instead, the transport was for fun or at least a dare, one that caused injuries and crop damage.[32] Separately, Britain led in the development of steam technology, but, as yet, it was not applied to transport.

It is useful to close on a comparative note, with Sir William Hamilton reporting from Naples in 1785:

'It is in vain to talk of extending the external commerce of this country … whilst the internal commerce remains in a state of total stagnation for want of communication from one province to another, in winter the roads are impassable, and scarcely passable in summer, even on horseback; in most of the provinces in this kingdom and in Sicily, except in the city of Palermo, wheeled carriages are unknown.'[33]

Chapter 6

Rail and The Rest, 1800–1850

'…with our steam engines we smile at the winds and disregard the operation of the tides.'

North Devon Journal, 2 July 1824.

'Coming slowly on *through* the forests of masts was a great steamship, beating the water in short impatient strokes with her heavy paddles as though she wanted room to breathe, and advancing in her huge bulk like a sea monster among the minnows of the Thames. On either side were long black tiers of colliers; between them vessels slowly working out of harbour…. The water and all upon it was in active motion, dancing and buoyant and bubbling upon.'
A sense of change was vividly captured in Charles Dickens' novel *The Old Curiosity Shop* (1841).

The scream of steam is the theme to the fore for this half-century, and, indeed, the steam engine made a major difference, both on land and on water. As a result of this combination, the steam engine was more significant than previous innovations. Moreover, steam was used to move both passengers and freight, and produced hitherto unprecedented speeds, on both land and sea. At sea, there was not the reliance on wind that had hitherto been to the fore. On the land, engines had feeding (coal), watering and repair requirements, and crucially required a well-maintained permanent way. However, in most respects, engines were more efficient than horses, not least as a measure of the load that had to be pulled, although not with regard to the gradients at which they could operate easily. However, that restriction was progressively overcome.

In general, the metrics of transport were those of expansion. Liverpool's docks expanded ninefold from 1756 to 1836 to cope with a 30-fold rise in tonnage, with St George's Dock (1771) and Duke's Dock (1773) part of the process. Elsewhere, there were also highly impressive increases in scale, both aggregate and relative.

We will focus on steam, but it is also necessary, as usual, to note the continuance of earlier transport techniques and routes. Although public hire sedan chairs in London, where they were introduced in the 1620s, were replaced by horse-drawn vehicles, they continued to play a role elsewhere, including in Bath, Edinburgh, Exeter, Newcastle, Norwich, Peterborough, Taunton and Weymouth. One-man powered Bath chairs also played a role, as in Bath and Weymouth.[1]

Rail did not conquer everyone. In 1839, John, 6th Duke of Bedford wrote to Lady Holland: 'I am once more "over the hills and far away" without the slightest accident or even alarm from the dangers of the Rail-road [because] we did not go by Rail-road, but took the old-fashioned mode of travelling with post horses.'[2] Furthermore, rail at first was restricted to freight. Thus, looking back to the 1820s, Anne Brontë in her novel *The Tenant of Wildfell Hall* (1848) referred to 'those slow travelling days' by coach, one in which one needed to consider food and accommodation.[3]

There were also improvements to earlier techniques. Indeed, this half-century saw a continuing enhancement of the canal and turnpike systems. In the case of the former, there were also attempts to improve river navigation, for example on the Ribble from Preston to the Irish Sea. Due to sandbanks and a changing river channel, both frequent problems, a company of merchants and townspeople backed by the Corporation acquired parliamentary backing in 1806 to take over and improve the navigation. Subsequent legislation in 1838 and 1858 created new companies and in 1883 handed the task to Preston Corporation. This costly responsibility of improvement involved stabilising and straightening the channels of the Ribble and building walls in the estuary to restrict sand movement. The task was made more difficult by the greater size of sailing ships and the introduction of iron steamers, but there were complaints to Parliament about the costs of the works.[4] This issue tends to be underplayed in accounts of transport history.

There was also much work on canals. Delayed in part by the need to build many locks, the Birmingham to Worcester Canal was finished in 1815. The 60-mile Caledonian Canal (1804–22) had 28 major locks, but it took 18 years, not seven as planned, to build and faced very major cost overruns. Steam engines were used for pumping and dredging this canal.

Thomas Telford's other works included the 2920 yard long Harecastle Tunnel on the Trent and Mersey Canal, the Pontcysyllte cast-iron aqueduct (1805) over the Dee on the 68-mile Ellesmere Canal joining the Mersey, Dee and Severn, the Birmingham and Liverpool Junction Canal, the Birmingham Canal improvement and the canal-seaport warehouse interchange at Ellesmere Port.

Moreover, alongside the new turnpike and canal routes, there were better means for moving freight and passengers along them. Indeed, linked to these, as well as to the limitations of the early rail system, the latter did not see any automatic conquest of the transport system. As with railways, successful canals could serve essentially one market, but also might provide for a number of tasks. Thus, the Rochdale Canal brought grain to the workforce, building materials to Manchester, and Lancashire cotton textiles to North Sea ports,[5] which greatly increased coastal and export markets.

In 1834, when the Parliamentary Bill for the construction of the Great Western Railway was in committee stage, some of the strongest opposition came from the Kennet and Avon Canal. The GWR directors, however, lined up a number of speakers to complain about canal transport. Samuel Provis, formerly a freight carrier by canal between London and Bristol, told the committee that the fastest trip between the two cities was around three days, but that frequent seasonal delays, shortages of water in the canal in summer, and winter floods and frosts, meant that the journey could take two to three weeks or longer. Richard Mills, a barge master from Reading, told MPs that the longest frost on rivers and canals he had encountered had stopped passage for nine weeks. Separately, canalmen often had a dark reputation as marginals, outside the constraints of society, who were prone to irreligion and crime.[6] This prefigured the response to the navvies who built the railways.

The Grand Western Canal, for which a parliamentary Act was passed in 1796, was planned from Topsham to Taunton, providing a route on to the Bristol Channel, but only the section from Tiverton on was built, that to the Somerset border being completed in 1814 and that to Taunton in 1839. The opening of the Bristol and Exeter railway in 1844 superseded this canal route and the Somerset section was closed in 1867. Other canals in Devon included the Tavistock Canal in 1817 between the town and Morwellham Quay on the Tamar, which included a tunnel nearly a mile and a half long, a branch to Millhill Quarries opened in 1819; a canal from Great Torrington to near Bideford opened in 1827; and the Bude Canal, also providing a route to the Atlantic coast, opened in 1823 and 1825, but not reaching Holsworthy as intended. The canal had been intended to bring sand inland in order to improve the hill soils. More successfully, although an attempt to extend it to Crediton had failed in 1810, the Exeter Canal was lengthened (and its banks raised) in 1825–7, enabling ships of up to 400 tons to sail up to Exeter, where a basin was opened in 1830. However, Devon's canals, and indeed those of a number of English counties, did not join to form part of a regional or national system.

To meet the competition from rail, canal companies drastically cut tolls in 1840. This was of value to freight-shippers but not passengers. The use of steam tugs instead of horses speeded up canal transport. The *Gloucester Journal* noted on 9 April 1836:

'The formation of a Steam Boat Company, for the purpose of facilitating the passage of vessels bound to or from this port, is a matter of such paramount importance to the mercantile classes connected with Gloucester, that we feel it is only necessary to direct attention to an advertisement which appears in an adjoining column.'

Steam boats were also used on rivers to transport passengers or freight, for example on the River Wear. From 1827, a steamboat began operation on the Severn ferry crossing from Aust to Beachley, another one being added in 1832, although sailing boats continued to be employed. However, the Severn Railway Bridge (1879) and the Severn Tunnel (1886) helped end the traffic.

Steam also played a role at sea. As an instance of the number of factors that affected routes, Parkgate, an outport on the Wirral for Chester had developed in the late seventeenth century as a port for passengers to Dublin, but this role ceased from the 1810s as a result of improved road links to Holyhead, steam ships from Liverpool, and human interference with the Dee causing the main channel to move from Parkgate.[7]

Relative predictability, combined with only limited risk, distinguished rail from steamships, ensuring that insurance costs were lower for rail. For long, steamships still carried sails. The difficulties of applying steam technology at sea were compounded by the problems of providing sufficient coal and the extent to which carrying coal reduced the space available to transport cargo. There was also a lack of sufficient coaling stations and of cargo space for coal. The impact of the weather reduced the reliability of timetables for steamship travel. Nevertheless, these difficulties were lessened by the development in the late nineteenth century of the high-pressure steam engine, and the increase in efficient power it offered.

Separate to that, shipping continued to benefit from the coastal nature of much of the British population, as in the Bristol Channel where the first packets from Bristol to Ilfracombe began in 1824 and a more regular service from Swansea in 1826.[8] Most shipping continued totally reliant on sail, with shipbuilding often linked to coastal trade. The latter included such basics as timber and also limestone for processing into fertiliser.[9]

The architect Gilbert Scott was told by his father Thomas (1780–1835) about Gawcott close to Buckingham: 'he found the road to it rendered impassable by a large hole dug across it in which the inhabitants were engaged in baiting a badger.' Furthermore, as a reminder of varied purposes, the Royal Military Canal was dug along the inner edge of Romney Marsh as a preparation to resist Napoleonic invasion.

Turnpike construction continued, sometimes bringing to fruition earlier plans as with the Princes Risborough-Thame turnpike that had been proposed in 1794 only to be abandoned due to the difficulty of negotiating a route. In 1825, the Risborough Road Turnpike Trust obtained a parliamentary Act for the road, which was finished in 1830 in the face of opposition from Thame. The road was part of the changing landscape seen with widespread enclosure.[10]

A series of often quite small-scale changes, notably the straightening and draining of roads and the strengthening of foundations, greatly improved the turnpike system. In Devon, turnpikes were constructed from Yarde to near Ilminster in 1807–12 and from near Broadclyst to near Cullompton in 1813–16. There were also improvements to existing roads. In the 1820s and early 1830s, the worst routes of the Exeter Turnpike Trust were replaced. All these small developments led to smoother and more level roads, and thus to an ability to pull heavier loads. By 1830, about 1,000 horse-drawn goods wagons left or entered London weekly, and some could carry loads of six tons.[11] The widening of Devon roads in the 1820s helped in the replacement of packhorses by wheeled traffic, while that decade the turnpike through the Snake Pass from Glossop to Sheffield helped open up the northern Peak District. By then, London mail coaches could reach Manchester in one day and up to 13 coaches daily went between Leeds and Manchester.

More generally, many roads were improved by resurfacing. Scottish-born John McAdam (1756–1836), General Surveyor of Roads for the Bristol Turnpike Trust from 1815 until his death, experimented with consolidating a layer of small, broken hard stone to form a very hard surface. Unlike Thomas Telford, who emphasised stronger foundations, macadamised and cambered roads gave a harder and drier road surface, and this permitted greater speed. His simple and relatively cheap system spread, being used on the Exeter to Exmouth turnpike in 1819. His family were surveyors to almost 150 turnpike trusts by 1861. The later use of tar, in large part a response to cars, the dust they caused and their tyres, was to lead to the term tarmac.[12]

Nevertheless, although other parts of Cheshire were better served early on, the Wirral did not get most of its turnpikes until after 1820. The *Taunton Courier* of 13 February 1823 criticised the Taunton Turnpike Trust for the state of the road between Taunton and Langport. Yet, criticism of roads has to address the issue of different requirements. Alongside those who wanted them improved, or, indeed, wanted the contracts to build or improve them, were others, notably drovers, for whom the roads were good enough. Wheeled vehicles, however, were a different matter.

It is necessary to remember that the social context continued to be problematic as was forcibly demonstrated in the widespread disturbances in west and mid-Wales in 1839–43, notably 1839 and 1842–3, the Rebecca Riots. These often involved attacks on toll-gates, which were seen as a form of exaction particularly in the late-1830s when the toll-renters greatly increased the number of side-bars or toll-gates on by-roads that bypassed the main toll booths. These hit the farmers, not least the transport of lime for fertiliser. The riots led to the Turnpikes, South Wales Act of 1844 which greatly cut the toll on lime movements as well as consolidating the trusts.[13]

En route from London to Oxford in 1806, John Lee noted a different issue with carriage traffic and horses:

> 'Having in this stage from Hounslow to Slough two leaders very unequal to each other, their traces were observed to be crossed and the coachman informed us that they by that means *would* enable the horses to draw better together. I doubt it very much.'

Pressing on from Oxford to Worcester, he found the coach slower. Leaving Oxford at seven in the morning, Lee did not arrive in Worcester until a quarter to six in the evening.[14]

There were also improvements in bridging. The Bridges Act of 1803 provided a national regulatory framework by declaring that no bridge could be built and taken as a county bridge unless built under the direction of the County Surveyor, a measure seen as ensuring adequate bridges. Non-suspension bridges were opened over the estuaries of the Teign and the Plym in 1827, making much of South Devon accessible to road traffic. Steam and chain floating bridges followed at Dartmouth, Saltash and Torpoint. Such improvements served to integrate regions into the national economy, and to create demand for further such development.

In addition, there was technological change. The Union Chain Bridge, opened over the Tweed near Berwick in 1820 for the Berwick and North Durham Turnpike Trust, was the first British suspension bridge able to carry loaded carriages. Turnpike roads focused on new crossing places, such as the suspension bridge across the Tees at Worlton opened in 1831. The Conwy Suspension Bridge, built by Thomas Telford and completed in 1826, replaced the ferry that had previously been the sole means to cross the river Conwy. It was part of an improvement to road transport that helped open up North Wales, ensuring that Holyhead became a more important port for Dublin, thus rivalling Liverpool. The opening of the Menai Suspension Bridge also in 1826, contributed to bringing about the end of ferries at Porthaethwy (1826), Beaumaris (1830), and Abermenai (1840s). There were also transport improvements to open up the slate mining district, especially in the 1820s, and in the early 1840s a regular coach service was established from Caernarfon to Harlech. Telford, Engineer to the Highland Roads Commissioners from 1803 to

1821, built about 1,200 miles of well-drained new or improved roads to the north and west of the Great Glen.

Alongside stone bridges, there were now also iron ones. The first, at Coalbrookdale, was heavy and had a modest span, but those that followed were lighter. The second, at Trentham, built in 1794, was less important than that at Buildwas (1796), which was much lighter and wider than Coalbrookdale, establishing a pattern that could be followed. There were also different types of bridge. The cause of suspension bridges was put back in 1830, however, when the newly-completed one over the South Esk at Montrose partially collapsed, when 70 spectators rushed from one side to another during a boat race. As a result, the proposal to build a similar structure across the Tamar was abandoned. Nevertheless, suspension bridges continued to be built. The design submitted in 1831 by Isambard Kingdom Brunel for a suspension bridge over the Avon at Clifton near Bristol was accepted as the most mathematically exact of those tendered. Brunel was appointed engineer and work began in 1836, but remained unfinished in his lifetime due to a lack of funds. The bridge was eventually completed in 1864 according to Brunel's plans, and using chains taken from the Hungerford suspension bridge which he had constructed over the Thames in 1841–5. Far more than trial and error was involved. Thus, for Robert Stephenson's Britannia Bridge for trains (1846–50) over the Menai Strait to Anglesey, a tubular form was used in order to provide stability. The carefully worked out designs were tested by experiment including the construction of a scale model that was tested with weights.[15]

Steam-power was also an important aspect of the construction of bridges, as with Stephenson's High Level bridge (1847–9) over the Tyne at Newcastle: steam hammers were employed for driving the foundations into the river bed.

On both the domestic and international levels, the key developments in Britain were those involving rail. These brought together technology, entrepreneurial drive, financing and demand possibilities, as well, less clearly, as the extent to which there were not comparable options for expansion in canal or road transport. The key technology was steam power, but this was not a magic bullet but, instead, the product of a number of innovations in usage and application. Furthermore, other technologies played a role, not least those of rail manufacture and usage. The turn to steam power was helped by the ready availability of coal and the extent to which it was inexpensive and more easily moved than wood which had a lower calorific value and was less easily used. The availability of coal was matched by the early use of rail in order to move coal, principally to ports from which it could be transported to London. This synergy helped in the financing of rail construction, for risk had to be contained and likely investment returns favourable if money was to be provided: aside from the cost of running and maintaining the system, it was necessary to construct it in the first place and to provide the relevant equipment. Entrepreneurs played a major role in capital formation and early joint-stock enterprise.

Self-propelled steam locomotives made long-distance movement by rail possible. In South Wales, horse-drawn tramways became more common from the 1780s. In 1802, George Overton built a tramroad between ironworks at Merthyr and Abercynon on the newly-built Glamorgan Canal in South Wales upon which in 1804 Richard Trevithick tried the first steam railway locomotive engine, pulling ten tons of iron and 70 men, although, due to its weight, breaking the rails, which was always a problem with heavy loads. Trevithick, a Cornish mining engineer, in the late 1790s improved boiler technology to produce a high-pressure steam able to move a piston. The key development was the use of materials capable of containing this steam. In 1801, he built a steam road locomotive, *Puffing Devil*, in 1802 an effective high-pressure steam engine and in 1803 the London Steam Carriage. Trevithick pressed on, providing the designs in 1804 for a locomotive for Christopher Blackett who owned the Wylam colliery. Built at nearby Gateshead, it was probably the first locomotive to have flanged wheels, but was too heavy for the existing rails. In 1808, Trevithick built another locomotive, *Catch Me Who Can*, that was displayed in a 'steam circus' near Euston, with admission of one shilling including a ride along the circular track. This did not prove a great success, and Trevithick moved on to other initiatives with steam power.

The next step forward was taken by Matthew Murray who in 1812 designed and built *Salamanca*, the name a tribute to Wellington's recent crushing victory over the French in Spain. This was the first commercially viable steam locomotive. Born in Newcastle, Murray was active in the

1790s in new machinery for flax-spinning and moved on to improve steam engines, an aspect of the ready transfer of expertise that was important to early rail development. He took Trevithick's work on high-pressure steam further by using two cylinders rather than one, and in 1811 also patented a toothed wheel and rack rail system. Murray made four locomotives, which were used on the Tyneside coal wagonways, also benefiting from the development of malleable iron rails in place of the cast iron ones that could not take the same weight. As a reminder that the story of progress should attract caveats, as well as the silences involved, two exploded, killing their drivers, the other two became unreliable and the Middleton Colliery turned back to horse-drawn wagons.

Locomotive technology achieved a breakthrough in the 1820s. The development of the locomotive from the stationary steam-engine provided the technology for the rail revolution, and industrialisation supplied the necessary demand, capital and skills. George Stephenson, who was in favour of locomotive engines not fixed ones, built the eight-mile Hetton Colliery Railway in 1820–2. The more famous Stockton and Darlington Railway followed in 1825, opened with a ceremonial journey from Witton Park colliery to Stockton. Commercial extraction of coal from the Witton Park Estate, near Bishop Auckland, had begun in 1819, and the railway increased its profitability.

Economic considerations and financial return were foremost for the early railways. Thomas Meynell, a wealthy local merchant and landowner who was a leading promoter of the Stockton and Darlington Railway, had argued that a railway was preferable to a proposed canal, as it was likely to yield a better return, and could be less expensive to build: a canal would not pay 'a reasonable interest to the subscribers, whereas it appears to me that a railroad affords a flattering prospect of indemnifying the proprietors.' The technical survey he organised led to support for a railway.[16] The 25-mile long line was designed to transport coal from the coalfields near Bishop Auckland to the port of Stockton, carrying 10,000 tons in the first three months and leading to a fall in the price of coal in Stockton. Again, a port link was crucial. The Stockton and Darlington was extended in 1830 to Middlesbrough, which became a major industrial centre, and a suspension bridge took the line across the River Tees.

A system would have developed in the region at this early stage had some other planned routes not failed to gain parliamentary approval. These included a 1819 proposal by William Salvin, a local landowner, for a line from Stockton to Cockfield with a branch to Tudhoe, followed by a 1823 proposal linking the coalfield around Willington with Billingham on the Tees, the line passing through Sunderland Bridge. Subsequently, he developed in effect the former backing the Clarence Railway Company which skirted Darlington en route to the coalfields and was thus shorter.[17]

Meanwhile, Stephenson had received approval in 1826 to tackle the Liverpool and Manchester, but faced the challenge presented by rivers, valleys, hills, and the waterlogged parts of south Lancashire, notably Chat Moss, a four-mile stretch of more bog that swallowed the tracks. He overcame the bog by floating the track on empty tar barrels, tree trunks and shingle across its length. The other natural obstacles ensured that the line required 63 bridges to traverse the terrain. Each increased costs, but linking the two cities and opening the railway in 1830 was a great prize and very newsworthy.[18] As with the earlier construction of canals, once they broke away from being a matter of enhancing rivers, railways were projected in a fashion separate to existing transport routes. That offered possibilities in terms of a relative flexibility, but also constraints with reference to the attitudes of landowners as well as terrain.

In many respects, railways represented an improvement on roads comparable to that of canals on rivers, but it was more than that, as well as posing particular difficulties. Like rail, canal construction was more impressive than river improvement because it created completely new links. Yet, it was also expensive, as large numbers of 'navigators' or navvies had to dig canals and railways by hand, with tunnels being especially difficult prior to high explosive and mechanical drills. Moreover, railways had the special costs of making the track that were absent with the inherited road network.

Railways, like, earlier, canals, were a response to deficiencies in existing transport arrangements, to powerful new demands, and to the availability of considerable resources. Moreover, for Britain, both canals and railways were to provide comparative regional and international advantages. Notably, there were cheaper transport costs, leading to lower production costs, enabling competitive advantage resulting in a high volume of production that drove further investment.

The Liverpool and Manchester Railway was the world's first steam-powered, inter-urban railway designed to transport both passengers and goods, notably raw cotton shipped into the rapidly growing port of Liverpool and turned into textiles in Manchester's mills. These crucial cities of economic development could help establish a model.

While encouraging the significant development of linked local horse-drawn transport, railways offered new routes and cut journey times for both freight and passengers, hitting coastal traffic as a result. With the benefit of a multiple-tube boiler, as well as a blastpipe pulling air through the fire, the *Rocket* locomotive, designed and built by Stephenson in Newcastle in 1829, could travel at 30 miles an hour. The following year, *Rocket* won the Liverpool and Manchester Railway's locomotive trials at Rainhill, trials that emphasised speed as the intention was to carry passengers. Direct drive from the cylinders and pistons to the wheels increased efficiency, as did an engine design that boiled water more rapidly. One of the rivals, John Ericsson and John Braithwaite's *Novelty*, the first tank engine, was quick to raise steam, but defective parts led to failure. A contemporary lithograph showed that locomotive in about 1830 pulling wagons that carried private carriages, a form of motorail. Improving performance made it possible to go for steeper gradients, as in the Sheffield to Manchester line built in 1838–45. Stephenson himself was against difficult gradients that might require two engines.

The success of rail helped see off the challenge from steam carriages, which had some parliamentary support and were backed by Telford. These carriages, however, suffered not only from mechanical issues, but also from different road interests which, for example, helped ensure high tolls for them.

With rail, a new Iron Age was in progress. Completed in 1823, the 50 foot long Gaunless Bridge on the Stockton and Darlington Railway was one of the first railway bridges to be constructed of iron and the first to use an iron truss. Aside from new bridges, wooden bridges were replaced by iron, as on the North Midland Railway at Belper. Existing ironworks began to produce for the railway. The Britannia Foundry at Derby came to make railway bridges and turntables, carriage wheels, locomotive tenders and steam engine castings. The Foundry was linked by sidings to the Great Northern Railway, and another site for the Foundry linked to the Midland Railway system was built. Train works were opened across the country, including in Newcastle, Gateshead, Crewe, Derby, Swindon and Wolverton.

Tunnels were blasted through hills: the Kilsby tunnel (1834–8) between London and Birmingham. With gunpowder, tunnel construction, like that of cuttings, was readily possible but it was costly, particularly the movement away of rubble. Costing about £200,000 and taking 157 tons of gunpowder, the Woodhead Tunnels (1838–45), over three miles long was necessary for the route between Manchester and Sheffield.

In many senses, there was a perfect financial moment for rail. The availability of inexpensive money had been limited by the long period of warfare that closed with the final defeat of Napoleon at Waterloo in 1815. Thereafter, government expenditure was low, and there was no resulting upward pressure on taxation or interest rates. The postwar recession of the late 1810s was a problem. But there was economic growth from the 1820s. Furthermore, Britain's commercial position made it possible to accumulate profit and loan-capacity. Both could be spent on railways, and improving capital-markets helped facilitate the situation. So also with the lack of comparable other investment opportunities: the Stockton and Darlington yielded a dividend of five per cent in the late 1820s and 15 per cent in 1841, and at a time of low inflation. The Liverpool and Manchester regularly paid out dividends of 9½ per cent.[19] There was to be further liquidity as a consequence of the mid-century gold rushes in America and Australasia.

In turn, the costs of rail were cut by the cheapness of the labour force, particularly the 'navvies' who built the railways, while the presence of a large metallurgical industry helped greatly in the provision of rails and other infrastructure, such as iron bridges. By modern standards, moreover, land was inexpensive, not only for the lines but also for the stations and for the marshalling yards that required much space. In the latter, rail benefited from an absence of any equivalent of modern zoning restrictions.

Rail provided a sense of transformed opportunities. Indeed, in 1842, the Reverend Sydney Smith observed 'distance is abolished.' 'Hyde Park as it will be,' a cartoon produced by John Leech in about 1845, showed locomotives used by children and the life guards and pulling the royal family, although in 'The Railway Juggernaut of 1845,' published in *Punch* of that year on 26 July, he attacked the speculation that led to 121 railway Acts being passed that year. The sense of promise, and the profits involved, helped ensure multiple disputes – over routes, propulsive systems, notably the locomotive as opposed to the atmospheric system, and the battle of the gauges, with Stephenson's narrow gauge opposed to Brunel's broad gauge. Stephenson backed a standard gauge with a rail spacing of 4 foot 8½ inches, arguing that different gauges would raise transhipment costs and therefore affect costs to customers.

The early railways were often task-specific, as with the 1834 Stanhope and Tyne Railway to link the limestone quarries of Upper Weardale to the port of South Shields. However, this could mean that the failure of businesses that it was hoped would use a line spelled trouble. This affected the Clarence Railway, which was hit by competition from the Stockton and Darlington, and by over-ambition. More generally, the ease with which joint stock companies could be formed contributed to speculation that was frequently unmerited not least due to a competition from other lines. This rivalry frequently related to expectations from differing routes and markets. Thus, James Rendel proposed an inland route from Exeter to Plymouth in 1840, one that required 18 river crossings. It was not pursued, unlike Brunel's longer coastal route which faced engineering issues but linked to growing settlements such as Dawlish, Teignmouth and Torquay.

Best practice developed through trial and error, although both involved political and social as well as financial considerations. Thus, a stationary engine house was built at Camden Town for the London and Birmingham Railway. The engine, which pulled trains by rope up the incline from Euston to Camden Town, was only used for six years, until 1844. It has been said that early locomotives were not powerful enough to haul trains up the slope, especially as it had to rise high enough to pass over Regent's Canal near Gloucester Road, but this was not the case. Instead, Parliament had not allowed the railway company to operate steam locomotives closer to the city, a restriction that was soon relaxed and then ignored completely. Adapting to regulations but also adapting regulations were both key aspects of the development of rail systems, not least in experience and expertise. The learning curve had to be a steep one, as an entire infrastructure had to be designed and operated, as had the relevant organisational structure, operating systems and finances. Ticket prices and freight rates were affected by competition, or the lack of it, between values, and by the customer's own judgment of value in the setting of cost, speed and reliability between rail and other modes of transport. Entrepreneurial consolidation and additional construction helped in the establishment of networks offering an inter-operability that affected these questions.

Rail redefined urban hierarchies and offered new routes. For example, established in 1844 and based in Derby, the Midland Railway was one of the largest in the country. The company originated as a merger of the Midland Counties Railway, the North Midland Railway, and the Birmingham and Derby Junction Railway. The Birmingham and Gloucester Railway was added in 1846 as part of the frequent process of acquisition that was characteristic of rail. Derby was extremely well-connected in terms of regional and inter-regional routes: it was important that it was north of Birmingham. Moreover, the Derbyshire coalfields provided a significant source of income, a position consolidated in 1845–7 by subsequent acquisitions, notably the Sheffield and Rotherham Railway.

The *Staffordshire Advertiser* of 14 October 1848 reported the opening of the Crewe branch of the North Staffordshire Railway 'which will give the district an outlet to Liverpool, Chester and Holyhead as well as for the present to Manchester and the north.' Rail linked the local to the national, a process taken further with special trains for particular purposes as when the London and North Western Railway laid on one in 1848 for a cricket match in Leamington between locals and an all-England team. Thomas Cook arranged excursion trains to the Great Exhibition in 1851. On 11 July 1855, the first number of Chudleigh's *Weekly Express* provided the London-Plymouth timetables. Rail was key to family economies and national investment. By cutting transport costs, rail lowered production costs, and the resulting profitability encouraged fresh investment.

Initially, rail was a product of the need for moving coal. This was a reflection of the earlier initial use of steam engines for a limited range of tasks, principally pumping water out of mines. Moving coal meant relatively short lines that essentially went with the gradient, the return journey being one of moving empty wagons back to the mines. There were also railways within the mines themselves, along which wagons for the coal once mined could be pulled. These saw the use of pit ponies, but also of human labour, particularly, and increasingly, women and children, as men tended to focus on cutting into the coal seams. The first public railway in the Midlands, the Leicester and Swannington of 1830 was designed to help Leicestershire coal compete with canal-carried Nottingham and Derby coal in the Leicester market and paid a dividend of eight per cent in 1839.

In contrast to canals, there was a rapid shift also to passengers. That had not appeared obvious at the outset, not least because there was only limited need for passenger transport in the area of maximum coal movements. However, the locomotive-rail technology was speedily improved in the late 1820s to permit higher speeds, and that made it more attractive as an option for passengers. The most important early route for that was from London to Birmingham and the success in developing such a long route so quickly encouraged much interest. This was separate to the potential for rail indicated by the suburban lines that were opened, notably to Greenwich.

The sums invested could be considerable as with the Chester and Holyhead Railway which was incorporated in 1844 with a capital of £2.1 million. On 18 January 1847, *Besley's Devonshire Chronicle* devoted two-and-a-half columns and an editorial to a meeting of the proprietors of the Exeter and Crediton Railway, and another two columns to an Extraordinary General Meeting of the South Devon Railway's shareholders.

The Joint Stock Companies Act of 1844 had replaced company formation only by royal charter or Private Act of Parliament. Moreover, whereas canals had generally only had investment in the form of large shareholdings, railways attracted small ones. The attraction to shareholders was greatly increased by the Limited Liability Act of 1855 which increased the possibilities for capital formation for new projects.

The pace of development saw 54 Railway Acts passed by Parliament in 1825–35, and another 39 in 1836–7 alone. Speculation, both sensible and less so, was attracting liquidity to the railways, and railways became the prime form of domestic and international investment, although the Bristol and Exeter Railway found it difficult in 1836–7 to get subscribers to pay for the shares they had committed to purchase when floated in 1835. By 1841, 1,696 miles was complete and the authorised capital of rail companies was £78 million, but, by 1846, the figures were 3,036 and £296 million, and the more capitalised nature of the industry was linked to the amalgamation of and expansion of the system, so that in 1845–6, in the 'Railway Mania,' the building of another 7,000 miles was authorised by Parliament. As part of the expansion, harbours were developed for coal movements, for example Hartlepool, and the linkage was clear at the company level, in this case with the Hartlepool Dock and Railway Company authorised by Parliament in 1832. So also with ports such as Cardiff, Seaham, and Sunderland.

The prospectuses for new lines clarified what was thought desirable. That of 1845 for the London and Manchester Direct Independent Railway, with a branch to Crewe, claimed that it would offer an important route to Scotland, adding:

'not by means of a route made up of circuitous segments of various undertakings, already overworked with a patch of new railway between, to make up a solicitor's line, but by one continuous railway.'

That for the London and Holyhead Direct Railway noted: 'The line will be, for the most part, of easy construction, as abundance of building materials exist over a part of the line.'

The building and operation of railways attracted fraud, notably with George Hudson, the 'Railway King,' whose speculative schemes left him controlling over 1,000 miles of track by 1844 but contributed to a general financial crisis. In 'The Hunting of the Snark,' a nonsense poem written between 1874 and 1876 when it was published, Lewis Carroll referred to the Snark's life being threatened 'with a railway-share.'

Like most issues of planning involving vested property interests, the emergence of railways, with their attendant companies, boards of directors, agents, surveyors, promoters, shareholders and speculators, encouraged both advocates and opponents for particular proposals. The number of railway bills and the number of committees to investigate proposed new lines (particularly committees of the House of Lords) was a major occupation of the 1830s and, especially, 1840s. Some MPs like Hudson and Trollope's fictional Melmotte were railway entrepreneurs who entered Parliament; but many other MPs were involved as directors, lobbyists (unpaid or otherwise) and, in some cases, opponents. Some aristocrats disliked lines crossing their prized acres or spoiling their view. As far as rail plans were concerned, politics hardly mattered in the sense of political parties, but very much did so in the case of private or corporate interests. Some parliamentary boroughs wanted lines. In contrast, the City of London kept the early lines outside its boundaries, as did the wealthy of the West End. Engines and stations were unattractive in terms of social and environmental amenity. But the likely profitability of lines attracted many, including some City bankers who helped to promote the companies.

All these interests had influence in Parliament, some of the individuals involved were members of one House or the other, and every new line required a private Act of Parliament for both the company's incorporation (until general legislation facilitated the formation of joint-stock companies with limited liability) and the construction of the line. It meant that, unless all the interests were squared beforehand, a railway Bill could be defeated or at least held up in Parliament. Most of the negotiation went on off-stage, but some debates on the Bills reveal the underlying tensions. On the whole, the aristocracy and other big landowners did very well out of the process. In Brighton, there was opposition to the route planned for the railway from London finally opened in 1841, with concerns about the station being near an affluent area. However, the railway was also seen as a way to provide coal from the port of Shoreham to where a branch line was opened in 1840.[20]

North of there, the Reading, Guildford and Reigate Railway Company was designed to provide a local solution offering a national outcome, by connecting the Great Western, London and South Western (which regarded the new line as an unwelcome incursion), London and Brighton (which had a similar view), and South Eastern lines; ensuring that traffic from the West Country, Wales, the Midlands and the North could reach the Channel ports. While this was not a difficult line as there were not troublesome landowners or unforeseen engineering issues, there were still local difficulties, as with the interests of the Countess of Warwick in Reigate, and there was also the plentiful legal, construction and operating work of even a relatively short railway, with each parish posing issues of location and maintenance. Completed in 1849, the line was taken over by the South Eastern Railway in 1852.[21]

There was regulation, with the Railway Department of the Board of Trade established in 1840 and Railway Regulation Acts passed in 1842 and 1844. 'Parliamentary trains,' those, referred to by Gilbert and Sullivan in their operetta *The Mikado* (1885), operated to comply with the Railway Regulation Act of 1844 which obliged train companies to provide inexpensive rail transport for the less affluent:

> 'The provision of at least one train a day each way at a speed of not less than twelve miles an hour including stops, which were to be made at all stations, and of carriages protected from the weather and provided with seats; for all which luxuries not more than a penny a mile might be charged.'

Thereafter, however, government control did not increase until the Regulation of Railways Act of 1868, and the opportunity for a government guided rail network, avoiding over-capitalisation and competing lines, was not taken.

Meanwhile, services from London had reached Birmingham in 1838 (with part of the line opened in 1837 to facilitate travel to London for Victoria's coronation), Southampton in 1840, Exeter and Oxford in 1844, Norwich in 1845, Ipswich and Bury St Edmunds in 1846, Plymouth and Portsmouth in 1847, Banbury and Holyhead in 1850, and Truro in 1859. Glasgow and Edinburgh were linked by rail in 1841.

Opened in 1837, the Grand Junction Railway ran from Birmingham via Crewe and Warrington to join the already-established Liverpool and Manchester Railway at Newton Junction. The northern end of the route to Newton entailed purchasing in 1835 the Warrington and Newton Railway which had been opened in 1831. This was ambitious but also highly profitable, the Grand Junction becoming through merger the basis of the London and North Western Railway formed in 1846, on the axis of the later HS2 plans. With some, the profitability was more dubious. Thus, the Manchester and Milford Haven Railway was planned in 1845 to give Manchester access to other ports so that it could compete with

Liverpool. Going through Shrewsbury, Aberystwyth and Cardigan, the route was connected for through traffic by 1867.

Commuting into London rapidly developed, as an extensive network spread over nearby areas. Rail services from London Bridge reached Deptford in 1836 and Greenwich in 1838, while the London to Croydon line opened in 1839, followed by lines to Margate in 1846, and to Southend in 1856. By then, the tolls on turnpikes no longer appeared viable and, in 1857, the Toll Reform Committee recommended their abolition on all tolls within six miles of Charing Cross. Their abolition rapidly followed.

Completed in 1838, the London and Greenwich Railway was the first steam railway in London and the first entirely elevated railway. Floated in 1831, the key element was a viaduct of 878 brick arches, and an Act of Parliament was obtained in 1833 with the first section opened in 1836, and the railway rapidly became very busy, although the high costs of building the line ensured that the company was not profitable. The line posed many problems, notably crossing Deptford Creek so that ships could pass under it. There was also experimentation on the line with the locomotives, which saw for the first time horizontal cylinders mounted at the front outside the frame.

The number of passengers on the line rose to over two million in 1844, indicating the commercial appeal of suburban rail services, but the line made a loss due to its heavy indebtedness from the original capital expenditure, which was a problem for all rail companies.

The plan had been to press on from Greenwich to Gravesend and also, separately, to Dover, but this was rejected by Parliament in 1836, which limited prospects, and therefore the possibility of raising fresh equity. As earlier with river improvements, turnpikes and canals, Parliament proved the major arbitrator of the new system, which helped stabilise the action-reaction processes of policy formation and also shape both lobbying and government responses, making recourse to Parliament more predictable and attractive for rail companies. More generally, public policy was important as offering a safe context for the time horizons required by investment in significant infrastructure. In turn, that policy, which helped sustain low interest rates, hinged greatly not just on the law but on its enforcement via the courts and parliamentary scrutiny and observance.

Urban street patterns were focused on the new railway stations. The major ones, such as Isambard Kingdom Brunel's Paddington (temporary station opened 1838, main train shed 1854) and Gilbert Scott and W.H. Barlow's St Pancras (opened 1868), were designed as masterpieces of iron and glass, in effect more lasting versions of the Crystal Palace built for the Great Exhibition in 1851. The stations each also had large railway hotels, such as the Great Western Royal Hotel at Paddington, opened in 1854. In a piece of 1860 decrying 'Refreshments for Travellers,' Dickens had an interesting reflection on the new impersonality of society with reference to:

> the great station hotel....Where we have no individuality....We can get on very well indeed at such a place, but still not perfectly well; and this may be, because the place is largely wholesale, and there is a lingering personal retail interest within us that asks to be satisfied.'

The major rail lines also had a great impact on what became London suburbia, opening up areas for development. Thus, in 1838, the line to Southampton reached what is now Surbiton, leading to the building of housing estates around the station. The suburbanisation was to be a continual feature of rail passenger developments, and notably so when combined with loose planning restrictions and easy access to land purchase. At the same time, the suburbanisation was much denser than that which was to follow with cars. Alongside increased specialisation of function, as well as the clearance of rookeries (slums), suburbanisation played a big part in the decline of population in the central areas, not least the City, from the 1850s onwards.

The railways needed a standard time for their timetables, in order to lessen the risk of collisions and to make connections possible, thus ensuring that railways and timetables could operate as part of a system. This characteristic was important to effectiveness and profitability. In place of the previous variations of time in England from east to west, with the Sun, for example, overhead at Bristol ten minutes behind London, the railways adopted the Greenwich Observatory standard as 'railway time.' In 1840, the Great Western Railway, that to the West of England, became the first railway to adopt London time and, by 1847, most British rail companies had followed suit. From its offices on the Strand in London, the Electric Telegraph Company communicated Greenwich Time from 1852, the entire process reflecting the centrality of London. More generally, the fixing of time and time-based practices were very important in changing the nature of the world of work. Clocks were kept accurate by the electric telegraph that was erected along railway lines largely to that end. The electric telegraph was patented in Britain in 1837, with an electromagnet utilised to transmit and receive electric signals. The telegraph was initially used by private companies to transmit information about trains.

There was massive destruction involved in the building of stations and lines, with trains proving the strong 'iron monster.' Dickens discussed this destruction in his account of north London. Camden Town and nearby areas was transformed by the building of Euston, King's Cross and St Pancras stations, and their extensive supporting marshalling yards and lines. This was the biggest concentration of major stations and railway facilities in London and the country. In *Dombey and Son*, Camden Town is the epicentre of change:

'The first shock of a great earthquake had … rent the whole neighbourhood to its centre… Houses were knocked down; streets broken through and stopped… Everywhere were bridges that led nowhere…. mounds of ashes blocked up rights of way, and wholly changed the law and custom of the neighbourhood… the yet unfinished and unopened Railroad was in progress, and, from the very core of all this dire disorder, trailed smoothly away, upon its mighty course of civilisation and improvement.'[22]

It is understandable that much of the emphasis is on lines built from London. However, this can lead to an underplaying of the role of many local and regional initiatives, often in the context of competing rivalries. Thus, in Norfolk, rail began by the linkage of local towns, notably in 1844 with the line from Great Yarmouth to Norwich, which competed with the water route. The following year, a connection to London was established through Ely and Cambridge, but a direct link to Liverpool Street did not come until later.[23] At all stages, it is necessary to counterpoint the lines that were built with both delays and those that did not move beyond planning or just speculation.[24]

The separate financing of individual lines encouraged what might appear a fragmentation, but this also meant a possibility for attracting finance to what seemed most profitable. The fragmentation was most apparent in the different lines running into London with their separate stations. However, the scale of London and the density of its built up area did not lend traction to ideas of a central London terminus. There was a rapid connection of major cities within England as well as the construction of a link between England and Scotland. The last required an impressive bridge over the Tweed at Berwick which was an aspect of the large-scale bridge-building that rail entailed. So also with embankments and cuttings: the limited power of engines ensured the need for only gentle inclines for the railways. This also meant that stations had to be kept outside town centres that were on a hill, as at Lincoln and Axminster. This situation increased the need for feeder services to the stations, and that need underlined a classic feature of transport systems, their consequential impact on other means of transport. Indeed, one of the major drivers of road transport in the later decades of the century was to focus on the requirements for rail, both for freight and for passengers. The latter helped ensure that this knock-on impact was far greater than in the case of canals.

Organisational change was also significant. Thus, in 1829, George Shillibeer introduced to London the Paris system of omnibuses. He ran two from Paddington along the New Road to the Bank of England. In each omnibus 29 passengers could be carried, at a fare of one shilling. In 1834, Shillibeer established services to Greenwich and Woolwich. He was ruined by railway competition, which was much better capitalised (a factor that separately blocked steam carriages), but in 1856 the London General Omnibus Company was founded, and horse-drawn buses became a key element, not least linking the railway termini. In turn, trams, horse-drawn buses operating on rails, appeared in London in 1869 and by 1874 over 60 miles of track had been laid there. In the 1880s, horse-drawn omnibuses were largely replaced by trams which, from the 1890s, were electrified.

Population growth, industrialisation, the coal economy and regional differentiation all helped drive demand for transport. So also did other factors. For example, the development of leisure landscapes such as the Lake District helped encourage and focus particular requirements for a major strand of transport, that of domestic tourism.[25] Yet, the terrain ensured that this was met by carriage services on turnpikes rather than by railways. The latter very much sought nearly level routes, which eased construction and operating costs. In contrast, escarpments posed the challenges of gradients and tunnelling and igneous rocks were harder to work. The first locomotives had relatively little power compared with what was to come, and they could not haul trains up steep gradients.

However, rail offered attractions that other systems did not. For example, droving was both slow and the animals used up much of their energy on the move. Wagons and carts often provided merchandise with inadequate shelter, and the methods of packing and of moving heavy goods on and off carts were primitive.

It is always necessary to remember the cost. In 1848, in response to railway competition, the last Whitmarsh went into the wine trade, bringing the prominent Somerset carrying company to a close. Dickens was well-aware that the railways relied on continual hard work, and that they affected the health of the workers, which was true for both the construction of railways and their operation. In his novel *Dombey and Son* (1846–8), Mr Toodle is a stoker: 'The ashes sometimes gets in here' – touching his chest – 'and makes a man speak gruff, as at the present time.'

Thanks to steam, both steamships and trains, the sense of time and space changed. Moreover, steam-powered travel provided a potent experience, one of new knowledge and its application serving to remould the environment and end previous constraints. This was modernisation in process and the basis for a new sense of development, one that powerfully contributed to ideas of evolution.

In practice, alongside great plans, shifts and expedients were repeatedly significant in the building of rail stations, as with battles between English and Irish workmen at London Bridge where expenditure on the line itself meant that, although services began in 1836, the station buildings came later. Railways, indeed, were by their nature really or potentially interim, as lines, as well as stations, could be extended or added. Far more mileage was to follow.

Chapter 7

Speed and Volume, 1850–1900

'I quite concur in the opinion that the permanent presence of a large military force at Hull is not requisite: that inland concentration, with rapid means of distribution by railroad, is the right system.' Sir James Graham, First Lord of the Admiralty, to Fitzroy, Lord Raglan, Master-General of the Ordnance, 1854.[1]

On 29 August 1850, in one of the public displays of ceremony that the era greatly loved, Queen Victoria opened the Royal Border Bridge over the River Tweed at Berwick. Designed by Robert Stephenson (1803–59), one of the greatest engineers of the day, this viaduct of 28 arches cost £253,000, and is still impressive today, the height of the bridge and the curve of the approach providing a fine vista. This was a man-made vista, as those of Victoria's reign increasingly were, and notably so with the railway. The bridge provided the last railway link between London and Edinburgh, one that enabled Victoria readily to go to Balmoral, her home in the Scottish Highlands, whereas George IV had gone to Edinburgh in 1822 by sea; now aircraft and helicopters are used to take the monarch and ministers to Balmoral, while it would be possible to circumvent some of the process by the use of video-conferencing. Stephenson was to be buried in Westminster Abbey, a recognition of the importance of engineering.

Far less prominence and recognition were given to the labourers. Many were Irish, a large number of whom had responded to the appalling crisis caused by the lethal Great Famine of the late 1840s by emigrating to England and Scotland. They were particularly important in construction projects, such as the railways. The largest Irish communities were always in London, even though, in percentage terms, many other places were far more Irish.

In the second half of the nineteenth century, there were new developments aplenty, with urbanisation and economic growth, and innovations in transport, particularly motorcars and safety bicycles. Moreover, there was the continuation of earlier systems. Thus, horse-drawn transport remained important and not simply as a residual feature. Indeed, it was greatly expanded both as a feeder to rail systems and as a way to meet the growing need for transport within expanding urban areas. In George Gissing's novel *New Grub Street* (1891), the poor protagonist's property is moved to his room in Islington by cart. In 1902, the number of working horses probably reached a peak of 3.5 million. The transport system was part of this equation.

Allowing for all that, the emphasis has to be on the expansion of rail and its ability both to create and meet new demands but also to attract transport from other forms which, accordingly, declined, notably canals. In this, Britain was in line with international trends and indeed helped finance them as well as provide major technological and skill transfers. If any age of transport was the British age, it was that of rail. Lines were added in many ambitious, even questionable, directions.

The belief in the beneficial impact of the train and the atmosphere of boosterism that surrounded the development of rail was captured in Charles Dickens' *The Uncommercial Traveller* (1860). The traveller was pressed by the landlord of the Dolphin's Head to sign a petition for a branch line: 'I bound myself to the modest statement that universal traffic, happiness, prosperity, and civilisation, together with unbounded national triumph in competition with the foreigner, would infallibly flow from the Branch.' In *Middlemarch* (1871–2), the novelist George Eliot has Caleb Garth, the wisest and finest character in the book, remark 'Now my lads, you can't hinder the railroad: it will be made whether you like it or not.' A sense of change was captured in Charlotte Brontë's novel *Villette* (1853), in which Lucy Snowe referring to 'a time gone by' when she, now old was young, notes that 'fifty miles were then a day's journey,' a reference to coach travel.[2]

The drive to the sea was the key element for much rail freight, not least coal exports. Thus, Hull had gained a rail link in 1840, with the terminus adjacent to the Humber Dock. In turn, the Victoria Dock Branch Line opened in 1853. As a major game changer, the very large Alexandra Dock opened in 1885 served the new Hull, Barnsley and West Riding Junction Railway formed in defiance of the North Eastern Railway's attempt at control. Steam-powered excavating machines were used. The King George V Dock, completed in 1914, competed with the Great Central Railway's Immingham Dock on the other side of the Humber completed in 1912 and involving new connecting lines. In addition to public railways, there were many that were used solely for particular commercial and industrial concerns and companies such as the Penrhyn slate quarry.[3]

The rate of construction was not consistent, but reflected financial circumstances as well as particular needs and possibilities. The finances tightened as a whole, in part due to periodic crises from the 1870s, but also arose from the possibilities for rail investment abroad. Indeed, in comparison with the bold scenarios outlined for rail investment in North America, there was not the same enthusiasm or interest for some of the cross-lines that attracted attention in Britain once the main network had been put in place. There was no national political pressure for such lines. Indeed the extension of the rail system did not attract much interest at the national political level, and this was also the case in Ireland. The lack of a regional practice in politics, governance and lobbying was a key element, a reminder of the extent to which transport so often depends on the absence of factors.

In the second half of the century, the national network of main lines and their connections were filled in, notably in Cornwall and Scotland. In Devon, the railway reached Ilfracombe and Sidmouth in 1874, Budleigh Salterton in 1897, Lynton in 1898 and Westward Ho in 1901.[4] These were linked to the rise of leisure travelling notably to seaside resorts, initially by paddle steamers, with the consequent building of piers, and later/concurrently by rail. The building of a short branch line to Brixham, authorised by Parliament in 1864 and opened in 1868, was intended to enlarge the market for Brixham-landed fish, but the line bankrupted its projector and owner, Richard Wolston, who had put in about £40,000. Taken over by the Great Western Railway in 1883, it was closed in 1963, although the access route to the station cut through the cliffs remains.[5] In Berkshire, branches were built to Faringdon (1864), Abingdon (1873), Wantage (1875), Wallingford (1886) and Lambourn (1898).

There was also, as a century earlier with turnpikes, a filling in with cross-lines. In part, this reflected competition between different companies, although the latter was lessened by a degree of consolidation. Another cause of extension was the increase in commuting not only into London, but also into other cities. The major growth in population encouraged this increase, as did a move by the relatively affluent out of the crowded city centre.

Commuting and rail travel as a whole had an effect in developing an infrastructure from station snack facilities and train dining cars to newsagents. Whereas the bumpy and dark nature of carriages had not encouraged reading, the situation was very different for trains once lighting was provided. They offered a relatively level speed. In turn, there was the need to develop conventions of behaviour. Some were matters of safety, such as not leaning out of windows and waiting for the train to stop before getting on or off. There was also the requirement for care at crossings, with many animals in particular killed. Other conventions related to human interaction, notably conversation, flirting, smoking, eating, and drinking; as well as to urinating. There was an attempt to police the system with regulations, guards, and differentiation by class of service; but the extent to which harmony arose is problematic. Rail travel was a cause of many anxieties, including attacks on passengers by criminals and the insane, who were supposed to use railways to move around the country. There were also more general fears that rail travel might accentuate or contribute to instability.[6]

As writers noted, rail produced a host of new experiences and assumptions. Oscar Wilde satirically observed some of these in his play *The Importance of Being Earnest*, written in 1894:

'… a cloakroom at a railway station might serve to conceal a social indiscretion – has probably, indeed, been used for that purpose before now – but it could hardly be regarded as an assured basis for a recognised position in good society.… I never travel without my diary. One should always have something sensational to read in the train.… we have already missed five, if not six, trains. To miss any more might expose us to comment on the platform.'

Yet, during this half-century, although it developed an impressive underground system in London, Britain itself became less significant as the rail innovator. In part, this was simply a loss of relative advantage, but there were also problems more specific to Britain, including a duplication of lines and therefore over-capacity. However, the labour issues that were to be very serious by the early twentieth century were not yet a major challenge to profitability and, therefore, the liquidity necessary to encourage investment.

Rail was the major feeder of trade and this expanded greatly, not least with new facilities, including, to serve London, the Poplar (1852), Royal Victoria (1855), Millwall (1868), Royal Albert (1880) and Tilbury (1886) docks. Dating from 1915, the splendour of the Port of London Authority building captured the significance of trade. In London, as elsewhere, factories were located near the quayside. The efficiency of coastal and other shipping improved. By 1900, over 90 per cent of all registered tonnage was steam-powered, sail being much reduced in significance, and in 1884 the first efficient steam turbine was developed by Charles Parsons. In 1893, Britain imported 3.9 million animal carcasses for meat and by 1909 four-fifths of the bread consumed was made with imported wheat.[7] Once landed, this food became a prime commodity for transport.

The use of railways became more central to the economy and to society. Coastal travel was shadowed by railways, but the victory was often hard-fought and took time. In 1855, three million tons of coal were moved by sea to London, and only 1.2 million by rail, only in 1869 was coal brought by sea matched by that moved by rail, and, in 1879, although 6.6 million tons were transported to London by rail, some 3.5 million still entered the Thames by sea, and coastal shipping from the Tyne was still indeed a major means of coal movement in the 1960s. Coastal shipping remained important for certain commodities, such as coal and grain, or, for Poole, clay, but the relative role of such shipping markedly declined, while the hinterlands of lesser ports contracted. The decline of coastal shipping meant a fall in the economic impact of the sea.[8]

Canals and rivers remained important, albeit overshadowed by the railways. Not all canals were in difficulties. In 1853, the Oxford Canal Company was able to give its staff a 20 per cent wage rise and to declare a 11.5 per cent dividend. At this stage the Buckinghamshire Railway did not appear serious competition. There was a large staff with wharfingers responsible for collecting canal dues, lock keepers, foremen, labourers and craftsmen.[9] The Oxford Canal Company in mid-century developed a number of quarries to provide paving for towpaths and wharves.[10] This was an instance of a more general tendency of transport concerns to provide for their needs, as builders, operators and employers. Indeed, they were often the major enterprises in particular centres. There were also challenges for other institutions, as with the churches introducing railway chaplains. There was also a need for security.

There were attempts to create an inland port at Peterborough, but the railway had a major impact on many canals. In Plym Bridge Woods, the railway was built on the canal towpath, to bring stone and peat from Dartmoor to Plymouth. The canal from Carlisle to Port Carlisle closed in 1853 and was converted into the Port Carlisle Railway.

Others, nevertheless, remained significant and benefited from the use of steam technology. Thus, in 1871–97 the Weaver Navigation was rebuilt with the locks replaced by turbine-operated hydraulic lock gates, a hydraulic boat lift to link the Weaver to the Trent and Mersey Canal, and a dredging of the main channel of the Weaver. At the same time, there was co-operation as well as competition between rail and shipping.

The impact of rail was very varied. Deaths in train crashes played a significant role in fiction, as in Wilkie Collins' *No Name* (1862).[11] On a lasting pattern, change in transport affected urban and rural activities and lifestyle. Thus, in Banbury, industrial activity increased with the canal and, subsequently, the railway, while social conditions and norms changed, as with an increase in the number of prostitutes.[12] At the same time, Banbury remained a focus of horse transport, for example both for carriers' routes and for mounted postmen.[13]

With the railway, public health could change, notably due to the possibility of infection. As an instance of the contingency that affected transport, a serious cattle plague in 1865–6 led to the closure of fairs and markets and to restrictions on the movement of cattle. A key long-term consequence was the end of urban cowhouses and dairies which had been particularly vulnerable. In place of these local supplies, railways became the key providers to the towns. They opened up urban markets for liquid milk, encouraging dairy farmers to produce 'railway milk,' rather than farmhouse cheese. Horse race meetings, such as those at York and Stockton, benefited from 'specials' and came to enjoy a national or regional following. So also with the Derby and other major races. In contrast, football, and rugby, like department stores and music halls, encouraged transport into the cities. Thanks to the railway, habits and hobbies changed. Thousands of visitors used the railways to 'view' great houses and their parks, a hobby that attained great popularity by the 1870s.

In areas with limited rail penetration, such as Cumbria and South-West Scotland, scheduled country carriers remained very important. In many respects, their business supplemented the rail system, providing cartage focused on railheads. Even in Cumbria, however, rail links spread. The Eden Valley Railway (1862), the Cockermouth, Keswick and Penrith Railway (1864–5), and the Cleator and Workington Junction Railway (1880), all aided the development of the West Cumberland iron industry. Routes were also planned into the Lake District, to further quarrying in Borrowdale and into Ennerdale and Ullswater. William Morris complained, 'You will soon have a Cook's tourist railway up Scawfell – and another up Helvellyn – and another up Skiddaw. And then a connecting line, all round.' This was unduly pessimistic, as a public campaign blocked the Borrowdale, Ennerdale and Ullswater plan. The 1881 advert for the Borrowdale Hotel noted 'An omnibus meets all trains at the Keswick station.' The cultural commentator John Ruskin was also concerned about rail:

'There was a rocky valley between Buxton and Bakewell ... divine as the vale of Tempe; you might have seen the gods there morning and evening – Apollo and the sweet Muses of the Light... You enterprised a railway ... you blasted its rocks away.... And now, every fool in Buxton can be at Bakewell in half-an-hour, and every fool in Bakewell at Buxton.'[14]

Elsewhere, the arrival of the train led to the decay of existing routes and of related facilities. Food for horses had been a major overhead for wagon and carriage services. Coal for trains was less expensive. Transport networks, moreover, changed. Crawley had been an important town on the London to Brighton coaching route, but the train went via Three Bridges instead. Again, it is necessary to remember the hard work involved. Northamptonshire-born Tom Masters (1878–1973), recorded in 1963: met 'the navvy boys' building the Daventry to Leamington railway, leading to his going to work when 15 on widening the London-Brighton railway. He started work 'stopping wagons – putting a piece of wood in the wheels to brake them. We were making a cutting 80 feet deep at Merstham Tunnel. Later I worked all down Surrey and Sussex.'[15]

The coaching town of Honiton was hit by the opening of a rail route to Exeter from London via Bristol, only, in turn, to benefit when a new line from London via Honiton began operating in 1860. Some turnpikes were bankrupted; for example, in Dorset, the Wimborne to Puddletown was hit by the introduction of the Southampton and Dorchester Railway. At the same time, there were improvements to the existing road network, including new bridges. Thus, the Workman Bridge was built over the River Avon at Evesham in 1866. The establishment of county councils in 1889 was accompanied by the winding up of turnpike trusts, as in Devon. Prior to that the trusts had been overseen by Parliament, to which annual accounts were submitted, and by the county Quarter Sessions, which oversaw the parishes.

There were other areas of new technology. Thus, the demand for bikes grew greatly as a result of the introduction of safety bikes in the 1880s and of the comfort and ease of maintenance resulting from the invention of pneumatic types. The 1890s saw a boom in cycling, with individuals, including young women, free to wander freely and flexibly. The press runs of Bartholomew's cycling maps rose from 2,000 in the early 1890s to 60,000 in 1908.

The pressures of urban transport were captured by writers. Of the lower-middle class, George and Weedon Grossmith observed in *The Diary of a Nobody* (1892): 'the Pooters rent a house in Holloway rather too close to the railway line (the landlord lets it go cheap because of the noise)'. In his 'The Third Generation' (1894), Arthur Conan Doyle referred to 'The dull roar of the traffic which converged all day upon London Bridge,' following in 'The Story of the Sealed Room' (1898) with: 'A four-wheeled cab, that opprobrium of London, was coming jolting and creaking in one direction, while in the other there was a yellow glare from the lamp of a cyclist.' The following year, Sir John Barry estimated that eight horse-drawn buses a minute would pass an observer on Tottenham Court Road,[16] an intensity that posed the problem of disposing of manure. Indeed, the more general removal of waste was an essential part of urban transport, one made more necessary by the rapid growth in population. This helped ensure a three-dimensional transport as sewage systems developed alongside the Underground. Robert Lowe spoke at the lunch served on Farringdon station on 9 January 1863 to mark the opening of tube services:

'The traffic of London has long been a reproach of the most civilised nation of the world, and the opprobrium of the age. Dr Johnson used to say that if you wanted to see the full tide of human life, you must go to Charing Cross, but Dr Johnson would have to raise his estimation of the full tide, or rather of the close jam of the full tide of human life, many hundred per cent before he could arrive at the state which the traffic of London has now reached.... Through gas-pipes and water-pipes and sewers, ... and ... the Fleet Ditch.... The line has had to worm its way through a complicated and intricate labyrinth under difficulties almost insuperable.'

There was another branch of three-dimensionality with the transport upwards of coal dust, pollution, smoke and surplus heat, such that Manchester acquired the description 'chimney of the world.' High chimneys were an important aspect of the resulting transport system. As with other aspects of transport, there was controversy, with arguments that smoke was linked to prosperity countered by others emphasising poor-health and wasteful inefficiency.[17] As with other forms of transport, the topography had a significant role in affecting the impact of high chimneys, not least in interaction with the weather. Temperature inversions in valley bottoms could trap smog.

Meanwhile, what Arthur Conan Doyle referred to in 'The Sealed Room' (1898) as 'the red brick tentacles of the London octopus' and in *The Sign of Four* (1890) as 'monster tentacles' were made possible by commuting.

Tram systems were frequently run by town councils and, from the 1890s, they subsidised fares in order to encourage people to move away from crowded residential areas in city centres. They had larger houses plus gardens in suburban areas or nearby settlements, for example Exmouth for Exeter, and the train gave them the advantage of regular and short journeys into the city. In Bradford, Leeds and Sheffield, tramways were built into open country in order to encourage development. Electric trams, of which the first in London was established in 1901, running from Shepherd's Bush to Acton, were quicker and carried more passengers than horse trams. They cost less than motor buses of which London had 1,000 by 1913, the first being introduced there in 1905. In Newcastle, where the first electric tram ran in 1901, the new system rapidly affected rail receipts from commuting.

Due to the pressure of transport, city streets became essentially means for circulation, rather than for sociability, household tasks, leisure, manufacturing, trade and shopping. People were subordinated to outside purpose, with the utilitarianism of improved traffic taking precedence over other goals. Local communities were hit in a system of the regulation of public space and activity by the police and local authorities. At the same time, horse-drawn wagons continued to be important in urban areas as well as their rural counterparts.

In 1886, Parliament repealed the legislation that had obliged cars to follow a man carrying a red flag and, instead, allowed them to drive at up to 14 mph. The Motor Car Act of 1903 extended the rights of the motorist but also introduced car registration, a very unpopular step; that of heavy road vehicles had been introduced with the Highways and Locomotives Act of 1878.[18]

The imaginative impact of transport in the late nineteenth century was very much focused on rail. This downplayed the extent to which other forms of transport were very important, notably walking. The significance of the latter emerged clearly in a number of novels that dealt with the poor, but these did not have a traction comparable to the depiction of rail. Instead, the latter was seen as necessary not only for the élite, but for the bulk of the population. Indeed, the successful pressure for working men's trains, those with less expensive tickets essentially for commuters, underlined the extent to which rail, unlike cars at the same stage, did not have an élite image; although this comparison was complicated by the role of buses. It was possible for the monarchs to have their own train, and for others to hire 'specials' just for themselves, while some landowners had gained in effect private stops in return for granting permission for the railway to be built across their land. However, essentially rail was a collective form of transport, albeit complicated by different classes of passengers. This was very different from walking, cycling and cars.

The century closed with a great variety of means of transport. At Exeter, a major rail hub for regional and local lines, there was also in 1900 six vessels weekly carrying goods to and from London, the movement by ship of much coal into the city, with coal yards near the busy quay, and a horse tramway from 1881 with eight horse trams from 1884. More traditionally, there was still an important cattle market.

In Bram Stoker's novel *Dracula* (1897), as an instance of variety, there is 'a little crowd of bicyclists and others who were genially noisy' at a Hampstead pub, a 'patrol of horse police going their usual suburban round', a 'four-wheeler' cab in London, carts moving Dracula's boxes round London, and Dracula owning a Bradshaw railway guide to help him navigate the rail system. It was extensive enough to require such assistance.

Chapter 8

The Age of the Motorcar, 1900–1950

Born in Felling, County Durham in 1894, Ella MacLean, long after described transport before World War One (1914–18). She went on family outings in a pony and trap, as so many families who could afford to did, only to meet:

'our first motor-car ... at Gosforth.... Ginny [the pony] was terrified and reared up, and Tom and Stuart had to jump out and hold her head. She was shaking with fear at the monster she had met.... Transport in those days was vastly different from what it is today [1986]. The horse-drawn vehicles were slow, but the trains were prompt to the minute and very clean – you could set your watches by the trains... one journey to Durham, when on arrival at the station there was a line of prisoners chained together waiting to be taken by horse-drawn vehicles to the prison.... A railway ran from Heworth down a steep hill to the Tyne where ships were waiting to collect the coal.... A coal-load was emptied at the back of the house near the coal-house.'[1]

Horses being terrified by cars was very much a feature of the overlap period, and a cause of frequent accidents, with casualties on both sides, but principally those of the more vulnerable riders. This was an aspect of the extent to which the existing lack of a segregation of use and space on the roads created problems as the range of users increased, a situation also seen today with pavements.

As a very different moment of memory, the crashing of the 1.25 pm from King's Cross, London, to Leeds express into the 1.10 pm King's Cross, London, to Leeds train at Balby Junction near Doncaster on 9 August 1947 led to 18 deaths and 51 injured passengers being detained in hospital among the about 1,400 passengers. The public inquiry revealed that the signalman made two mistakes, but that one of the engines being unable to start from a stop was a problem, the driver of the 1.10 blaming 'A heavy train, a rising gradient, and the bend of the road. It was nothing to do with the coal,' the last a reference to the poor quality of much coal in this postwar period, one that affected the running of trains. The Chief Inspecting Officer of Railways established that the signalmen did not leave the box nor read a newspaper,[2] both serious offences.

Meanwhile, alongside novelty, the persistence of reference to traditional means of transport was suggested by Thomas Hardy in his 'A Trampwoman's Tragedy' (1903) which depicted a murderous quarrel on an English road with the trampwoman left alone 'haunting the Western Moor,' a reference to 'sad Sedge-Moor' in Somerset. In practice, the 'true case' was based on the long-dead Mary Ann Taylor, and Hardy set the story in the past.

Again, there is the question of balance. In terms of new developments, this was the age of aircraft, with the new technology leading to regular services within two decades. Moreover, the lack of a need for a permanent way comparable to canals, rail and roads helped ensure that aircraft services were more similar to those of maritime transport: airports providing nodes where different environments met, like harbours, but no need for a fixed route. Both maritime and air transport were also subject to the weather. However, by 1950 only a small fraction of Britain's domestic passengers and, even more, freight traffic was by air, and the international equivalent, while greater, was still very modest compared to what was to follow from the 1960s.

Moreover, the high cost of air travel to passengers made significant expansion appear unlikely. The major changes that were to be brought by jet aircraft, package holidays, jumbo jets, and budget flights were all in the future.

Separately, Mr Toad in Kenneth Graeme's novel for children *The Wind in the Willows* (1908) with his zeal for novelty captured an appeal of the motorcar. It appeared to offer unconstrained power and to give individuality its head: 'the magnificent motor-car, immense, breath-snatching, passionate, with its pilot tense and hugging his wheel, possessed all earth and air for the fraction of a second.'[3] Toad becomes:

'the Terror of the Highway … as if in a dream, he pulled the lever and swung the car round … all sense of right and wrong, all fear of obvious consequences, seemed temporarily suspended.… he was only conscious that he was Toad once more, Toad at his best and highest, Toad the terror, the traffic-queller, the Lord of the lone trail, before whom all must give way or be smitten into nothingness and everlasting night.'[4]

Graeme presented a transport system in transition, which has been the situation from the end of the seventeenth century. Thus, the story begins with Mole going on a walk, continues with Mole and Rat boating by means of rowing (their own efforts), and then moves to their visiting Toad who presents a horse-pulled caravan, Toad declaring a commitment to travel:

'There's real life for you, embodied in that little cart. The open road, the dusty highway, the heath, the common, the hedgerows, the rolling downs! Camps, villages, towns, cities! Travel, change, interest, excitement! The whole world before you, and a horizon that's always changing!'[5]

Their journey works well when 'along narrow-lanes,' but disaster ensues at the hands of a fast car when they meet 'their first high road.'[6]

There are other means of transport in the story. After the horse-caravan is ruined as a result of the car terrifying the horse, the travellers go to town to pick up a train to take them to a station near their homes, walking Toad thence to Toad Hall. Later, having escaped prison, he appealed for a journey to an engine-driver, the description of whom captured the hard work involved: 'the engine, which was being oiled, wiped, and generally caressed by its affectionate driver, a burly man with an oil-can in one hand and a lump of cotton-waste in the other.'[7] The driver does not 'hold with motor-cars.'[8] Toad jumps from the train, which is being pursued by another, and takes refuge on a canal barge; in turn, stealing the barge-horse and going down 'a rutty lane.'[9] Selling the horse to a gypsy, he gets a lift in a car, drives it too fast, causing it to crash into a horse-pond and escapes anew.

Toad does not travel by sea, but coastal and overseas freight traffic continued to be dynamic. For example of the three million tons of traded goods crossing the Devon county boundary in 1913 only just over a million tons were carried by rail, and coal in particular came from South Wales. Far more coal came to Devon by sea than rail; although, as an instance of the problems posed by statistics, coal, minerals and other goods landed at ports were moved on by rail.[10]

In the early years of the century, there was still extension to the rail system, in part under the Light Railways Act. Thus, the line that killed river traffic on the Tamar was not opened until 1908, while light railways in Essex to Tollesbury and Thaxted were opened in 1907 and 1913. Most of these later lines were not very profitable, which helps explain why they were built so late. Nevertheless, the absence of large-scale car ownership meant that other transport systems played a role to a degree that might appear surprising given the later stress on cars. These systems were generally characterised by an emphasis on group transport by a variety of means. The form of propulsion was less significant. Thus, in 1897, the 'Hundred of Manhood and Selway Tramway' opened, running the eight miles from Chichester and carrying holiday-makers, local passengers and agricultural freight. In service till 1935, when it fell victim to more reliable bus competition, the 'tram' was one of the numerous schemes of Colonel Holman Stephens who created rural services by using low construction, rolling stock and maintenance costs, and simple methods. In fact, this 'tram' was a railway that bypassed the safety requirements of a Light Railway Order by using the private purchase of land. There were numerous derailments which led to the death of one fireman, and an absence of level crossing gates.[11] Light railways often dispensed with crossing gates, but this meant that the train had to cross the crossing at walking speed and led to grindingly slow journeys. Thus, trains took over three hours to cover the 58 miles from Carmarthen to Aberystwyth. An instructive indication of change away from rail was the 9.5 mile North Holderness Light Railway from Beverley to North Frodingham, approved under the Light Railways Act in 1897, but never built and instead replaced in 1903 by a road service.

The profitability of recent and new lines focused in particular on the expansion of the London underground system, especially to the north of

London until World War Two and of Southern Railway services south of London. However, Green Belt legislation was to transform the context by controlling demand through the geographical expansion of the city.

At the same time, aside from new lines, new services offered significant possibilities. The most recent mainline, the Great Central Railway, which opened for passenger travel to Marylebone in 1899, ran a nonstop service from London to Sheffield from 1903, with slip coaches (carriages designed from 1858 to be uncoupled from the rear of a moving passenger train) for passengers to Leicester and Nottingham, and also, from 1903, a through express from Dover and Folkestone over South Eastern Railway track to Reading, Great Western to Banbury, and then on to Leeds and Manchester, thus avoiding a break-of-service in London. There is no comparable service today. In 1902, the company had also introduced a Southampton to Newcastle express.

The drama of rail was present at the outset of John Buchan's successful adventure novel *The Thirty-Nine Steps* (1915), with Richard Hannay boarding a moving train at St Pancras, a staple of such works, and then 'roaring through the northern tunnels' of London. Reaching Scotland he steals a car, as Mr Toad had recently done, only to discover the 'risk of getting on to a farm road and ending in a duck pond or a stable-yard.' Hannay is tracked by an aircraft and he runs his car into a hedge to avoid another one.

The financial situation had already caused a crisis for British rail prior to the outbreak of World War One in 1914 and, therefore, prior to the major expansion in car, bus and lorry use in the 1920s and 1930s. The fragmentation of the railway industry was a cause of difficulties as the resulting companies often lacked the necessary capital base and liquidity to provide investment or to attract it from elsewhere. In part because the time horizons were inappropriate, the regulation of fares and freight rates exacerbated this problem and also made it harder to cover running costs. These costs were a matter not only of maintenance and the purchase of coal, but also of the wages demanded by workers, wages that the industry could not manage.

Indeed, in 1901, a labour dispute between the Taff Vale Railway Company, a key carrier in South Wales, and the Amalgamated Society of Railway Servants, a union founded in 1871, led the House of Lords, where the law lords made judgments, to decide that unions could be liable for damages resulting from their actions, a decision that was reversed by the Liberal government that came to power in 1905 with the Trade Disputes Act of 1906: the previous Conservative government had rejected trade union pressure to change the law. The Liberal government enjoyed parliamentary support from Labour. Alongside the coal miners, the railway workers were to be the most militant of the trade unions, and the two unions were joined in their activism. The low rate of return on capital hitting share prices and investor returns would not have been of interest to the workers, but it was a crucial issue, one that discouraged investment.

In 1911, against the background of earlier industrial disputes,[12] the first general rail strike in Britain, a strike that arose from anger with the Conciliation Board established in 1907, led to intimidation and the deployment of troops who killed two people at Llanelli where the Great Western Railway line had been blocked. These deaths were followed by riots that included the vandalization of the station. Supporting the government and worried about radicalism, George V referred to 'what was fast becoming a terrible calamity.'

This strike was an aspect of the political role of rail, one differently seen in the significance of trains for electioneering. Just as Queen Victoria was able to travel by rail around Britain in a way not open to her predecessors, regularly going to Scotland as a result, so politicians such as William E. Gladstone employed the train to reach out to the electorate in a fashion that had not been possible hitherto.

In the face of the more general difficulties of rail, there was talk of nationalisation and certainly of the consolidation of ownership among fewer companies, a form of corporatism. The latter was backed by David Lloyd George as President of the Board of Trade (1905–8). A radical moderniser, he argued that consolidation would enhance profitability and efficiency. However, the measure lacked political traction at this point. As a different aspect of corporatism, most of the rail unions merged in 1913 to form the National Union of Railwaymen.

There was in economic and financial terms an over-provision of services and spare capacity, which contrasted with the situation in Germany where provision was more efficient. On the other hand, not that this was the intention, this spare capacity enabled Britain during World War One to maintain existing rail services while also adding new ones. Germany lacked comparable flexibility then, not least due to pressures on resources, including coal supplies.

Meanwhile, the capital of empire, London, had been given added transport flexibility, as well as distinctiveness, by an underground railway system. No other British city had an underground until Glasgow opened one in 1896, providing the third oldest in Europe after London and Budapest, where the first line, an electrified one, was opened in 1896: Istanbul had an underground funicular railway, built in 1875. The Glasgow underground was powered by a steam-driven clutch-and-cable system until converted to electricity in 1935; while the 15 stations had island platforms.

London was in a different league at this point, as Paris did not follow until 1914. Train services, both over and under ground, were crucial to London's character and sense of identity, and important to the city's expansion. The great success of the Central Line between Shepherd's Bush and the Bank, opened in 1900, encouraged the building of other underground lines, notably the Bakerloo, Piccadilly, and Hampstead to Charing Cross (part of the Northern Line), with the key figure being Charles Tyson Yerkes, an American financier of dubious practices but boundless energy who had been responsible for the Loop in Chicago. Opened in 1906, the Piccadilly initially ran from Hammersmith to Finsbury Park, making it the longest line that fed commuters and shoppers from West London into the West End. Sensing the possibilities of expanding London, Yerkes planned an extension for the Hampstead Line to Golders Green, which opened in 1907, offering the prospect of expanding past the obstacle of Hampstead Heath and thence across rural Middlesex. However, there was no large-scale expansion of the system into less prosperous Dockland, although, in part, that was catered to by overground services. The 'tube' was particularly significant as London had the largest underground railway system in the world and this system came to affect the imagining of the city.

Built underground, including by cut and cover methods, the tube caused less destruction than the establishment of main line rail services. Massive demolition resulted from the construction of London's stations, culminating with the building of Marylebone in 1893–9, the last of the termini, which led to the destruction of Blandford Square and the eviction of over 4,000 mostly working-class people.

Whether by tube or by other means, commuting was scarcely value-free, and this was notably so in terms of provision and costings. In London, the Cheap Trains Act of 1883, passed against the wishes of the railway companies, obliged them to operate more cheap trains and, by 1914, had ensured that 1,000 cut-price trains daily were taking workers into London. The parliamentary debate on a Cheap Trains Bill in 1900 indicated the different views at play. Charles Stuart-Wortley, Conservative MP for Sheffield Hallam, who opposed the extension of such measures, emphasized the need to treat railway companies 'in a reasonable manner, so as to induce the investing public to come forward when their money is required.' Lieutenant-Colonel Amelius Lockwood, a Director of the LNWR as well as Conservative MP for Epping, also spoke in favour of the shareholders:

'It would appear that when some enterprising individual wants to enter upon private legislation, the railway companies are to be his favourite hunting ground … a Cheap Trains Bill … secures a certain amount of popularity in the constituencies…. The railway companies having large capitals are looked upon as fair game for any attacks made upon them. When the representatives of the railways attempt in the constituencies or in the House of Commons to defend the companies from these continual attacks they are called bloated capitalists or the railway ring… The two largest items which have affected the net revenue of the companies are the increased wages, curtailed hours of labour, and increase of local taxation.'

As was invariably the case, the rail system included much that was less impressive. Arthur Conan Doyle noted, in his non-Sherlock Holmes short story 'The Brazilian Cat' (1898), when a character goes to the fictional Clipton-on-the-Marsh in Suffolk: 'After changing at Ipswich, a little local train deposited me at a small deserted station.' Such unmanned stops became more common as the network expanded.

In 1910, the Committee of Imperial Defence expressed concern that war with Germany, which had the second largest navy in the world, would affect the movement of supplies, notably from the ports on the North Sea coast. A sub-committee took evidence from the general managers of the leading railway companies and in 1911 concluded that the closure of these ports would create grave problems for feeding Londoners. These managers pressed for a central body to respond in wartime, not least by coordinating government requirements from rail. In the event, in the face of German submarine attack, notably, but not only, on the vulnerable North Sea coastal shipping that was additionally exposed by the German seizure of Belgian ports, and the possibility of attack by surface warships, the war created problems for British coastal trade which forced more goods onto the trains. This concern had led in 1912 to the establishment of the Railway Executive Committee (REC) and in 1914, with the outbreak of war, to the railways coming under government control, an Irish REC following in 1917. In practice that meant control by a committee of prominent railway managers and its range of sub-committees.

In order to focus on the war effort, and to save on coal and locomotives, 601 of which were sent abroad to help the war effort there, there was a reduction of services deemed unnecessary, such as dining cars, express speeds, and provision to many stations, all also seen in World War Two. The Bideford, Westward Ho! and Appledore Railway was pulled up for transfer to the Western Front, only for the freight ship carrying it to be sunk by a German submarine. The majority of locomotives remained in Britain but there was not the usual pattern of replenishment, and the unprecedented amount of work contributed to worn-out engines. This created major operational problems for the postwar railways. Separately, motor transport and knowledge, from driving to repairs, greatly increased during World War One, with many lorries, and eventually tanks, used in the war.[13]

So also with knowledge of aircraft. The postwar establishment of air services led to competition for rail, for example on the London-Paris route. This began in 1919 from Hounslow Heath Aerodrome, where Heathrow now is, to Le Bourget in Paris. From 1920, Cricklewood Aerodrome, where the Golders Green Estate was to be built, was also the base for Paris services, as was Croydon Airport which opened in 1920 on the site of Beddington and Waddon aerodromes and became Britain's leading airport. By 1921, six companies operated a London to Paris service and the Croydon-Le Bourget route became the busiest in the world. There were also flights from London to Amsterdam and Rotterdam from 1920 and to Berlin from 1923. The airport was greatly expanded in 1926–8.

However, the London-Paris example of successful operation in part was a matter of competition with the cross-Channel ferries which were linked to rail services. In contrast, overland, rapid train services benefited from their city-centre-to-city-centre character, and from the small carrying-capacity of aircraft, which were also vulnerable to weather conditions, and far more so than trains. Moreover, air services were more expensive than trains, and had a higher accident rate. Airships appeared to offer potential for longer-range services, but accidents, especially the crashing of the poorly-conceived R101 in 1930, on its first flight, helped ensure failure.[14]

At the same time, railway companies tried to benefit from the growth of air services. In 1933, the GWR Air Service began a twice daily weekly service between Plymouth and Cardiff via Haldon airfield near Exeter, a service extended that summer to Birmingham. In 1934, the Big Four railway companies and Imperial Airways formed the Railway Air Service, which linked with the international flights of the latter. This company continued until nationalised in 1947. The main base was Croydon Airport, and the major route was from London to Glasgow. This was competition with rail, but competition that was effective only because this was a long journey.

Over-ambitious expansion in the nineteenth century compounded by a lack of investment in World War One left the railways in the 1920s in a difficult position, not least with a lack of recent investment or of the replacement of locomotives and rolling stock, both of which had been put under heavy strain due to a massive rise in usage to meet wartime requirements. These difficulties were exacerbated by interwar economic problems,

The war had seen national wage bargaining for rail workers rather than at the level of individual employers. This situation continued postwar, as did the implications of a rise in union membership from 43 to 60 per cent of railway employees. The wartime situation was consolidated as a result of the 1919 national rail strike, which was called in response to the government wish to cut pay rates, which had risen greatly during the war. Finding himself cut off in Balmoral in Scotland from all London letters and newspapers, George V felt his royal office drifting out of control, and returned to the capital by car.

The strike, and the subsequent Railways Act of 1921, led, in the settlement, to full union recognition, a new wages board, and an eight-hour day. Helped by the strength of the National Union of Railwaymen and the wartime acceleration of the development of railway trade unionism, the railwaymen had done better than the miners were to do when faced with significant wage cuts in 1921. On the other hand, fares rose as a result, which challenged the competitiveness of the industry. Moreover, in 1919, without resorting to violence, the government had shown an ability to cope with the strike that indicated that rail was not as essential as hitherto. Emerging road transport ensured food deliveries, and aircraft, both military and civil, provided capacity, while volunteers from the public helped keep transport moving. Yet, there was still a need to face immediate problems as Sir Eric Geddes, the Minister of Transport, pointed out in a Cabinet memorandum of March 1921:

'the Coal Strike, the disturbances in Ireland, and more recently the sudden and sharp depression in trade have exercised a disastrous effect on Railway Revenue and the hopes of financial equilibrium have not been realised.... In order to secure the permanent financial stability of Railway Companies, a consolidation of railway interests is essential.'

In Ireland, both the largely successful rebellion outside Britain and the subsequent civil war beteen Irish nationalists saw enormous damage to the rail system.

In 1918, there had been government consideration of nationalisation, and, although that did not happen, the Railway Act of 1921 ensured large-scale reorganisation, such that in 1923, when the railways were returned to their private owners, they were grouped by the amalgamation of more than 120 companies into four large companies, a radical, and oligopolistic, change from the pre-war situation. Originally there had been proposals for five or six companies for England and Wales and one, later two, for Scotland; but there was opposition in Parliament to a separate system for Scotland. Geddes had supported this separation as he did not see why Scottish railways should be cross-subsidised by English customers. The four companies competed. In place of a range of earlier regulations, a Rates Tribunal established a target return on capital in what was now a highly regulated industry, which, however, took away flexibility and made it very difficult to stem the speedy loss of freight traffic to the road. As a result, railway companies pressed for the revision of the regulatory framework.

In Agatha Christie's novel *The Secret Adversary* (1922), a meeting of political agitators reveals links with the unions, notably the miners and the railwaymen. The General Strike of 1926 saw the railways again a centre of union opposition, whereas road freight was more flexible. The transport system was at the forefront of tension with some workers striking, others continuing work, and the use of troops and volunteers to maintain services, the former particularly conspicuous in moving flour from the London docks. Reporting varied greatly, with the *British Worker* writing of large-scale support for the strike as in the issue of 5 May: 'The strike early laid its paralysing hand on the great railway station at Carlisle, where seven important lines converge... Within a few hours the usually animated platforms were deserted and desolate.' And so on for transport at Middlesbrough, Hull, and Birmingham. As a result, there was a reliance on road transport, as with fish from Hull. That issue reported hostile demonstrators including tramwaymen preventing the use of volunteers to run tram cars from the Camberwell depot in London. On the 6th, there was violence in both Edinburgh and Glasgow as demonstrators attacked tram and bus services leading to police charges. The *Flying Scotsman* ran off the line between Morpeth and Newcastle, wrecked as the result of the sabotaging of the track.[15]

The consolidation of rail companies in 1923 offered the scale seen as necessary but was challenged by labour issues and, more significantly, by the reduction of carriage due to the economic problems of the 1930s, especially in their traditional freight markets of coal, metallurgy and heavy engineering. The General Strike had proved that the nation could live without railways, and much of the lost high-value traffic never returned after the strike. In part, this was a reflection of the extent to which the rail system revealed inflexibility in meeting changing patterns of passenger and freight demands.

In the interwar period, 240 miles of track and 350 stations were closed completely and another 1,000 miles and 380 stations were closed to passenger traffic but remained open for freight. Among the 'Big Four' railway companies, the Southern Railway was alone in paying a regular dividend to shareholders before 1948. This was the only company that electrified on a large scale and that did not serve depressed industrial areas; instead, as a reminder of the regional character of transport, it catered to London's massive expansion south of the Thames. There were also important steam services on the Southern.[16] The other three were the London, Midland and Scottish; the Great Western; and the London and North Eastern.

The lack of profit reduced investment, and there was no supporting government finance, a marked contrast to the situation as far as roads were concerned. The financial hit to rail, a hit that affected investment possibilities, were referred to in Ernest Bramah's short-story 'The Knight's Cross Signal Problem': 'City and Suburbans [a fictional rail company] … after their late depression on the projected extension of the motor bus service, had been steadily creeping up on the abandonment of the scheme.'

Under-investment, over-capacity and a massive wages bill were major interwar issues, as was economic transformation: the newer consumer industries tended to have lower-bulk freight needs, many of which were met by road transport. Whereas access to rail needed special facilities, notably passenger stations, freight sidings or marshalling yards, road transport was different. It offered access at every point along a road. In addition, the vehicles were far less expensive and easier to maintain than those required for the rail system, the majority were owned by individuals, and they did not require comparable training in their use. Lorries served many of the booming industries of the period. For example, they could readily move housing materials such as bricks from central sites. The 1933 Road and Rail Traffic Act provided inadequate assistance for the railways, while price increases in 1937 hit rail freight.

Owing to regulations, rail companies were not allowed to become road hauliers other than at their railheads. Inexpensive lorries and petrol, low taxation on wages, capital and profits, and no need to pay for road construction or maintenance, provided the road hauliers with major advantages. So also with their ability to set their own prices and wages, and the lack of an obligation to be common carriers, which could entail unprofitable loads for rail companies. Separately, lorries could readily move materials from warehouses, and the latter proved more efficient than marshalling yards many of which had legacy problems including cramped sites and unionised workforces. Road freight warehousing required less space. In addition, buses competed with railways to transport people. Buses offered a flexibility that trains generally lacked, not least with special services, and the resulting possibility for tapping potential demand. As a result, the trains had to share excursion business. Buses competed with railways to take people to the new holiday camps, such as the Butlin's camp opened at Skegness in 1937.

The reorganisation of 1923 certainly led to a measure of rationalisation. Standardisation of locomotives and rolling stock cut maintenance costs and helped efficiency. Freight handling improved thanks to the gradual introduction of containers and mechanised marshalling yards such as Whitemoor. Opened in 1929, on the site of an old yard, this had Frohlich hydraulic brakes, the first time they had been used in Britain. Whereas the previous yard had 24 sidings and could take 1,265 wagons at any one moment, such that about 3,000 could be handled daily, the replacement had 43 sidings and room for 4,000 wagons at any one time, and, by 1939, 8,000 wagons were sorted each day. The down yard, added in 1933, was closed in 1972, and, from 1982, there was scant use of Whitemoor.

Freight handling is important in terms of the efficiency and security of rail transport. Aspects include developing wagons and infrastructure for each of loading bulk products and their automatic unloading, and also containers that reduced product handling and improved security in order to prevent theft.

Furthermore, an attempt was made to project a modern image. LNER used Gill Sans lettering, which was invented for it, on publicity. Its posters continue to be impressive, as with Frank Newbold's 'Take Your Car by LNER' (1935), for which the rates were 3d per mile for the car for a single journey if accompanying one first or two third class ticketholders, and, for a return, 3d per mile outward and 1½d per mile return. Much building on the rail network used modern architectural techniques, for example Surbiton station and SR 'glasshouse'-style signal boxes. More generally, there was a lot of streamlining. F. Tennyson Jesse, in his short story 'The Railway Carriage' (1931), referred to moving from a third-class carriage of the closed type to 'a modern corridor train.'

Nevertheless, despite cuts in services, the rail reorganisation of 1923 had not produced massive cost savings, nor the necessary investment, for example in large railway wagons able to carry 20 tons of coal. More generally, once built and then consolidated, there was very little new investment in railway lines and marshalling yards. Road, air and sea transport had some limiting factors of infrastructure, but their routes and flows could be adapted much more easily than rail.

Meanwhile, while the bicycle and the car had brought a degree of flexibility, speed and range for travellers not seen for walkers and horse-drawn buses respectively, the motor buses and taxis that in turn appeared from 1898 and 1904 added capacity. Economic activity followed these new vehicles. By 1907, the Britannia Foundry at Derby included a motor cylinder line making 400 to 500 parts a week for car manufacturers, such as Jowett Motors of Bradford. Aside from professionally-made vehicles, many do-it-yourself motor cycles and cars appeared, including the three-wheelers: the Shotwell Junior made in 1903 in Rothwell was fuelled through a lampwick carburettor, but lost a wheel when tested.[17]

Car production rose from 116,000 in 1924 to 341,000 in 1938, by when there were nearly two million cars, half a million road goods vehicles (some diesel-powered from the early 1920s), and 53,000 buses and coaches. George Bernard Shaw captured the appeal in the first Act of his 1929 play *The Apple Cart*: 'What Englishman will give his mind to politics as long as he can afford to keep a motor car?' Thanks to the Morris works at Cowley, Oxford had only 5 per cent unemployment in 1934, and the car factories in Oxford employed 10,000 in 1939, producing on the American model that William Morris sought to copy from Henry Ford. Morris was also influenced by all-steel car bodies.

'The sound of horns and motors' of T.S. Eliot's dystopian poem 'The Waste Land' (1922) was becoming more insistent. On 4 October 1923, the *Times* complained about the over-development of the seaside. At first:

'muddy paths were replaced by sound roads' but then 'The roads became asphalt esplanades... the same fate overtaking the use of the motor car. To that end better roads were needed; and first the greater, then the smaller roads were so improved that the Romans, even Napoleon, General Wade[18] and Mr Macadam, would have marvelled at them. And then, as with the seaside, the idea began to run away with its promoters. Little by little the greater roads began to lose all semblance of the rural.... A decade or two more, and we must search the wilds of distant countries for a truly country road.'

This was a foolish prediction and ignored the value of a hierarchy of roads, including through-routes. Nevertheless, the sense of overwhelming change was effectively captured.

Detective novels increasingly focused on cars rather than the more traditional trains. Edith Caroline Rivett, writing as E.C.R. Lorac, in her successful *Death on the Oxford Road* (1931), began the novel with Peter Vernon remarking:

'The only object of running a car nowadays is that it makes you independent of railway time-tables.... Motoring for pleasure is a contradiction in terms. Either you stick to the main roads and form one of a procession, – bonnet to tail – reaching from Land's End to John o' Groats, or else you take to the by-roads and rattle your car to ruin over ruts and pot-holes until its not worth anyone's while to salvage the remnants.... The roads at the present moment are a pleasure to drive on, but as it's past midnight, that fact can hardly be taken as a criterion of their state during the rush hours.... to be relieved of the burden of coping with time-tables.'

His driver, Chief Inspector Macdonald, Lorac's hero, adds a social dimension to commentary:

'Opinions nowadays are derived from two sources; one source is the car-owner, class-hogs to a man; the other is the pedestrian class, the back-bone of England, the fellows who get the work done, and, who ... can't own a car.'[19]

Very differently, in her *Impact of Evidence* (1954), set on the Welsh Marshes, roads were cut and bridges brought down by heavy rains and floods.

Major roads that had been overshadowed during the age of rail, such as the London-Brighton route via Crawley, revived in importance. Less prominent Victorian by-roads had frequently been poorly surfaced, but greater traffic flow led to pressures to improve them, not least by providing all-weather surfaces. In 1909, the national Road Board was founded to lend energy and cohesion to road construction. However, roads not adopted by county councils were neither asphalted nor looked after, and rapidly became tracks that were not accessible to cars.

Other transport systems were vulnerable, even if in 1911, Cadbury's established a new factory at Knighton on the Shropshire Union Canal, producing condensed milk which was moved to the Cadbury works at Bournville near Birmingham on the Worcester and Birmingham Canal. The company moved cocoa from London and Southampton by rail. Yet, rail and road hit canal traffic hard. Thus, in Berkshire, commercial traffic on the Wilts and Berks Canal stopped in 1906, the canal closed in 1914, and, on the Kennet and Avon Canal, traffic had all but ceased by 1939: it is now a major leisure canal. In his 'London is a Muddle' (1937), E.M. Forster commented on the largely disused nature of London's canals: 'Occasionally a string of barges passes through behind a tug, on its way to the docks.' Yet, canals continue to be significant in some areas, J.B. Priestley referring in 1929 to industrial Bruddersford [Huddersfield]: 'That streak of slime must be the Leeds and Liverpool Canal or the Aire and Calder Canal.'[20]

In response to wage cuts, the canal strike of 1923 saw about 500 boats on strike. On 13 September, the *Times*, observing 'The canals are relatively so small a part of the transport system of the country,' noted the difficult nature of the job, as well as it being separate to society:

'Canal boatmen are a class very much apart from others … a moving home … live on the boat … crew his wife and the children who are old enough to lend a hand.…The children have little or no schooling.'

The wages were 'downwards' from £2 a week and this meant that the boatmen could not afford homes on land. John Betjeman captured a sense of canals as past in his poem 'A Shropshire Lad':

'The gas was on in the Institute…
A lass was singing a hymn,
When Captain Webb the Dawley man,
Captain Webb from Dawley
Came swimming along the old canal
That carried the bricks to Lawley.'

The spread of motor vehicles also hit coastal steamship services by adding a dimension to the competition from rail and filling the gaps between railheads, reducing the opportunities for coastal services. As steamship services were cut, seaside settlements lost their function as regular ports. The weekly cargo and passenger service to Barmouth provided by the Aberdovey and Steamship Company ended in 1915.

The extent of overlap was shown in London, where the first horseless cab [a car] appeared in 1897, but the last horse-drawn cab was not removed from service until 1947. Trams overlapped with buses. In 1930, London introduced Felthams – comfortable, quick, trams, and a sign that trams were regarded as having a future. In *The Good Companions* (1929), Priestley provided a sense of the ubiquity of trams in writing of the Pennines 'not a dozen miles from where the Bradford trams end or the Burnley trams begin'. Subsequently there is reference to 'Ponderous trams loomed up, creaking and groaning … lumbered off.'[21] However, the greater flexibility of buses ensured that London was soon planning to close its tram routes by 1941. Trams ran on steel tracks and required a power supply, but buses did not need any route infrastructure separate to roads and could respond rapidly to changes in demand. In 1905, a new steel bridge was built across the Exe at Exeter, and an electric tram system, with twelve trams, began service that year. However, the last electric tram ran there in 1931.

The new roads led to new smells and sounds and affected the visual context of life, both in towns and in the countryside. Roads created new demands for signs, lampposts, manhole covers, and traffic lights. Roads led to new boundaries and commands, to zebra crossings and Belisha beacons, the second named after the Conservative Minister of Transport in 1934–7, Leslie Hore-Belisha: by 1941 there were 64,000 Belisha beacons.

The popular engagement with road transport brought many casualties, in part due to the commitment to speed. The ending of the 20 mph speed limit in 1930 caused an increase in fatalities, with the absence of regulations about car maintenance a contributing factor. In 1934, 7,343 road deaths and 261,603 injuries were recorded, with pedestrians accounting for half of the casualties. The government responded with the 30 mph limit in built-up areas (1934), the driving test (1935), the Belisha beacon (1934) and a rewritten Highway Code (1934). It was accused of 'pampering pedestrians' but the ideas of control and constraint became established before the wartime pattern of enforcement. Design changes were also important to reduced casualties, not least shatter-proof glass and cars with roofs as opposed to the open cars in which drivers were liable to break their necks if the car turned over.

There was also a more extensive use of pavements at least in towns. This was an instance of the degree to which transport segregation was a key to safety. Thus, zebra crossings became a regulated aspect of such segregation.

Travel by road led to the need for individual decisions which were not required when making journeys by rail, as road transport offered access at every point along the road. There was also a need for fuel, accommodation, refreshment and information, both en route and for planning. This led in 1905 to the first national road atlas for cars, *Pratt's Road Atlas of England and Wales for Motorists*. The Automobile Association, in turn, commissioned atlases including, from 1925, set itineraries along the major roads in the editions of the *AA Road Book of England and Wales*. *A-Z Street Atlases* followed from 1936, with Phyllis Pearsall playing the key role, notably in checking the streets of London. These A-Zs were a great commercial success and focused on transport to the exclusion of other elements. In the 'A-Zing' of life, differences within the city or town, for example of wealth, or environmental or housing quality (or presence/absence), are ignored. Political canvassers, estate agents, salesmen, police officers and residents are aware of detailed variations among streets, of a geography of zones and boundaries, of ownership and residence patterns, that do not appear on any street plan.

More generally, maps of transport systems neglect the perceptions that create and reflect senses of space, in favour, instead, of a bland uniform background that is described, and thus experienced, in terms of routes.

The latter, however, are not depicted with sufficient attention to their characteristics as routes, notably traffic density. This made the maps of rail use produced as an appendix to the Beeching Report (1963) so instructive.

Moreover, ignoring another form of transport, the maps of roads were very much ground level. There was scant sense of the vertical, and thus of the many who live and work in skyscrapers or more modest multi-storey buildings, and of the transport problems these buildings pose and the means used to tackle these: lifts and stairs.

Improvements to road infrastructure included in 1934 what was then the longest underwater tunnel in the world, the road link under the Mersey between Liverpool and Birkenhead. Devised in 1929, begun in the 1930s, in part to improve speed, notably for freight, and also to offer employment, and resumed in the 1950s, the Trunk Roads Programme prefigured the motorways in providing major changes to traditional local road patterns. Indeed, the programme anticipated the motorway system opened from 1958, not least in an earlier use of the word motorway.

Plans for bold road developments gathered pace, especially those focused on London. Sir Charles Bressey, a Ministry of Transport engineer, proposed a programme of massive building including large roundabouts and big flyovers. In the late 1930s, more fantastically, the Modern Architectural Research Group envisaged huge, raised arteries, more than 200 feet wide, crossing London at rooftop level, carrying trains and buses, while the streets below were to be handed over to private cars. Patrick Abercrombie's *County of London Plan* of 1943 proposed a large number of new roads, including three orbital routes, as well as radial roads to join these rings and provide links from the centre to the major trunk routes in South-East England. His *Greater London Plan* of 1944 proposed six ring roads, including E Ring, much of which is now followed by the M25, as well as ten radial roads. Abercrombie argued that fast through-traffic must be separated in order to protect local communities. The plans foreshadowed the Greater London Council's commitment in the 1960s and 1970s to a motorway box for London. Postwar reconstruction planning failed to make much of railways, but tended to focus on road flow.[22]

The impact of the environment on transport and of transport on the environment was readily apparent in cities, for example Norwich. In 1912, when 6 inches of rain fell there in 12 hours, there was a flood leading to the suspension of tram services due to a flooding of the main streets and serious damage to the electricity supply. Conversely, V.F. Soothill, the Medical Officer for the city between the wars, complained about the increase in cars, whose 'offensive gases' made some of the streets smell at times 'like the omnibus station outside Liverpool Street station' in London. As a result, he argued that the streets of the city centre should be built as wide as possible so that 'the wind has free entry either to remove the fumes rapidly or hasten the oxidation of any carbon monoxide to the less poisonous dioxide.'[23] As a reminder of the individual experience, steam left smuts aplenty to affect health and clothes, notably for the train crew. The situation was different with diesel and very different with electric.

Transport extended to completely new systems to a degree that is generally neglected. The Electricity Supply Act of 1926 established a National Grid for electricity, under the control of the Central Electricity Board. Schemes for supply areas were prepared by the Electricity Commission and adopted by the Central Electricity Board. Thus, in 1931, the North Wales Power Company erected an overhead line across the Menai Straits and Anglesey. Earlier steam-generating electricity power stations were closed. At the cost of about £29 million, a Grid of about 4,000 miles was completed by 1933, and, by 1938, 98 per cent of the population was supplied, with the price per unit half that of the early 1920s.[24]

So also with oil pipelines, with oil moved from landing places to refineries, and then on. The development of radio and television also ensured new transport needs and systems. The key characteristic of these forms of transport was that they related to freight not passengers, and had specialised means of conveyance. As such they were different from the movement of the post and (to a lesser extent) coal, both of which made use of existing services, thus coal being moved by coasters, rail, canal and lorry.

The hierarchies of transport need can be seen in the very different ways of viewing networks, both in terms of what is (and was) discussed, and at what relative length, and with reference to the relationship between national, regional and local flows, the latter, as with electric lifts, often very local. The car provided needs and possibilities for all three flows, but also a hierarchy in part mediated through the provision and purchase of different types of cars, and, separately, as a result of different funding sources for road programmes. Road use within towns owed much to commuting, the need for which increased greatly with the movement of people from crowded central areas. Often the cars (and buses) fed rail commuting, which had increased in scale as cities had expanded and rail networks developed in the suburbs. *Autocar*, however, estimated in 1936 that 60 per cent of Britons could not afford to run a car, even if one were given to them free.

In 1914, there had been 132,000 motorised vehicles in private ownership, while the comparable French number was 107,535. In the interwar period, those who could not afford cars were in the overwhelming majority, but vehicle ownership became a goal or model for many of them, creating a pent-up aspiration and ensuring that future affluence would lead to the purchase of more cars. The cinema helped to foster this romance.

So also with fiction. Although he could go by train on visits (albeit with a car collecting his luggage at the station),[25] P.G. Wodehouse's fictional Bertie Wooster, a wealthy young man, is readily able to go on 'a motor trip,'[26] and can drink plentiful brandy before driving.[27]

In World War Two (1939–45), state control was accompanied by German air and rocket attacks. State control was insistent, not least due to the allocation of resources, particularly coal, oil and labour in a period of rationing, conscription, and serious war damage and vulnerability. For rail, there was control over services and a usage that imposed heavy strain on track, locomotives and rolling stock. As a result, there was a deterioration that was not countered by investment or adequate opportunities for maintenance.

Rail facilities were difficult to disguise and protect. German air attacks on the British rail system were particularly acute in the winter of 1940–1, with major damage to stations in London and Liverpool. German aerial reconnaissance and other target-allocation made much of identifying rail facilities for bombing. Repair work, often by night, was crucial to the continual running of services, much of this work conducted while in danger of renewed attack.

Trains were used for the evacuation of civilians threatened by bombing. The evacuation of children and others from cities at the start of the war, with 1.3 million people moved by train in a fortnight, was an unprecedented movement. 118,745 children were evacuated from London, including my parents. This was achieved by special trains. There was no comparable movement by road. To deal with 'drift back,' parents were given special cheap train tickets (free if children were very ill) and special train deals for the summer holidays. There were fresh evacuations when VI and V2 attacks were launched on London in 1944–5.[28]

Meanwhile, the Allied wartime effort required a formidable transport effort focused on port facilities, airfields, depots and warehouses. Aside from the supply of British units, those of Allies had to be supported. The American air force in Britain, the 8th AF, was largely supplied through the port of Liverpool, near which there was a main supply depot at Warton. A series of depots and lorry transport stations provided the infrastructure for the lorry-borne movement of ammunition to the air bases in eastern England.

Road transport was hit hard with higher prices for petrol and limited availability of it. As a result, passenger usage of rail rose. In part, this also reflected the extent to which wartime disruption, notably to family life, and not only service leave, encouraged people to travel to see family and others. Yet, wartime usage for military and special purposes put a lot of pressure on train services. With many trains taken up for wartime tasks, other services were fewer, more crowded, and often subject to cancellation. Trains were slower and usually dark so as to prevent spotting by hostile aircraft. As with road travel which was greatly affected by the black-out, accidents increased, including falling on and off dark platforms. A lack of track maintenance led to slower running of trains over more uneven track, and this resulted in more delays.

Novels of wartime rail travel such as those of Edmund Crispin, were of dismal journeys, as in *The Moving Toyshop* (1946): 'I had a pretty bloody journey from London. Very slow train. Stopped at every telegraph pole – like a dog.' A more romantic context was provided by the British film *Brief Encounter* (1945) which was shot at Carnforth railway station, but based on a 1936 play. In it, Laura Jesson goes on a weekly train journey to a town for shopping and an afternoon film.

The war saw government control of railways in the Inter-Company Freight Rolling Stock Control. This control prepared the way for postwar nationalisation, not least by reducing the financial strength of the companies. In that respect, wartime was a continuation of the Depression. Companies were only allowed to retain a portion of their profits, while sources of income, such as first-class travel (1941) and restaurant cars (1944), were abolished in order to increase usage. In Raymond Postgate's novel *Somebody at the Door* (1943), which is set in January 1942, travel from Euston is bleak: 'The month before, a large number of trains had been taken off because of fuel shortage.... the train pulled in, dead and dark with all its blinds drawn.'[29]

Furthermore, routine maintenance decreased greatly, and there was no regular replacement of locomotives. It was not only that pre-war plans for improvement were abandoned, but also the practice of remaining fit for purpose. This had consequences in terms not only of wartime accidents but also a higher rate of accidents after the war than before it. So also with postwar breakdowns in locomotives. Obsolescence characterised the rail system, which was going to find the return of peacetime welcome but difficult.

There were also social tensions. Evelyn Waugh's novel *Brideshead Revisited* (1945) provided an account of how wartime road transport helped force through change, as with that to the fictional stately home Brideshead:

'We laid the road through the trees joining it up with the main drive; unsightly but very practical; awful lot of transport comes in and out; cuts the place up, too. Look where one careless devil went smack through the box-hedge and carried away all that balustrade.'

So also with geographical ones. A sense of tension between motorists and the local rural population, as well as the role of the topography, was captured by E.C.R. Lorac, who lived in the Lancashire area of Lunesdale, in her novel *The Theft of the Iron Dogs* (1946):

'The gradient was so steep that the roadway, though marked on the Ordnance Survey as a thoroughfare, was impossible for any wheeled traffic except farm carts, and even for these it was a heavy pull.... Had the gradient been less steep, motor tourists from Lancaster and the Lake District would certainly have taken advantage of access to the River Lune.... As it was, there was no metalled road ... motorists as a race do not like hilly walking. Giles Hoggett had sometimes watched with pleasure when some advantageous driver had risked a partial descent of the brow. Their "outfits" could be rescued by a couple of stout farm horses towing them up in reverse. Apart from that, only a caterpillar tractor could deal with the situation.'[30]

There was also a continuing gender dimension to transport. Thus, in 1949, cars were registered in the name of 13 per cent of men, but only 2 per cent of women.

The idea of a new postwar order seemed to presage more sweeping changes in transport, and under the Labour governments of 1945–51, civil aviation (1946), railways, including related assets such as shipping (1948), canal transport (1948), and some road haulage (1948) were all nationalised. The nationalisations of the period, however, subsequently were criticised from within Labour, with right-wingers arguing that free market solutions were better, while left-wingers were opposed to the top-down and bureaucratic method that was followed.[31] Under the National Dock Labour Scheme introduced in 1948, the power of the unions increased. Felixstowe, then a minor port, did not join, and this was instrumental to its eventual success.

At the same time, the pattern of daily travel remained dominated by the traditional means of walking and bicycle, and they were most under challenge from the rising use of the bus, rather than the car, the use of which had not changed since the 1930s. Petrol remained rationed until May 1950. In the meantime, there had been a stop of the basic petrol ration from mid 1947 to June 1948 when about 90 miles monthly was allowed.

Kenneth Graeme's novel *The Wind in the Willows* (1908) was very different from the community spirit that was to the fore in the Reverend Audley's presentation of train life on the fictional island of Sodor. Published from 1945, when *The Three Railway Engines* appeared, the Thomas the Tank Engine stories are benign and were first designed to comfort the author's son who was suffering from measles. The maps provide both the imaginary island, including its terrain (in height) and towns, as well as the lines, both the main line and the branch lines, as well as locating the episodes mentioned in the text as in 'Here Terry rescued Thomas from snow,' 'Gordon waited here for Duck and Stepney to bring Diesel's train' and 'Slate trucks ran into Peter Sam here.' It is possibly only on the imaginary island of Sodor that a recent British cartographer could map roads alongside railways and make the former far less prominent. In contrast, railways are less prominent in most modern maps, for example Ordnance Survey maps.

The second book, *Thomas the Tank Engine* (1946), was illustrated by Reginald Payne who was shown by Awdry, as a model, a photograph of a 0-6-0 E2 Class engine of the London Brighton and South Coast Railway. These locomotives were indeed then in service, but there was a historic dimension as they had been built between 1913 and 1916. They were to be withdrawn from service and scrapped between 1961 and 1963 which was further to date the stories.

In the chronology of the stories, Thomas arrives on the fictional Sodor swiftly after he is built in 1915, and seeks a major role rather than his part as 'a tank engine'. Eventually, he is given his own branch line. Wilbert Awdry wrote the stories from 1945 to 1972, his son Christopher following suit in 1983–2011. Christopher Wilbert Awdry's notes were the basis of *The Island of Sodor: Its People, History and Railways* (1987), which provided background details to aid consistency.

For the government, new initiatives were to the fore, notably nationalisations; but for the bulk of the population it was the grind of austerity, one underlined by continued rationing, that was the dominant note. This was captured in correspondence to newspapers and also in novels such as John Dickson Carr's *He Who Whispers* (1946), which referred to a country still recovering from war with 'erratic buses,' taxis and cars short of petrol, post-blackout 'motor-car lamps, odd in newness,' long passenger queues at Waterloo, and train journeys similar in their misery:

'It was not a long train, and not very crowded. That is to say, people were packed into seats trying to read newspapers with their hands flat against their breasts like corpses; dozens stood in the corridor amid barricades of luggage. But few were actually standing inside the compartments.'[32]

Chapter 9

Motorways, 1950–2000

'…all that remains
For us will be concrete and tyres.'
Philip Larkin, *Going, Going* (1972)
taking forward a theme from
T.S. Eliot's *The Waste Land* (1922).

Built in 1972–80 and opened in 1981, the Humber Bridge, built across the broad estuary, was the longest single-span bridge in the world, with an overall length of nearly 2220 metres (about 1½ miles), and 1,410 metres (4,626 feet) between the towers. Due to its length, the two supporting towers had to be set out of alignment by 36mm (1½ inches) to allow for the curvature of the Earth. The record length was only beaten in 1998 by the Akashi-Kaikyo bridge in Japan. Built to further Labour Party interests in Hull, the Humber Bridge helped make the new county of Humberside appear a more viable unit by ending the road distance from Hull to Grimsby, its two major towns. Yet, it was also a prime instance of poor public policy on transport. Its use by cars is low and by freight even lower. Instead, the east-west route to the A1 and the motorway network is mostly used, rather than a glorious bridge ending in rural Lincolnshire.

In 1952, in the worst peacetime rail crash in British history, due to one signal passed at caution and two signals passed at danger, the stationary Tring to Euston train was hit at Harrow and Wealdstone Station by a Perth to Euston service, with a Euston to Liverpool express running north then derailing due to debris, killing 112 and injuring 340. The accident speeded up the introduction of the Automatic Warning System on the tracks, with in-cab audible and visual warnings.

Most change was less dramatic, but it was still insistent. Demonstrating a need for railway consolidation, the *Beeching Report* (1963) observed 'Road competition has forced down rates on goods railway traffics to the point where they are quite incapable of subsidising the very costly provision of services to handle poor rail traffics.' As such, the report drew attention to a failure of cross-subsidisation, a practice central to rail traffic but one that now could be scrutinised with care and costed.

Railway nationalisation had certainly led to national processes and standardisation which was a key aspect of British nationalisations, also seen with the Health Service: the route taken was centralisation, the route favoured by the Labour government and the trade unions, and not decentralisation. Thus, there was the gradual standardisation of carriages with the introduction of the all-steel British Railways Mark 1 in 1951. The printing of tickets was concentrated on one site. The continued commitment to steam was seen with the new BR commissioning several classes of steam locomotives, and the construction of steam locomotives only ended in 1960. As BR hauled coal, and the coal mines had also been nationalised, there was a clear synergy. Looked at differently, there was a shared inefficiency in the absence of price signals and competition, indeed a cosy expensive relationship.

Alongside the continuing commitment to steam, there was change, although no sustained attempt was made to use the railways as instruments of broader economic planning and 'British Railways made its inadvertent contribution to the later general association of nationalisation with obsolescence and incompetence.'[1] Diesel offered major operating conveniences, not least in working gradients, which challenged steam pressure, and also in saving labour. In place of the substantial workforce essential in order to get steam trains to operate, especially firelighters, lubricators, drivers and firemen, it was necessary with diesel only to have drivers. From 1948 to 1962, BR staff fell by a quarter, which was an aspect not only of technological change but also of historic overmanning. However, despite the spread of diesel, the strength of union opposition to change, as well as firmness over pay differentials and working practices, as in the 1955 17-day national strike, helped undercut the investment that was made. At the same time, as a consequence of considerable investment, the percentage of traction-miles run with diesel and electric rose from 13 in 1955 to 62 in 1963.

Despite relatively strong freight and passenger usage in the 1950s, the operating deficit of British Rail increased from £16.5 million in 1956 to £104 million in 1962; although how much was lost would depend on which accounting convention is used, a point more generally the case when assessing rail financing. Yet, whatever the conventions, rail operations made a significant cash loss. Cashflow is more vital in some respects than profit: profit can be calculated in different ways and struck at different levels, but a loss of cash cannot be readily manipulated or hidden. By 1961, losses were running at £300,000 a day and it was no longer possible to pay the interest on loans.

In the early 1960s, the Treasury pressed for clear financial targets and for economic charges by nationalised industries, in order to limit and hopefully drive down their debt and investment requirements, and the pressure thereby put on the rest of the economy through higher public expenditure. This expenditure was facing difficulties, not least as economic growth was modest.

John Betjeman froze for posterity in his poems the way in which rail could capture the past, as in 'Pershore Station, or A Liverish Journey First Class' which begins

'The train at Pershore station was waiting that Sunday night
Gas light on the platform, in my carriage electric light,
Gas light on frosty evergreens, electric on Empire wood,
The Victorian world and the present in a moment's neighbourhood.'

Opened in 1852, Pershore was proposed for closure by British Rail in 1964 and again in 1967, and demolition started in 1968. In the event, the station remained as an unstaffed halt. Betjeman also wrote on the 'Great Central Railway,' offering an impression of triumphant rail:

'"Unmitigated England"
Came swinging down the line
…
As we hooted round a bend
…
Above the fields of Leicestershire

On arches we were borne
And the rumble of the railway drowned
The thunder of the Quorn [a famed hunt]'

Yet, that poem also captured change:

'We pounded through a housing scheme
With tellymasts a-row,
Where cars of parked executives
Did regimental wait
Beside administrative blocks
Within the factory gate.
...
And quite where Rugby Central is
Does only Rugby know.
We watched the empty platform wait
And sadly saw it go.'

The line had begun passenger service in 1899, but express services from London beyond Nottingham ended in 1960, the line was closed to passenger trains between Aylesbury and Rugby in 1966, and the last train at Rugby Central was in 1969, bringing to an end a service from Nottingham, one of the pattern of cross-services that was so important in the regions. The Betjeman poems are full of romantic nostalgia but also offer a clue to the then current and future decline of rail.

Continuing the interwar pattern, there were already cuts to the network in the 1950s, including, for example in Devon, the Princetown line in 1956 and the Teign Valley line in 1958, both rural lines that carried little traffic. 3,318 miles of railway were closed or converted to freight-only operation between 1948 and 1962 as a result of the work of the Branch Lines Committee of the British Transport Commission. At the same time, as so often, the process of closure was not immediate. Thus, the branch line to Moretonhampstead on Dartmoor, opened in 1866, was closed to passenger service in 1959, but freight continued. The line closed only in 1964, and a last special passenger train ran in 1970 after which part of the track was lifted.

Trains, including steam trains, were scarcely without multiple problems however much it is attractive to imagine that only poor policy led to their decline. The reports in the press in April 1955 noted not only the move toward a damaging national strike but also the death with severe burns of the fireman on the Luton to Leighton Buzzard train which had suffered a blow-back in the engine, the train running through two stations without stopping before crashing through level-crossing gates.

In the event, a major transformation of the rail system was proposed, by *The Reshaping of British Railways* (1963), a report better known after Dr Richard Beeching, the Chairman of the British Transport Commission, and the first Chairman of the British Railways Board (which operated from 1963 to 2001). This report has remained highly controversial to the present and is a standard point of reference. At the time, there was significant support for the essentials. Speaking for the government in the House of Lords, Viscount Hailsham, the Lord President of the Council, said that new investment, the approach outlined in the 1955 modernisation plan, alone was not the answer:

'a system which was built in the main about 1855 or before, and designed for purposes then, needs redesigning.... one-third of the system is not really being used adequately at all ... the people, whether they be consignors for freight or potential passengers, are voluntarily deserting the railways in droves and taking to the roads ... [for] the flexibility of road transport ... the danger is the force of inertia.... What we have to do is to design a 20th century rail system.'

The last theme, that of ensuring a modern system, was an established part of the rhetoric of rail, one that was frequently repeated. This theme was also important to the Macmillan government in the period, lying behind, for example, also in the early 1960s, both the first attempt to join the European Economic Community, the forerunner to the European Union, and the Macmillan government's drive for national economic planning. The Beeching Report should not be separated from this context nor from the earlier plans for rationalisation and improvement. Indeed, it was a systematic attempt to press forward the call for specialisation on bulk carriage seen in the 1955 plan, and similar to the 1955 report of the British Transport Commission on canals.[2]

The focus in the rail report was on a core network, largely radiating from London and the larger cities, one made possible and necessary by the move from steam to diesel and electric, and one designed to provide speed, efficiency and profit. Modernisation was to be focused on creating what was to be an effective and profitable system that was less dependent on Treasury support. The focus was to be on well-used lines and stations, and the supporting maps clearly differentiated between lines carrying zero to 5,000 passengers weekly, and 5,000 to 10,000, and grades above. The first two described most of the lines. So also with density of freight traffic, with most lines carrying up to 5,000 tons weekly or 5,000 to 10,000 tons. A map showing 'flows of freight traffic (excluding coal) favourable to rail but not on rail' was designed to show potential for enhanced rail traffic, and this was related to the proposal for 'liner train routes' and terminals

Branch lines that had survived earlier cuts were ruthlessly culled. Rural and smalltown Britain changed as railways that had integrated it into an urban-centred network were removed. As a result, largely rural areas, such as East Anglia, Lincolnshire, Mid-Wales, the Welsh Borders, north Cornwall and the Isle of Wight, were left with few or no services. In Devon, lines that closed included all those in West Devon, the Exe Valley Line to Tavistock and on to Exmoor, that from Exmouth via Budleigh, and those from Taunton to Barnstaple, and Barnstaple to Ilfracombe, although that from Exeter to Exmouth was saved by lobbying. In Scotland, there were extensive closures, including in the Borders, South-West Scotland, and North-East Scotland. The line north of Inverness was only reprieved through political lobbying. Some lines only survived by becoming private leisure lines of which there were 100 miles in 1970.

Yet, the lines themselves was not the sole issue with provision. In particular, on a longstanding pattern, and one that has continued to the present, the emphasis, in the links that survived, on routes into London, axial routes, was not matched by necessary attention to lateral ones, for example cross-country services. Thus, Trans-Pennine services are inadequate as are those, for example, from Bristol to Weymouth, Great Yarmouth to Liverpool, and Birmingham to Cambridge. There is a Norwich to Ipswich service but Norwich to King's Lynn is via Ely, changing there. Norwich to Lincoln via Peterborough takes two and a half hour's journey time, ie without waiting for the connecting train. North of Norwich there is only a branch line to Cromer and another to Yarmouth left, and other services were removed under the Beeching cuts. There are also problems due to the situation at Ely, a major junction where five lines converge: as laid out, it cannot cope with increased freight traffic to the port at Felixstowe, and goods and passenger trains tend to get in each other's way. An upgrade has been repeatedly promised since 2010 but has never materialised.

The capacity of the surviving system also saw cuts, as track was cut, thus reducing maintenance. So with the reduction of double track lines to single track, as with most of the Salisbury to Exeter line in 1967. Only passing places were left, which cut flexibility if one service was late, a situation that has continued to the present, as with waits outside Tisbury, constraining capability.

There was also devastation-style rebuilding, as at Euston, and threats to redevelop other stations, such as Liverpool Street. As a result of Beeching and other changes, many stations were closed during this period, for example in Manchester. In addition, railway works at major sites, such as Darlington and Swindon, closed. The last pick-up of mail by a moving train was made in 1971; thereafter, mail was only brought to rail stations by road, and aircraft and lorries were increasingly used to move post. Indeed, the motorways offered a network for postal distribution that was separate to that of rail. This was a major change as the post was an information system dependent on physical movement which was very different from the telephone. The switch for the post from stagecoaches to rail in the mid-nineteenth century was highly significant, and now the transition to road underlined the growing not so much marginality of rail but, rather, sectoral significance.

At the same time, the dramatic cuts to the rail system subsequently suggested as options in the 1982 report by Sir David Serpell, former Permanent Secretary at the Ministry of Transport, were rejected. One option, the headline one, would have reduced the system by 84 per cent, essentially to a few major routes, notably from London to Cardiff and Newcastle, and to Scotland only via Manchester, and not via Newcastle. That proposal contrasted with the map of 'principal services' in May

1982, in fact only services converging on London, which included Outer London pick-up set-down points (Stevenage, Luton, Watford, Reading, Woking, East Croydon and Bromley), and showed towns in terms of fastest journey from or to London.

The parliamentary discussion of the Serpell Report led Lord Underhill to claim that Britain seemed 'one of the few Western democracies which is behind in placing emphasis on the need for a strong rail system.' Lord Nugent of Guildford drew attention to the cost to the taxpayer of the rail system and to archaic working practices. He also commented on:

'...the sort of natural sympathy which most of us have for the railways themselves. I dare say that in my generation it dates back to our childhood wish to be an engine driver but, certainly, the sympathy is there and we do feel for the railways, especially if we could see a steam engine. That really does give us a thrill.'

The Serpell proposals were not pursued. Nor did the support of the rail unions for the coal miners' strike in 1984–5 lead to action against rail, which, indeed, survived the crisis of the coal industry, but in shedding a key legacy affected much of the viability of the freight business as then constituted. The rail freight business, seen as key in the Beeching Report, only really revived from the early 2000s.

This was an aspect of the degree to which the privatisation of electricity generation, coal and rail led to much improved freight handling and price competition on freight rates. So also with Royal Mail being able to move its post to more efficient road transport once it could terminate the expensive contract with rail that had been set in the days of shared state ownership.

Instead of additional cuts, the rail system, with passenger numbers reviving from the mid-1980s, stabilised at just over half the interwar mileage. This stripped out a lot of capacity, but also reduced the mileage that had to be maintained and the attendant costs, notably in wages where upward pressure was a major figure. Whereas the number of thousand million passenger-miles by rail had fallen from 24.2 in 1952 to 20.5 in 1976, it rose to 25.5 in 1990. This, moreover, was better than the figures for bus or coach: 50.3 in 1952, 32.9 in 1976, and 25.5 in 1990. Yet, these figures were totally dwarfed by those for car, taxi and motorcycle: 33.6 in 1952, 215.0 in 1976, and 352.9 in 1990.

Car ownership was seen as success, Margaret Thatcher, the Conservative Prime Minister from 1979 to 1990, suggesting that a 26 year old man who was a bus passenger could see himself as a failure.[3] John Prescott, the Labour Deputy Prime Minister from 1997 to 2007, claimed the car was the most democratic invention of the century, although this keen driver argued in 1997 that more people should be using public transport and driving their cars less. Road freight became more competitive to rail due to the relaxation of weight limits for lorries and the construction of motorways.

Air posed scant competition despite the development of domestic air services and a network of regional airports greater than that today. For example, in 1951, Don Everall, a Wolverhampton coach-operator, established an airline, Don Everall Aviation, which began scheduled services in 1953. Wolverhampton airport survived until 1970.[4] Passengers on domestic flights rose tenfold from 1951 to 1970 but in the latter only comprised 0.5 per cent of passenger-miles.

There were attempts at rail modernisation, including new trains. The tilting Advanced Passenger Train, however, did not prove a success. Tilting carriages, on which there were experiments from the 1950s, were designed to permit trains to go round curves on older and newer lines without reducing speed, notably on the West Coast main line and thus to prevent the need for fresh tracklaying. Prototypes were tested in the 1970s, but the first runs in service in 1981 did not go well. This led to a disproportionally hostile press response and a rapid withdrawal from service. A return of the tilting train to service in 1985–6 did not meet with favour, in large part due to the success of the reliable, more conventional high-speed diesel InterCity 125 introduced in 1976. The tilting trains were withdrawn from service; although the technology was to be used successfully for tilting trains in other countries. In contrast, on the East Coast Main Line from London to Edinburgh, fully-electrified 225s, introduced in 1991, ensured journey times considerably less than they had been in the days of steam. There were also extensions to urban railway systems, notably the Tyne and Wear metro system from 1980, and the Docklands Light Railway in London from 1987. The former linked to existing lines, but also provided new routes, notably to the airport.

Opened in 1994, the Channel Tunnel appeared a major new development of great promise, but has repeatedly found it impossible to meet financial expectations. The initial idea for a Channel Tunnel preceded the railway, with Albert Mathieu's suggestion to Napoleon in 1802 for a tunnel for horse-drawn carriages. Running from Cap Gris Nez to Eastwear Bay, this would obviously facilitate military intervention. From the 1860s, proposals became more frequent, but were repeatedly rejected by the British government as a result of invasion concerns. In 1948, at a time of good relations, when the cost, including modifications to Victoria Station, was put at £68.5 million, the Cabinet rejected the plan with scant debate. The idea was re-presented from 1957, when the government adopted a non-commital approach, to 1964 when it came out thoroughly in favour. In 1963, a report by Anglo-French officials had suggested a cost of about £143 million.

In 1966, the British and French governments announced that they would go ahead with the tunnel, but there was a lack of agreement in Britain over funding, with ministers divided over priorities. Meanwhile, projection costs rose, and environmental concerns emerged. In 1975, in response to an acute fiscal crisis, the tunnel, on which construction had begun in 1974, was dropped as was the plan for a air/seaport at Maplin Sands.

The situation changed when political support and financing both came into line, with the Thatcher government (1979–90) encouraged by the financial strength of the Eurotunnel Group. In 1986, an Anglo-French tunnel treaty was signed. The initial submarine investigations led to the designation of routes in terms of very good, good, medium or poor viability. Tunnelling was mostly through chalk marl which had the advantage of being malleable as well as impermeable. However, the French side posed more geological difficulties with more fractured and harder chalk. Surveying in 1958–9, 1964–5, 1972–4 and 1986–8 established the options and the possible routes.

Opened in 1994, the Channel Tunnel is a 50 kilometre rail tunnel, and the Eurostar rail service took nearly four-fifths of passenger travel from London to Paris and Brussels by 2019. The tunnel also carries cars on a train service, which provides significant competition to the earlier ferries. Construction began in 1988 and with an estimated cost of £5.5 billion.

In the event, £9 billion was spent, and the resulting financial burden created a difficult legacy, affecting the share value. In turn, the Covid pandemic of 2020–1 cut Eurostar's revenue by 95 per cent for 15 months. It responded by cutting services, including those to Disneyland Paris and to the south of France. However, there were serious problems even before the pandemic. Whereas in 1994, 22 million passengers annually were predicted, in 2019 only 11 million travelled. This cast a critical note on plans in 2022 for direct trains from London to Frankfurt, Cologne, Geneva and Bordeaux. The long promised through services from the English regions had never materialised.

Cost helped ensure that cross-Channel ferries continued in operation. As an earlier and more complete instance of a new technology that worked, but did not achieve financial breakthrough, the hovercraft was briefly effective as a cross-Channel service, with the first commercial service, from Ramsgate to Calais, beginning in 1978. However, the hovercraft neither sustained that position nor was used effectively for other transport tasks bar a service to the Isle of Wight.

As an instance of change to a much more longterm system, coastal shipping declined, but as late as the 1970s it was the least expensive way to move coal and was used, for example, to ship it from the North-East and Scotland to the gasworks and power stations in the Thames estuary. There was also the transport of coal to other ports, such as Exeter.

The closure of the mines ended the trade. Coastal shipping did not become a leisure activity as canals, with over two million people using them in 1973, had done. This was with the significant exception of cruises. Indeed, cruises round the British Isles were particularly attractive to the elderly as there was then no need to take a flight which had insurance implications. Furthermore, coastal shipping was hit by the marked decline in shipbuilding, in part due to international competition.[5]

Meanwhile, older transport systems were coming to an end. The last Newcastle, Gateshead, London, Aberdeen and Glasgow trams ran in 1950, 1951, 1952, 1958 and 1962 respectively, and the last London and Newcastle trolleybuses in 1962 and 1963 respectively, although from the 1990s there was a small-scale revival in Croydon, Manchester, Sheffield and Wolverhampton of trams, now seen as a viable alternative to buses. The cost of electricity and the maintenance cost of the wires had hit trolleybuses, of which London had had a maximum fleet of 1,811 and the largest system in the world. Trolleybuses also suffered from intermittent electricity supply.

In contrast, buses benefited from far greater manoeuvrability and did not require specialised track. They had problems, however, with reliability and speed. In Graham Greene's novel *The End of the Affair* (1951), Sarah explains 'I'm sorry. I came by bus and the traffic was bad.' His reply 'The tube's quicker,' leads her to observe 'I know, but I didn't want to be quick.'[6] En route from NW16 in London, the protagonist in Kingsley Amis' dystopian novel *Jake's Thing* (1978) noted:

'Every 6–7 mins was how often 127s were supposed to turn up at the stop by the Orris Park Woolworths, so to be given the choice of two after only 10–11 was rather grand and certainly welcome in the increasing rain and squirts of cold wind…. The conductor was one of the newish sort, which in this case meant that he chucked you off if you hadn't got the exact money.'[7]

Amis also used the novel to comment on the high cost of rail tickets.

Far more significantly, the creation of the motorway system provided a new set of links around the country, with nodes, services, issues, and problems accordingly. The development was part of an international change, one seen in particular both in Continental Europe, notably with the German *autobahns* and Italian *autostradas*, but also with the establishment in America of the interstate system, also a development from the 1950s, and one linked to a presentation of cars as democratic.[8] The funding in each case was state. In Britain, there were not the toll charges seen in some Continental European states, notably France and Italy. Instead, although there was no amortissement [fixing allocation] of the income, the motorways were in effect paid by the contribution made by road users through motor vehicle licence taxation and petrol duty. Both were considerable, which established a funding challenge in the 2020s as the use of electric cars increased, not least as measures were sought in order to incentivise the latter.

The motorways were also seen as a way to help the economy, both by facilitating freight movements (which greatly relied on predictable steady-speed journeys) and by encouraging the car industry. The greater prominence of this compared to that of railway-linked manufacture was very important to the political economy of transport in Britain. Moreover, unlike with the earlier establishment of railway works, which was essentially at the behest of the rail companies, car manufacturing became, notably from the 1960s, an aspect of regional policy, with the location of plants encouraged and subsidised on Merseyside and in central Scotland, and later at Sunderland. Such measures, and the more general investment and employment bound up in car and lorry manufacturing and in associated companies, made it difficult at the governmental level to oppose calls for the development of the road infrastructure and this was the case for all political parties. Crucially, the Conservative support for road interests was matched by Labour, which provided the government in 1964–70 and 1974–9, and that despite Labour's close links with the rail unions. In part, this matching arose from the prominence of road use and car manufacturing unions, particularly the Transport and General Workers Union. Moreover, the car factories were located in Labour-supporting areas, and not in Conservative counterparts, which was an important aspect of the regional politics of transport.

Motorways were regarded as aspects of a modernisation that was also pursued through civil nuclear power, corporatist industrial policies, and the attempts to join the European Economic community. Pump-priming investment such as motorways was praised as an economic, social and regional benefit. As a different form of benefit, allegedly gangland victims were buried in the concrete bridges. The first motorway opened, the eight mile Preston bypass, later part of the M6, in December 1958 by Harold Macmillan, the Prime Minister, was rapidly followed by the M1 from St Albans to Rugby, 50 miles, compared to the present 200. This was a tourist attraction for a while. Modern drivers are amazed by photographs and films showing how few vehicles were on the motorway. There was no speed limit until 1965 when one at 70 mph was introduced. The first motorway service station with food opened at Newport Pagnell in 1960.

The motorway system was to spread rapidly over succeeding decades, in part in order to provide comprehensive cover and in part to deal with unexpected heavy usage, not least for the M1 which started to crumble within three years, and not, as envisaged, twenty. By 1972, 1,000 miles of motorway were complete, by 1980, over half the population were within 25 miles of a motorway and by 1990, there were 1,919 miles of motorway, including, in 1986, the 118 mile round-London M25 which cost £909 million.[9] In contrast, in Wales, the continuing lack of north-south road infrastructure helped perpetuate 'North and South' Walian outlooks on the world.

Car use increased significantly. Although in the 1950s they were still essentially a middle-class means of transport, in the 1960s much of the working class bought them, a process greatly eased by the rise in average wage rates and by hire purchase systems, and one encouraged by the movement from inner-cities to new housing estates where parking was more plentiful. There were still major differences in how and when people from different classes acquired cars. In Birmingham in 1972, only 8 per cent of women in council houses had driving licences. Women had to negotiate buses, escalators and pedestrian bridges. The affluent knew little about public transport. Indeed, in 1975, most members of Birmingham council's transport committee had not used public transport in the previous four months.[10]

The private ownership of cars increased five-fold between 1950 and 1970, a rate that greatly outperformed that of commercial vehicles which, instead, doubled while that of buses and coaches essentially remained constant.[11] By 1966, half of all households owned one or more cars, which reflected both wider ownership but also its continued concentration in the hands of the better off. The cheap price of petrol in the 1960s encouraged the adoption of cars.

In contrast, other forms of transport declined. Whereas, in 1952, cyclists were responsible for more than 10 per cent of all British passenger miles, in 1970 the percentage was only one. For buses and coaches, the percentages were 42 and 15, for motorcycles three and one. Between 1975 and 1993, the number of those qualified to drive rose by 52 per cent so that two-thirds of those aged 17 and over were qualified. In 1966, developments in lightweight battery-powered cars led to much interest notably from the UK Electricity Council, but a lack of orders and problems with battery-charging ensured that no manufacturer committed to them.

Long-distance road haulage had been largely denationalised by the Conservatives in 1953 (one of the few earlier nationalisations reversed)[12] and there was interest in subsequent renationalisation by Labour, notably by the Transport Act of 1968 and its proposed Freight Integration Council. This affected investment in that industry.

The limits on work-time for lorry and bus drivers and the economic significance of freight encouraged measures to speed traffic, notably by improving roads. Being delayed hit the efficiency of lorries which otherwise had considerably increased due to their larger permitted length such that by the early 1970s lorries could be called HGVs, 'tics' for articulated lorries and juggernauts. The ton miles carried by lorry rose 343 per cent in 1958 to 1986.

A different form of freight was the long-established caravan, which had preceded motor transport, but became much more common from the 1950s with less expensive, assembly-line, mass-produced caravans. The use of lighter materials helped, and as the price fell the number of households using caravans rose from two million in 1955 to 4.5 million in 1967. Their use, however, was challenged by package holidays using jet aircraft.

The romance of the road now seems very distant, but at the time there was considerable enthusiasm for motorways and few protests. Indeed, Barbara Castle, Labour's determined Minister of Transport from 1965 to 1968, described sites such as the Almondsbury motorway interchange of the M4 and M5 (still a difficult one) in 1966 as 'the cathedrals of the modern world.' Both parties backed the motorways, the Conservatives implementing policies for trunk roads developed by Labour in the late 1940s. In 2022, 2,300 of the about 245,000 British road miles were motorway, which had been redefined in 1958 as 'limited access dual-carriageway road with grade separation, completely fenced in, normally with hard shoulders … for the exclusive use of prescribed classes of motor vehicles.'

The impact of major roads on established sites was amply displayed with National Trust properties. The M1 speeds past Hardwick Hall, the M54 past Moseley Old Hall. The six-lane Plympton by-pass was cut through the park at Saltram in 1970, largely obliterating the eighteenth-century carriage drive. The M4 was driven through the Osterley estate in 1965, the M5 through the Killerton estate, although the Exeter northern bypass scheme was not pursued.

Within cities there were also abrupt changes, and ones that were more profound than those with rail as major roads were wider. Thus, Birmingham's inner ring road was built between 1957 and 1971, while Wolverhampton's ring road was opened in stages between 1961 and 1986, clearing away established landmarks and residential districts. Carlisle's, opened in 1974, cut the castle off from the city, and was followed by the replacement of a long-established area by a shopping centre. Pressure for by-passes grew, and the towns that gained them, as with Honiton in 1966, became far more attractive places to live.

Also in Devon, the A30 further west bypassed Okehampton, while the A38 bypassed Ashburton and Ivybridge, before passing north of the centre of Plymouth and over the new Tamar Bridge. As a result, the route to the Southwest, which had hitherto been very slow, became swifter. In turn, however, there were new bottlenecks. To the east, the A303 was improved, parts becoming dual carriageway, while towns, including Ilminster, were bypassed. However, where the road was not 'dualled,' there were major issues, notably across the Blackdown Hills and near Stonehenge. In each case, other policy concerns and constraints, notably landscape and heritage, clashed with that of ease of transport, a clash that has lasted in these cases to the present.

So also with the A35 west across southern Dorset to Honiton. Dualled, as near Axminister which was bypassed as was Bridport, it sped along, but that was not possible in the hills between there and Honiton. Further east, near Charmouth, greater traffic flow on the A35 made village life unpleasant, leading to local activism, as in the form of continually pressing pedestrian crossing lights. Oliver Letwin, MP for West Dorset from 1997 to 2019, told me that calls for village bypasses set villagers against those who lived in more rural settings through which these would be built. The 1980 Highways Act maintained the local authority responsibility for highways. Where there was provision, it did not always work, in part due to rising demand. Moreover, some ring roads and bypasses were badly-planned and quickly became engulfed by the towns, for example the Newbury ring road.

Across the country, for the sake of speed and safety, roundabouts and junctions along trunk roads such as the A1 were replaced by slip roads. Demand more generally for road use, notably motorway use, rapidly increased, Thus, in Cambridgeshire between 1981 and 1995, traffic on the mostly new A14 and the new M11 increased by close to 300 per cent. In the same period, it grew there by over 100 per cent on the older established A10. Seen as a public service, motorways were toll-free, although there were to be exceptions, notably on the 27.6-mile M6 toll, finished in 2002, the Dartford Crossing on the M25, and major bridges.

There were very varied environmental consequences from roads. Cities that in the 1960s enjoyed far more sunshine hours from the clearer atmosphere after the declaration of smokeless zones subsequently noted a decline as a result of car exhaust. Concern about the health consequences developed and became marked in the 2020s, contributing to an increase in regulatory intensity in the cities. More immediately, rabbits, hedgehogs, badgers, deer, and birds were killed in large numbers each year on the roads. The extension of the M40 from Oxford to Birmingham, proposed in 1972 to take pressure off the M1 on the London-West Midlands route, was opened in 1991 after major battles over the route across Otmoor, an area of rural calm. Nearby Banbury became a major distribution centre making use of the M40 with for example a large Amazon depot.

At the neighbourhood level, major routes became obstacles in the second half of the twentieth century, as high streets were turned into through routes, as in London's South Circular Road. With roads busier and the traffic faster, they became barriers for pedestrians, the number of whom were killed rose by a third between 1950 and 1969; and cycling became more difficult. In response, zebra crossings were introduced from 1951, and lollipop ladies to aid pedestrians, especially children, to cross roads from 1954. Death rates among drivers were tackled with speed limits, breathalysers, and seat-belts which, eventually, became compulsory.

In turn, the danger of existing roads encouraged the building of new through routes unrelated to the existing neighbourhoods, as in Glasgow in the 1970s, the East Central Motorway in Newcastle in the early 1970s, and Newcastle's Western Bypass in 1990. In *A Certain Justice* (1997), the novelist P.D. James observed of the building of Westway in the late 1960s:

'Soon there would be nothing but tarmac and the ceaseless roar and screech of traffic thundering westward out of London. In time even memory would be powerless to conjure up what once had been.'

I was born in Edgware in 1955 north of the A41, which was domesticated as the Watford Way. The journey to school involved crossing this en route to Edgware tube station. That was done at the traffic lights at the junction with Edgwarebury Lane, although traffic flow could be so low that it was possible to walk across the A41 at other places. Cars could leave the northward side of Edgwarebury Lane at the lights and turn either way into the A41.

Subsequently, the pattern was to be one of continual restriction, with cars stopped from turning right. Later, the pedestrian crossing was removed at the junction and barriers along the A41 made earlier crossing impossible. Now there is a high bridge to cross, one impossible for prams or the infirm, and inconvenient for the fit.

There were also significant developments in this period in the movement of water, oil, natural gas, and telecommunications. Thus, the beginning of North Sea oil and gas production in the 1970s was followed by the building of pipelines to the coast and then across Britain. As with freight as a whole, there was insufficient public interest, but, in addition, in contrast to rail, canal and lorries, there was the underground nature of this supply routing. Indeed, an earlier instance was the major transport systems created in the late nineteenth century in order to remove human waste from cities to treatment plants and facilities. These also do not tend to be mentioned or assessed when people discuss transport systems. The success of these forms of infrastructure was linked to the *relatively* contained costs that they presented. In each case, these forms entailed considerable planning as well as engineering skills. Underground routes were aspects of the three-dimensional nature of transport that became significant from the late nineteenth century with the delivery of people, water and waste underground. Aircraft ensured that in the twentieth century, the dimension of height was generally considered in terms of above-ground, but below-ground remained highly significant and became more so as coal was in large part replaced as a power source by oil and gas. There was also pressure for environmental reasons to bury electricity cables.

As ever, transactional decisions could also be significant in terms of political contention, as with the drowning of Welsh valleys to take water by pipeline to English cities, long a matter of contention. Wales also reflected the significance of what did not occur, a key element that tends to be overlooked or ignored completely. The improvement in bridges, road and rail links brought Cardiff closer to Bristol and London, but not to Bangor which lay on the other side of a mid-Wales across which there were only slow links, notably from Aberystwyth. Already, in 1941, at the annual general meeting of the National Industrial Council of Wales and Monmouthshire, Councillor G.O. Williams of Flintshire County Council emphasised that postwar reconstruction must be considered by two regional, not one united, committee, 'stressed the difficulties of travelling from North Wales' and declared that 'very little consideration had been given to the convenience of North Wales.'

Telegrams were replaced by the use of the phone, which reached 80 per cent of households in 1985 compared to 20 per cent in 1965. In turn, mobile phones provided a new way to use phones, lessening the need for public call-boxes. Separately, courier services became more important, challenging the Post Office transport of parcels.

The public sector suffered repeatedly from issues over labour unrest, notably, but not only, on the railways. Thus, in 1969, an unofficial strike in London was a response to revised bus schedules that reduced overtime earnings. There were other problems in the public sector, not least inconsistencies in government policy, but, for the public and for industry, strikes repeatedly encouraged a reliance on cars and lorries, including by strikers, as with the 'Flying Pickets' of 1978–9 and 1984–5. Strikes did not tend to attract the attention of those who sought an optimum outcome for transport. However, reliance on public sector transport was repeatedly undermined by strike action.

In 1986, as a result of the 1985 Transport Act, deregulation of local bus services occurred outside London, such that no publicly-run bus services continued. Intended to encourage competition and to lessen the power of local councils, this deregulation was followed by a fall in operating costs, but not by a return to the bus. In Greater Manchester usage fell from 355 million trips annually in the mid-1980s to 182 million in 2019. Whereas buses and coaches were responsible for 15 per cent of passenger miles in 1970, the 1990 percentage was 7, while the rail percentage fell from 9 to 6.

Somewhat differently, problems with parking challenged car use and, indeed, the value of car ownership. Creating carparks led to contention over land use, visual amenity, capacity and charges, both amounts and length of period. For example, to provide parking spaces, there were plans, ultimately unsuccessful, in Exeter for the university to fill in part of Duryard Valley in front of the campus, plans that would have destroyed a natural habitat of note. More generally, multi-storey carparks are the source of great unpopularity with many urban residents. In the 2010s and 2020s, charging for parking at hospitals became a focus of particular contention and political promises. In practice, charges appeared a way to deal with serious demand pressures and to tackle the flow of traffic into the urban areas. At the same time, there were issues over the availability of parking for staff and its impact on staff safety, especially with reference to the need for staff to work at night.

Meanwhile, as earlier with rail, the language changed to take on board the use of cars, with motorway service stations, breathalysers, seat-belts, contraflows, motorway madness, and Flying Pickets.

By the end of the period, the Internet was transforming the transport of messages and documents. In 1731, the *Craftsman* had been accused of having 'a murmuring trumpet, which blows a political rumour in a few minutes, from Berwick to Cornwall.'[13] What might seem to have been the case in 1731 but was fantastical, was the reality for very many by 2000.

Chapter 10

Modern Discontents

'Nothing of the ancient bridge remains but the piles; nor is there anything in the structure of this, or of the other five Roman bridges over the Tiber that deserves attention. I have not seen any bridge in France or Italy comparable to that of Westminster, either in beauty, magnificence, or solidity; and when the bridge at Blackfriars is finished [which it was in 1769], it will be such a monument of architecture as all the world cannot parallel.'[1]

The confidence in British excellence expressed by Tobias Smollett in 1766 seems at one with the glory of Ozymandias mocked by Shelley in 1818.

Now, at times, it can vie with the weather, for transport is also a constant source of conversation and complaint in modern Britain, and this is so for road, rail, air and ferries. Congestion, cost and delay are the major issues; and the resulting pressures are collective as well as individual, and are year-round. There are frequent estimates of the total cost of delays. At the same time, more people than ever before are travelling within, from and to Britain, and more frequently. Indeed, travel is part of the culture. So also with the development of new forms of transport and speculation about many more, a trend that in 2023 included active planning for aerial taxis, planning in which regulatory issues were to the fore.

This contrast between complaint and scale, is scarcely new, but may now be more acute. The rapid rise in the population, and at all age groups, is accompanied by expectations of regular mobility far greater than in the case of former such rises. In part this is a matter of the democratisation of expectations, for the assumption is that all should be able to travel. This expectation is seen in planning and is met by a plethora of privileges so that elderly people need not pay for local buses, while there are reductions of the cost of rail and long-distance bus travel for the elderly, families and students. There are costs and transfers in all these systems, but these tend to be underrated. In part, the system is one in which benefits are conferred on the elderly and students, as part of a more general intergenerational transfer from the working population.

Separately, the aggregate population size is unprecedented, and growing at an unprecedented rate; and that creates pressures on transport of its own, not only in people flow but also moving goods in order to provide for this number. The goods include conventional ones such as food, but also demands for rapid information flows. Indeed, the availability and speed of internet connections were major issues of discussion and sources of political pressure and government promises, notably from the 2010s.

With new technologies, there was a sequence that included the provision of electric cars, hybrid cars, e-scooters, e-bikes, and drones, the last for freight. Alongside the attempt of government to retain control over the process, not least for safety and revenue reasons, there were expedients by which regulations were ignored, notably with e-scooters. So also with earlier vehicle types, as with bicycles being now frequently ridden illegally on the pavement. The episodic nature of governmental regulation and police action involved other underreported aspects of transport crimes, although cameras, notably speed cameras, increased the range of policing.

Aside from the regulation of road use, including speed and its consequences for safety, and the use of charging and taxation to create and reallocate regulatory revenue, there were those arising from concerns about pollution. These included attempts to control the type of vehicle employed, notably engine type, and fuel, as well as routes. This caused particular contention when pricing and control policies were introduced as in London and Oxford, but also more generally. Thus, to take the editorial for the September/October 2023 issue of *St Leonards Neighbourhood News*, my 'local' in Exeter, an issue fronted with a caricature deriding traffic planners as bullying obsessives heedless of all, the editor commented: 'the whole city seems currently in the throes of turmoil and anger over much bigger traffic changes, especially those designed to make the heart of Heavitree a ghetto.' This was not the view of Devon County Council which, in its 'Heavitree and Whipton Active Streets Trial' leaflet, explained the purpose of the relevant Experimental Traffic Regulation Order:

'To help create quieter streets for walking and cycling, a number of traffic filters and bus gates will be installed:

Traffic filters use bollards and planters to prevent the passage of vehicular traffic, except for buses and certain other exempt classes of vehicle, such as emergency vehicles and local authority vehicles. These restrictions will be enforceable by the Police.

Bus services and walking/cycling routes will be unaffected by the changes. All properties will remain accessible by car and taxi, but some people may need to use alternative routes for certain journeys.'

In practice, as the map made clear, the suburb of Heavitree would be cut off from neighbouring areas apart from if using the heavily clogged Fore Street, East Wonford Road route. To get in particular to the more northerly Pinhoe Road axis would be only possible by a very circuitous route. The leaflet's claim that 'Traffic volume will be significantly reduced on the residential streets, by removing most "through" vehicular traffic, ie traffic not travelling to or from properties in Heavitree and Whipton' is fanciful. In 2024, this low traffic neighbourhood was scrapped.

Reasonable or otherwise, similar comments can be found elsewhere. Popular views were indicated in September 2023 when a public consultation for the Greater Cambridge Partnership saw 58 per cent of respondents reject it. Car owners were to have had to pay £5 daily to drive at peak times, the revenue intended for the improvement of the local transport infrastructure. However, concern about the impact on low-income families led the Labour group on the Council to withdraw support and also affected the popular response. Cambridge itself indicates some of the problems with modern transport. There is prosperity-based congestion, despite the large number of cyclists, as well as a range of proposed solutions focused on public provision. Thus, the Cambridgeshire Autonomous Metro proposed in 2017 as a light rail scheme envisaged a 88 mile system, including seven under the city, initially costed at £4 billion, later £2 billion, was shelved in 2021 by Nik Johnson, the newly-elected mayor for the Cambridgeshire and Peterborough Council Authority. He had defeated the protagonist for the scheme, James Palmer, his Conservative predecessor. Johnson described the system as 'a white elephant' and it was rejected in favour of a 'revamped bus network.'

'Traffic calming schemes,' a classic instance of the misleading use of language in transport matters, pose particular problems with access for the elderly, the inform, those needing to transport loads and to work, and for deliveries; and there is also a reduction in choice as to how to travel. This is particularly problematic as the population is significantly ageing. The assumption that public transport, cycling and walking can deal with all needs is demonstrably foolish, as well as highly exclusionary and discriminatory toward the elderly, infirm, and those caring for young children. No- or low-car zones are based on flawed assumptions about the mobility of much of the population and their need to transport items that they require. No- or low-car zones are also dangerous because they preclude ready access for emergency services. Local authorities argue that speed restriction and access reduction programmes will make streets safer and tackle pollution by cutting car speeds and encouraging residents instead to walk or cycle. These measures drew on the 15 minute idea that people should try to live within 15 minutes of their work and shops, a phrase dropped by Oxford City Council in 2024 because it had become toxic and incendiary.

Each of these issues were and remain contentious and revealed the extent to which transport had become a cause of political contention in the wider sense of politics, that in which organised parties were not to the fore. In part this is a matter of the longstanding public lobbying seen in transport, as with the AA (Automobile Association), RAC (Royal Automobile Club), and the Motoring Defence League established in 1963. As a later instance of lobbying, and in large part due to popular activism, there was a refusal from 2011–12 to raise petrol tax in line with inflation. This freezing of petrol duty is estimated to have cost the Treasury around £80 billion. In contrast, fares for trains have continued to rise. The unexpected Conservative success in the Uxbridge and South Ruislip by-election in July 2023 was attributed to popular hostility to the Labour-backed ULEZ (ultra-low-emission zone). Very differently, access for walkers has been a contentious issue from the 1930s, but one that has become more so in the 2020s.[2]

The pace and scale of controversy, however difficult to measure, has increased of late. To a degree this reflects attempts at transformative legislation, notably in the cars that can be driven. Thus, the popularity of electric cars has declined, including as revealed in *Auto Trader* polls in 2019 and 2023 not least due to the cost of the cars, the lack of easy charging infrastructure, and worries about range and safety. These concerns compromised the attraction of the proposed 2030 ban on new petrol and diesel models and the issue came to the political fore in September 2023, when there were calls for delays in proposed changes. In the event, that month the Prime Minister, Rishi Sunak, declared that 80 per cent of all new cars would have to be electric by 2030, the ban on the sale of new petrol cars by 2030 was pushed back till 2035 (by when 100 per cent of all new cars were to be electric), with Sunak claiming that politicians had not been 'honest with the public' about the cost of net zero. Separately, investment in battery production attracted a government subsidy; while new hybrid cars, which use a combination of electric and conventional fuels, are to be banned in 2035.

The accumulated past of this form of transport, the petrol-powered internal combustion engine, is intended for the knife as swiftly as the steam engine, but with private ownership, the second-hand car market, and the cost to individuals of replacement making the transition for cars far more problematic. In the case of rail, labour issues and government intervention at least in the shape of financial support were more prominent.

Transport also repeatedly posed social issues. In 1971, 14 per cent of children at junior schools were driven to school, but in 1990 64 per cent. This was linked to a decline in children's health, notably a fall in exercise and a rise in obesity.

In 2015, British motorists bought 2.6 million new cars; there were also many purchasers of second-hand cars, a practice made much easier by online information which transformed that market. The average distance travelled each day per person had risen to about 20 miles by 2000, which was an increase of three-quarters over a quarter century. This increase helped a drive not only for more cars (including per family) but also for more space, for both roads and associated infrastructure, such as garages and parking. The rise in the number of cars per family put more pressure upon parking. In suburban areas, this problem resulted in the paving over of front gardens, a household design and land use consequence of transport developments. There was also the misguided drive to increase motorway capacity by the use of 'smart motorways' in which hard shoulders were used as a running lane. Begun in 2006, the scheme was halted in 2023.

In addition, many cars became larger, notably on the American model and especially as SUVs (Sports Utility Vehicles) enjoyed great popularity from the 2000s. There were particular problems for parking with SUVs, not least the obsolescence of existing garages, many of which were therefore used for other purposes, as well as major problems in car parks.

SUVs affected other road users whether cars, cyclists, riders or pedestrians. There was a social as well as regional dimension in the response to them, as in their description as 'Chelsea tractors,' a term that captured antipathy, indeed hostility, towards wealthy Londoners with second homes in the countryside. This underlined the degree to which discussion of transport generally had a wider dimension. This dimension was frequently spatial, as in parking restrictions and charges for outsiders, social and political.

The attempt by planners to limit car usage by authorising new developments in which houses or flats had no or few parking spaces proved of only limited effectiveness. Quarrels between neighbours over street parking increased greatly and offered a variation on 'road rage,' which, itself, became a problem. Indeed, a classic cause of small-scale altercations, brawls, and vandalism arose from homeowners or tenants assuming (wrongly) that parking at the streetside curb outside their dwelling should be used only by them. Residents' parking permits did not solve this issue.

Another aspect of road rage developed from cyclists breaking traffic regulations, especially driving through lights. In turn, cyclists complained about other road users and demanded special lanes, not that this stopped some from riding on the pavement. The net effect was more acrimonious individual relations and a marked rise in tension. Cyclists became more effective in their lobbying because young, affluent Londoners increasingly cycled to work in the 2010s; their deaths in accidents attracted very favourable treatment of the victims, and cycle paths were installed there in the 2010s, considerably reducing the space available for cars and buses, notably in Central London.

Car speed also became a major issue. Although the earlier move in Scotland attracted less opposition, the move to 20 mph speed limits on residential roads in Wales in 2023 caused controversy and was unpopular. The law of 2022 making this possible prompted protests, with motorists in Wales tying red ribbons to their cars, a reference to the Locomotive Act of 1865 known as the Red Flag Act, which imposed very strict speed limits and requiring a person waving a red flag to walk in front of vehicles.

In London, also, the speed limit on more than half the roads were cut to 20 mph, with 125,000 speeding fines issued in April and May 2023. Average speeds on A roads across Greater London fell to 14.4 mph in 2022. There was a clear political dimension, with only Conservative-run outer London councils, such as Bromley, against low traffic neighbourhoods and 20 mph limits except outside schools and in high streets. Enforcement of the law raised multiple issues. Wandsworth's trial of civilian-run cameras was deemed unlawful by the Department of Transport as enforcement can only be done by the police. There are such speed limits across many urban areas and they are designed to cut pedestrian deaths, which were over 2,000 in 1998–2002. Defenders of the schemes say that because traffic flows more smoothly, average journeys are not greatly increased.

By 2022, there were 33 million cars registered in Britain. Drivers in the ten most congested cities spent an average of 80 hours in traffic jams (London, 156). Traffic projections are projections, not least because of issues of energy availability, but traffic could increase, the Department of Transport suggests by as much as 54 per cent by 2060 because of population growth and cheaper-to-run electric vehicles. For any form of road vehicle, the marginal cost of driving is relatively low once the vehicle is owned: the key cost is the purchase.

Very differently, the impact of the car was also particularly apparent in rural areas. It facilitated the mobility of most rural consumers but was also linked to the closure of many rural schools, shops, pubs, churches, and post offices, greatly affecting the fabric of rural life and the nature of community; potholes on rural roads were also generally the last to receive attention. Conversely, these closures, and the fact that, by 2000, 75 per cent of rural parishes had no daily bus service (while those that existed were generally infrequent), encouraged dependence on cars. There was also a class element. The wealthy could afford to take taxis to and from pubs and thus observe drink-driving laws. Yet, it is also appropriate to devote due attention to other factors than transport and, in doing so, make it less credible to explain change solely or largely in terms of transport. For example, the increase in minimum wage levels makes some activities less financially viable, for example running pubs.

For both the state and for individuals, costs could be formidable. By 2015, London-wide passenger usage was growing by 3 per cent per annum, and Transport for London, which ran the tube and bus services, was taking up £10.7 billion of the Greater London Authority's budget of £17 billion. This percentage made the high pay of tube drivers particularly contentious.

At the same time, the rate of growth in cost could be affected by contextual and contingent factors. Thus, the Covid pandemic in 2020–2 smashed government finances, leading to the cancellation of the HS2 leg to Leeds, and hit the revenues of transport operating companies from airlines to motorway service stations. The pandemic also led to a marked reduction in transport, which increased the state support required by the railways, and at a time when state revenues were falling greatly. The railways were then seriously hit by industrial action in 2023–4. Working from home ensured that whereas cars were driven 263 billion miles in 2019, by 2022 the figure was 244 billion. Traffic peaks also changed from before 9 am on weekdays to later in the day and at weekends. Homeworking also meant a slump in rail season ticket sales and in rail (and non-rail) travel on Mondays and Fridays. Home working, however, also encouraged the move of some work processes to foreign countries with lower living costs and wages, which increased the nature of information transported.

Fiscal crisis, which gathered pace from 2022, was a major departure from the earlier era of quantitative easing, low interest rates, inexpensive Chinese imports, and much political bombast. This crisis has played a role in the downscaling of plans. This was particularly the case with HS2. Driving new lines through densely populated areas is costly. Tunnelling in particular is very expensive, whether to achieve speed through straightness or to shield trains from view. In 2006, a government-commissioned report by Sir Rod Eddington rejected Britain's need for new high-speed links, but, though accepted then by the Blair government, the conclusion was subsequently rejected by the Labour government of Gordon Brown (2007–10) which opted in 2010 for HS2 on the basis of highly-speculative estimates for future (crucially not immediate) expenditure for what was seen as a way to counter Conservative support for such links. In the 2010 election, the Labour manifesto declared for 'a new high-speed rail line, linking North and South,' the Conservatives even more boldly opting for 'a national high-speed rail line.' At their 2008 party conference, the Conservatives had supported the idea of speedy trains to Leeds and Manchester, which, it was declared, would cost £16 billion and be ready by 2027.

From the outset, the project, in part a vanity project that David Cameron (2010–16) and Theresa May (2016–19) could not bring themselves to cut, was totally out-of-control. The end result of the HS2 planning was over-engineered and not what was needed, a combination of intervention by politicians and overly bold projections by the rail industry, neither party being sufficiently mindful of the financial situation. Indeed, there was almost an enormous jointly-shared comfort with deluding the public and thwarting financial accountability, one that was characteristic of British public projects in the period, as with the Elizabeth Line across Central London or the building of two large aircraft carriers.

The HS2 project had bold specifications. Thus, by 2023, the London to Birmingham stage included 25 miles of tunnels while much of the route was built in cuttings, with the track effectively below ground. With its lower population density, the original TGV line in France cost £15 million per mile at 2022 prices, but HS2 could cost just under £400 million a mile. And that at a time when long-distance rail journeys represent only 0.17 per cent of journeys. The business case presented by the government for HS2 saw a steady deterioration in outcomes, so that a benefit-cost ratio initially estimated as £2.40 and still in 2019 as £1.30 was by 2023 estimated as 0.92, such that it would cost more to build than the advantages it could bestow. These figures were contested as estimates of likely constructions costs varied.

Moreover, the 2019 assessment, in the Oakervee report (commissioned from a former chairman of HS2), assumed wrongly that HS2 would cost no more than £69 billion in 2015 prices and that the link to Leeds would be built. Supporters of the scheme argue that the benefit-cost ratio is assessed over a period of 60 years whereas the railway will last for longer, and they also claim that the line will help Britain meet its net-zero targets. The underlying claims, for example that the line would create half a million jobs, were groundless although the case offered by capacity pressures on the London to Scotland lines remains pertinent, not least as improving existing lines is both costly and highly disruptive. By constructing in effect a new line for long-range passenger services separate to the existing one that would be for local and freight services, speed and capacity would increase, and it might be possible to move freight from the roads. Boris Johnson, Prime Minister from 2019 to 2022, was a keen advocate for the scheme despite strong opposition from key advisors.

By March 2023, the estimated cost of what was then the largest, or at least most costly, infrastructure project in Europe, had risen from £32.7 billion, when it was approved in 2012, to £72 billion, and the opening of the line to Birmingham pushed back from 2026 to between 2029 and 2033, with the second part of the line, to Manchester, and a truncated eastern leg from 2033 to 2035–41. In 2022–3, inflation hit hard as the cost of timber, steel, aggregates, fuel, energy and labour all rose considerably, materials-price inflation peaking at 26 per cent in 2022. This led to an increase in anticipated costs, possibly to £106 billion, a figure already offered in 2019 by critics of the Oakervee report. Furthermore, cost overruns usually come on the signalling and that work had not yet started. There were suggestions of changed specifications, fresh delays, or a HS2 route that was further slimmed down, with the line possibly reaching Euston only in 2041. Postponements, which was an option, however, push up the long-term cost.

In September 2023, plans were prepared to axe the second leg of HS2, that between Birmingham and Manchester, while there were questions over HS2 East, the planned link from Birmingham to East Midlands Parkway southwest of Nottingham, and over terminating trains in London at Old Oak Common, not Euston. Johnson told the *Times* that the new plan was 'desperate' and 'Treasury-driven nonsense,' leading to a:

'mutilated HS2. We need to connect the Midlands with the North with HS2 because that is the way to deliver Northern Powerhouse Rail.... It is no wonder that Chinese universities teach the constant cancellation of UK infrastructure as an example of what is wrong with democracy.'

Cameron and George Osborne, who had strongly backed the project when in government in 2010–16, both opposed the changes, as did Michael Gove, the Levelling-up Secretary. The government, instead, considered a new line between Leeds and Manchester, from the latter of which there was the suggestion that the northern section of HS2 between Manchester Airport and Manchester Piccadilly be prioritised as that would be instrumental as a part of an east-west route: Northern Powerhouse Rail, which had been brought to the fore in 2019. In practice, there was an obsession with new lines with all their costs as opposed to improving existing ones. The example of HS2 is of particular significance given Britain's role as the original trendsetter and power of rail.

In October 2023, Sunak axed HS2 north of Birmingham arguing that 'the facts have changed,' and saying that the £36 billion saved would be spent on other transport plans, including £1 billion on travel between Liverpool and Manchester, the electrification of the line to Hull and of that from Holyhead to Crewe, reinstating a passenger service between Stocksbridge and Sheffield, a new station for Bradford, all part of a new 'Network North,' work to improve the M6, A1 (the long-promised dual carriageway from Morpeth to Ellingham), A2, A5, and A75, funding for the Shipley bypass, the Blyth relief road, and £2.5 billion for trams for Leeds and extensions to the West Midlands metro and Nottingham tram network. Bus fares were to be capped at £2 until the end of 2024, while £8.3 billion was to be spent on pothole repairs. In total, out of the £36 billion savings, £20 billion were to be spent in the North and £9.6 billion in the Midlands. HS2 is still due to be extended to Euston, but under a new development authority and dependent on private investment. Moreover, Euston was only to have six high speed rail platforms, not eleven as originally proposed and ten as decided in 2020: Old Oak Common could take eight trains hourly. HS2 officials revealed the hope that a Labour government would revive the northern leg and in 2024 this was discussed by the new Starmer government. There was considerable opposition to the abandonment of the northern link of HS2 and HS2 East, not least in the areas immediately affected. Notably so at Crewe which had been chosen for a new HS2 station, that was to be enveloped by a commercial hub and new houses, as well as a nearby major train depot. In practice, despite impressions to the contrary, the HS2 service would not stop at Birmingham. It would connect to the West Coast Main Line at the Handsacre junction near Lichfield from which HS2 trains could run north.

In light of the estimated cost of HS2, it was, indeed, instructive that in 2023, there was an estimated repair backlog of £14 billion for potholes which reflected the general reduction in road improvement work. The Local Government Association (LGA) said this huge backlog was caused by years of funding cuts followed by more recent inflation in cost of repairs. Many local authorities are currently doing no resurfacing. Whereas in 2006, £4 billion was spent on UK local road maintenance, the figure for 2019 was £2 billion. Moreover, the latest LGA residents' satisfaction polling found that only 34 per cent of residents were satisfied with how well their local roads were maintained. The financial problems of many councils are also pertinent.

The problems of rail were systemic, but varied. For example about 38 per cent of the UK system is electrified compared to a European Union average of 60 per cent, and the resulting diesel usage contributes to pollution. Very differently, the government sets regulated fares, which cover about half of all journeys in England, including season, anytime urban, and off-peak long-distance tickets, and finds itself ultimately responsible when franchises fail. Thus, in May 2023, services run by TransPennine Express were brought under government control, that of the Operator of Last Resort, when its contract expired. This was a response to a very high rate of cancellations, in part due to industrial action: that February, nearly a quarter of its trains were cancelled. At a more modest level, in April 2023, plans to reintroduce a passenger service (closed in 1961) on the freight-only Isle of Grain branch on the Hoo Peninsula were postponed, Medway Council citing 'high inflation, significantly increased construction costs and pressures on public spending.'

More impressive, not least because far less resources are at stake are recent developments in Scotland, where the emphasis has not been on exorbitant blue-skies conventional new construction as with HS2. Instead, with the Scottish government arguing that regional-inclusive growth is held back by poor infrastructure links, the major change from Beeching has been the (re-) opening in 2015 of the 35-mile Borders Railway, closed in 1969, that connects Edinburgh to Galashiels and Melrose.

Moreover, from the opening of Transport Scotland in 2006, there has been a focus, imperfect but present, on integrated services reflected in subsidiary commuting developments. Another line reopened was the Stirling-Alloa-Kincardine line in 2008. The Edinburgh tram, light-rail system faced numerous problems but has been completed. Railways in Scotland were renationalised in 2022 as Scottish Rail Holdings Ltd and the Crossborder Sleeper service was nationalised in 2023.

Issued in July 2023, the Strategic Business Plan for Scotland's Railway set out the challenges of providing effective maintenance of rail assets in the context of decreased use as a result of the Covid pandemic. The contrasting nature of maintenance between high-speed, high-tonnage and high-service intensity routes, and low ones characterised by 'historic low levels of renewal' notably the Far North, emerged.[3]

The (relatively) highspeed train from Dublin to Belfast, the 'Enterprise,' has to slow down when it enters Northern Ireland because the infrastructure cannot support the speed. Motorways in the Republic have been funded by European money, and sport large signs to that effect. Motorways in Northern Ireland, which are focused on Belfast, did not meet the bold plans of the 1960s for eight in total. They have been criticised on the grounds that the roads allegedly run out with the Protestant population. There are plans now to extend the rail network on both sides of the border. Announced in 2021, the All-Island Strategic Rail Review reported in 2023 identifying inadequate coverage, low service frequencies and slow speeds. Rail took about 1 per cent of all trips and around 3 per cent of passenger mileage. The Report recommended increased connectivity, more tracks, faster speeds, and increased frequencies, and a potential reunification of the rail network.

The frequency in Britain of rail strikes in 2023–4 led to grave doubts about rail as the remedy. However, rail still offered much for particular groups, and not only non-drivers. The theme of vulnerability was to the fore in 2023–4 when the closure of most ticket offices was proposed as labour saving measures. The rail operators argued that they were not necessary as most passengers purchased tickets online. However, advocates for the elderly and disabled pointed out their need for advice and assistance. The debate was closely interlinked with the politics of an industrial dispute. Such interlinking has been more frequent in the history of transport than the standard emphasis on technology might suggest,

Meanwhile, whatever the scale of the discussion of HS2, the popular emphasis remained that on road. In the year to April 2022, rail carried 2 per cent of journeys by volume and 9 per cent by distance, while road had considerably more than 80 per cent for both. And yet, that year, £5.8 billion was spent on roads, national and local, and £5.6 billion on HS2 alone. The 'road lobby' was in practice that of the bulk of the population.

For international transport, in contrast, the emphasis remained on aircraft. Other than serving islands, such as the Outer Hebrides, and Scotland and in Northern Ireland, it continued however, to be of little importance within the country, and the limited opportunities for profit were shown by the collapse of Flybe and the withdrawal of British Airways from Bristol. In contrast, air transport continues to be the dominant form of international passenger movement.

Aircraft were also significant for freight. Primarily, they are used for high value products that are needed in tight deadlines. However, the value of the product itself, or its perishability, can be the reason for shipping by air, as rapid shipping of high value products reduces the need for working capital. High value products include flowers from Kenya and vegetables from Guatemala. Much air freight is shipped on passenger flights, but there are also many purely freight flights. Ferries (carrying lorries) and other shipping, however, remain crucial for freight movements.

Chapter 11

Postscript: Into the Future

'Every road leading to the Terminus was thronged by pedestrians and vehicles.... Thousands were assembled on the green slopes west of the railway.... At about 12.20 pm a thousand cries of "Here they come!" announced the fact to those from whose sight of the train was yet hidden by the winding of the hill ... the train was seen gliding swiftly along the line.... The train having reached the terminus, the National Anthem was played and sung.... Bands continued playing for half-an-hour, when the National Anthen was again sung..."

London in 2030? No, Brighton in 1841 when the train arrived from London.[1]

Problems with HS2 as well as the contemporaneous disputes over runways at Heathrow and Gatwick led to considerable debate over whether the British were incapable of seeing through major infrastructure projects. Much was made of the complexities and delays of the planning system, and of the propensity to appeal against projects, of 'short-termism' and 'nimbyism' [Not In My Back Yardism].

In practice, aside from securing funding, the difficulty of obtaining and maintaining project consistency, in what is a crowded country with clashing interests, is the key problem. In 2023, as the estimated costs of HS2 rose further, there was the risk that all other plans by the Department of Transport would have to be shelved, a point underplayed by HS2 advocates who instead presented HS2 as not only necessary but also an essential prequel to other schemes. This underlined the varied nature of the regional and local 'pulls.' The 'North' was not united. In Birmingham and Manchester there was support for HS2 not seen, for example, in Newcastle or Stoke-on-Trent. When HS2 was finally given the go-ahead in February 2020, it was supposed to reduce overcrowding on the existing network and triple capacity between Birmingham (second to London in the number of rail passengers) and Manchester (fourth), but 'jam tomorrow' for others was not central to those facing repeated delays and serious overcrowding on Trans-Pennine services, and the Yorkshire stake in HS2 was severed in 2021 when the projected line was cut.

The nationwide failure of the British air traffic control system in August 2023 illustrated the fragility of the transport system. Many buses in London were delayed that September when Tower Bridge was stuck open for over half an hour causing traffic chaos. Fragility was shown very differently with the closure of nearly sixty per cent of the bank branch system in 2015–23 as the cash infrastructure was hit by digital alternatives. There was worry about utility transport networks. Concerns about the capacity to move water to shortage areas led to the building of a pipe to take surplus groundwater in northern Lincolnshire and from the river Ancholme and Covenham reservoir, and pump it down to the south. In 2022–3, the companies that owned the gas networks wanted to repurpose the pipes to carry hydrogen but the government cooled on the idea of using hydrogen for heating.

The electric solution to domestic heating and to cars led to questions about the energy infrastructure, not least the danger of serious overloading and also, more positively, the development of new systems including rooftop solar panels, electric vehicles, electrolysers and local energy communities. Yet, the anticipated cost of the last as a national system was high and unpredictable, while, in its absence the actual electricity available was inadequate. There was the anticipation of a significant increase in the quantity of electricity used, both in absolute terms and as a proportion of the energy mix, with consequences for the National Grid aside from its likely decentralisation. The pressure for heat pumps for domestic properties limits the electrification possible for electric vehicles. In Britain in 2022, cars and taxis drove about 240 billion miles, light commercial vehicles 57.5 billion, heavy goods vehicles 17.4 billion, buses and coaches 2.1 billion, motorcycles 2.8 billion, and pedal cycles 3.9 billion.[2]

Separately, the rise of renewable energy sources which, by the first quarter of 2023 supplied a third of UK electricity, changed energy flows. The 'Holistic Network Design' plan for rewiring the National Grid to accommodate 50 GW of offshore wind by 2030 has an estimated cost of nearly £54 billion. Moreover, the bill for new cables will be higher if buried underground, an issue that brings together public health, heritage, and house value anxieties and considerations. Proposals for interconnectors to bring electricity into Britain have encountered significant public disquiet, notably in Portsmouth and Suffolk. There has also been controversy over building pylons for 112 miles from north Norfolk to the Thames estuary at Tilbury via Suffolk. Carrying offshore windfarm-generated electricity, these are the East Anglia Green proposals. There was pressure instead for undersea offshore routes for electricity, as with the Eastern Link from Scotland to northern England. The costs of offshore or underground routes are far higher.

Cars going fully electric would increase demand by around 24 per cent, although that does not make allowance for the heavy electricity needs of SUVs. The comparable percentage for all road transport would be around 40 per cent. Electricity is more efficient in converting energy into motion than petrol.[3]

Considering the prospect for electric vehicles in the absence of sufficient electricity underlines the significance for the earlier development of rail of the plentiful availability of coal. The absence of such coal had not prevented the construction and running of rail services in many countries including Denmark, the Netherlands, Norway and Portugal, but for Britain, as for America, France and Germany, large supplies of coal had been a major advantage.

The global nature of transport technology (and of the major challenge from pollution) is such that there will not be a specific technical solution or path for Britain's transport future. The more distinctive nature of the political character of consumer demands and funding policies ensure that a national outcome will be more to the fore in transport policy, and that may be more the case having left the European Union. Yet, it is not easy to anticipate the likely direction of this outcome. Transport is not to the fore in national party political contention, which reflects in part the extent to which widespread public concern, indeed irritation, has not been politicised, or at least pushed to the fore in party politics, although that may change.

At the same time, the delegation of government powers, both within the United Kingdom and inside England, is such that there will be more policy initiatives in transport, as it is a responsibility, or at least opportunity, for these agencies, for example elected mayors. The powers handed to them under devolution legislation in 2017 included the ability to create a franchised bus service. In 2021, by when there were fewer local bus journeys in the remainder of England combined than in London, the government criticised recent neglect of the buses and offered extra funding to local authorities that submitted bus service improvement plans which would include lower and simpler fares, faster and more reliable services, and better connections with the railways.

In 2023, the first to do so, Andy Burnham of Greater Manchester, established the Bee Network, a franchised system akin to that in London, and with fares, routes and timetables set by politicians. A fleet of 50 yellow electric vehicles are initially running in Bolton, Wigan and parts of Salford and Bury, with a wider rollout across the region to be completed by 2025, as part of a network designed to integrate buses, trains and trams. However, cross-subsidy is expected: Greater Manchester is paying for the initial £134 million costs until 2025, but Burnham then wants central government to take over the funding which he somehow presented as Greater Manchester 'retaking control of its buses.' Such rhetoric often means that someone else should pay.

For transport systems, there are also the potential legal constraints arising from the possibility of judicial decisions on points such as liabilities over pollutant levels. The latter underline the extent to which politics should be understood in a broad sense. Moreover, the nature of consent to any particular transport process, situation or agency is undercut by the possibilities of legal and extra-legal challenge, from judicial review to obstruction. The practice of blocking traffic, notably by Extinction Rebellion, became commonplace in the early 2020s with environmental issues to the fore as the explanation. There was a regional emphasis in this action on London, which is the news-centre. The possibility of a future intensification of this process is unclear.

So also with changes on the 'demand' side. The Covid pandemic of 2020–2 hit not only the profitability of transport industries, notably air and rail, but also the practice of regular commuting. There was a more lasting shift to working from home and, linked to that, when commuting revived, it was frequently only for part of the former working week, notably Tuesday to Thursday. There were consequences for demand, not least for season tickets, and for existing patterns of provision and anticipations about revenue flow.

The role of the consumer in formulating the need and desire to travel and for transport can and should lead discussion of transport that, however, tends to centre on public provision and focus on state investment.[4] Indeed, the social pressures for individual transport are strong. Having provided the wider context for the growth of car use, these pressures remain invested in cars emotionally and practically. Moreover, the role of organised labour in lessening public support for public transport increased for many in the early 2020s.

At the same time, for most transport, it was a different type of unpredictability that was to the fore, that of the weather. Indeed, there is a kind of almost perverse continuity in the way in which transport falls victim whatever the technology. Thus, on 7–8 October 2023, nearly a month of rain fell in a weekend causing many mudslides which left most rail lines at a stop and many trunk roads impassable. The east coast main rail line was shut north of Montrose because it was under water, while the A83 in Argyll was blocked by six landslides and vehicles were stranded on other major roads such as the A84 as they were under water.

The range and variety of changes and possibilities in the early 2020s undercut any simple pattern of drawing consequences, as in Covid caused x, or the shift to electric cars will probably lead to y. The nature of government policy, public responses and popular attitudes were far from uniform and fixed, and this helped create multiple influences and pressures. That also reflected the numerous constituencies of interest, commitment and emotion bound up in transport, and that irrespective of the complicating feature of rivalry between different forms of transport.

Rivalry, moreover, was not constant in its causes, course, scale, intensity and consequences, but rather varied as such across time. It is all too easy to look back and ignore, or at least underplay, the extent of controversy over the means, routes, ownership, costs and much else of transport. Thus, when considering the development of canals it is worth noting the bitter public rows that were matched by private political and legal pressures. For example, in 1766, proposals to link the North and Irish Seas by a Calder-Mersey Canal touched off a controversy in the *Leeds*

Intelligencer.[5] So in the period did canalisation schemes in the Thames Valley system as well as the road network in the area.[6]

This cross-sectional view of transport underlines its complexity. That situation also amplifies the problems with looking back and readily arguing in providing explanations from changes to causes and/or prioritising among either. The nature of transport, whether continuity or change, will continue as multivalent and as reflecting a range of factors and contexts, from demand to technology, profitability to regulation. It would be foolish to anticipate the consequences with any certainty. The ride will be exciting.

Notes

Preface
1. Montagu-Douglas-Scott, later Countess of Courtown, to Lady Mary, Countess of Courtown, 13 July 1780, Beinecke, Osborn Files, uncatalogued, prov. 80.6.33. For other sources, see J. Parkes, *Travel in England in the Seventeenth Century* (Oxford, 1925; reprint, Oxford, 1986); E. Moir, *The Discovery of Britain: The English Tourists 1540–1840* (London, 1964); C. Zacher, 'Travel and Geographical Writings,' in A. Hartung (ed.), *A Manual of the Writings in Middle English, 1050–1500* (New Haven, Conn., 1986); R. Gard, *The Observant Traveller: Diaries of Travel in England, Wales and Scotland in the County Record Offices of England and Wales* (London, 1989); I. Ousby, *The Englishman's England* (Cambridge, 1990); A. Timiswood, *The Polite Tourist: Four Centuries of Country House Visiting* (London, 1999).
2. N. Humphreys, *Lost Women* (London, 2023), p. 53.
3. J. Langdon, 'Horse Hauling: A Revolution in Vehicle Transport in Twelfth and Thirteenth-Century England?,' *Past and Present*, 103 (1984), pp. 37–66.
4. As argued by Julian Munby, for example, 'Men in the Saddle and Women on Wheels: the Transport Revolution in the Tudor and Stuart Courts,' *The Court Historian*, 24, 3 (2019), pp. 205–20.
5. *Sherborne Mercury*, 7 June 1737.
6. J. Sigurosson and T. Bolton (eds), *Celtic-Norse Relationships in the Irish Sea in the Middle Ages, 800–1200* (Leiden, 2014); H. Clarke and R. Johnson (eds), *The Vikings in Ireland and Beyond: Before and After the Battle of Clontarf* (Dublin, 2015); C. Cooijmans (ed.), *Traversing the Inner Seas: Contacts and Continuities in and around Scotland, the Hebrides, and the North of Ireland* (Edinburgh, 2017).
7. D. Bates and R. Liddiard (eds), *East Anglia and its North Sea World in the Middle Ages* (Woodbridge, 2013).
8. César de Saussure, *A Foreign View of England in the Reign of George I and George II*, edited by Madame Van Muyden (London, 1902), pp. 146–7.
9. Horace Walpole, *Memoirs of King George II*, ed. by John Brooke (3 vols, New Haven, Conn., 1985) II, 26.
10. P. Colquhoun, *The State of Indigence and the Situation of the Casual Poor in the Metropolis Explained* (London, 1799), p. 5.
11. J. Barnes, *Metroland* (London 1980; 1981 edn), pp. 34–7.
12. *Ibid.*, p. 60.
13. *Ibid.*, p. 61.
14. See also for London, F. Staples, *Fifty Years in 'The Milk Game'*, (Cheltenham, 1996).

Chapter 1
1. A. Cooper, 'Once a highway, always a highway: roads and English law, *c.*1150–1300,' in W. Allen and R. Evans (eds), *Roadworks: Medieval Britain, Medieval Roads* (Manchester, 2016), pp. 50–73; J. Campbell, *The Anglo-Saxon State* (2000), pp. 182–4. For all the lesser

tracks, lanes and pathways which did not come under the category of 'King's Highway,' C. Taylor, *Roads and Tracks of Britain* (1979). For visual evidence of them, M.W. Beresford and J.K. St Joseph, *Medieval England: an aerial survey* (2nd edn, Cambridge, 1979), pp. 273–84.

2. H. Summerson, 'The enforcement of the Statute of Winchester, 1285–1327,' *Journal of Legal History*, 13 (1992), pp. 232–50 at 233.

3. C. Taylor, *Village and Farmstead: A History of Rural Settlement in England* (1983).

4. Information derived from N. Saul, 'Thoughts on the Gough Map.' I am most grateful to Nigel for providing a copy.

5. A. Roberts, 'Late Upper Palaeolithic and Mesolithic Hunting-Gathering Communities 13000–5500 BP,' in R. Kain and W. Ravenhill (eds), *Historical Atlas of South-West England* (Exeter, 1999), p. 50.

6. R. Madgwick et al, 'Multi-isotope analysis reveals that feasts in the Stonehenge environs and across Wessex drew people and animals from throughout Britain,' *Science Advances*, 5, 3, 13 Mar. 2019, DOI:10.1126/sciadv.aau6078.

7. T. Driver, *The Hillforts of Iron Age Wales* (Eardisley, 2023).

8. F. Pryor, *The Fens: Discovering England's Ancient Depths* (London, 2019).

9. S. Harrison, 'The Icknield Way: some queries,' *Archaeological Journal*, 160 (2003), pp. 1–22; Taylor, *Roads and Tracks*, pp. 36–8.

10. J.P. Roth, *The Logistics of the Roman Army at War* (Leiden, 1999); S. Stallibrass and R. Thomas (eds), *The Archaeology of Production and Supply in NW Europe* (Oxford, 2008).

11. For a different take, Taylor, *Roads and Tracks*, pp. 190–1.

12. P. Bidwell and N. Holbrook, *Hadrian's Wall Bridges* (London, 1989).

13. H. Davies, *Roman Roads in Britain* (Stroud, 2002); J. Poulter, *The Planning of Roman Roads and Walls in Northern Britain* (Stroud, 2010).

14. *Journal of Computer Applications in Archaeology*, https:/doi.org/10.5334/jcaa.109

15. B. Jones and D. Mattingly, *An Atlas of Roman Britain* (Oxford, 2002); D. Sim and I. Ridge, *Iron for the Eagles: The Iron Industry of Roman Britain* (Stroud, 2002).

16. B.B. Simmons, 'The Lincolnshire Car Dyke: Navigation or Drainage?', *Britannia*, 10 (1979), pp. 183–6.

17. S. Rippon, *The Severn Estuary. Landscape Evolution and Wetland Reclamation* (Leicester, 1997).

18. A. Everitt, *Continuity and Colonisation: the evolution of Kentish Settlement* (Leicester, 1986).

19. T. Tatton-Brown, 'The Evolution of "Watling Street" in Kent,' *Archaeologia Cantiana*, 121 (2001), pp. 121–4.

20. M. Hyer and G. Owen-Crocker (eds), *The Material Culture of Daily Living in the Anglo-Saxon World* (Exeter, 2011) and (eds), *The Material Culture of the Built Environment in the Anglo-Saxon World* (Liverpool, 2015).

21. R. Fleming, *Britain After Rome: The Fall and Rise 400–107* (London, 2010); D. Griffiths, *Vikings of the Irish Sea* (Stroud, 2012)

22. J.R. Maddicott, 'Prosperity and Power to the Age of Bede and Beowulf,' *Proceedings of the British Academy*, 117 (2010), pp. 49–71.

23. D. Hill and A. Rumble (eds), *The Defence of Wessex: the Burghal Hidage and Anglo-Saxon Fortifications* (Manchester, 1996); J. Blair, *Building Anglo-Saxon England* (Princeton, NJ., 2018), pp. 232–5.

24. P. Hindle, 'Roads and Tracks in Anglo-Saxon England,' in M.C. Hyer and G.R. Owen-Crocker (eds), *The Material Culture of the Built Environment in the Anglo-Saxon World*

(Liverpool, 2015), pp. 37–49; S. Brooks 'The Place Name Evidence for a Routeway Network in Early Medieval England', *Medieval Archaeology*, 58 (2014), p.428.

25. G.B. Grundy, 'The ancient highways and trackways of Wiltshire, Berkshire and Hampshire and the Saxon battlefields of Wiltshire,' *Archaeological Journal*, 75 (1918), pp. 69–104.

26. J. Blair, *Building Anglo-Saxon England* (Princeton, NJ., 2018), pp. 189–90, 220–2; A. Cooper, *Bridges, Law and Power in Medieval England, 700–1400* (Woodbridge, 2006).

27. J.R. Maddicott, 'Trade, Industry and the Wealth of King Alfred,' *Past and Present*, 123 (May 1989), pp. 3–51.

28. A. Cooper, 'The Rise and Fall of the Anglo-Saxon Law of the Highway,' *Haskins Society Journal*, 12 (2002), pp. 39–69.

29. H. Fairbairn, 'Was There a Money Economy in Late Anglo-Saxon and Norman England?,' *English Historical Review*, 134 (2019), pp. 1081–35, esp. 1115, 1108, 1107.

30. L.J. Downer (ed.), *Leges Henrici Primi* (Oxford, 1972), pp. 109, 249–51; A. Cooper, 'The King's Four Highways: Legal Fiction meets Fictional Law,' *Journal of Medieval History*, 26 (2000), pp. 351–70, and 'Extraordinary privilege: the trial of Penenden Heath and the Domesday inquest,' *English Historical Review*, 116 (2001), pp. 1167–92.

31. T. Tatton-Brown, 'Evolution,' pp. 122–3.

32. R.H. Hilton, *English and French Towns in Feudal Society: A Comparative Study* (Cambridge, 1995); J.L. Bolton, *The Medieval English Economy, 1150–1500* (London, 1980), pp. 132–6.

33. H.S.A. Fox, *Dartmoor's Alluring Uplands: Transhumance and Pastoral Management in the Middle Ages* ed. M. Tompkins and C. Dyer (Exeter, 2012).

34. J. Langdon, *Horses, Oxen and Technological Innovation: The Use of Draught Animals in English Farming from 1066–1500* (Cambridge, 1986), 'The Economics of Horses and Oxen in Medieval England,' *Agricultural History Review*, 30 (1982), pp. 31–40, 'Horse Hauling: A Revolution in Vehicle Transport in Twelfth and Thirteenth-century England?,' *Past and Present*, 103 (1984), pp. 37–66.

35. P. Nightingale, *A Medieval Mercantile Community: The Grocers' Company and the Politics and Trade of London, 1000–1485* (New Haven, Conn., 1995).

36. G. Platts, *Land and People in Medieval Lincolnshire* (Lincoln, 1985), pp. 135–44.

37. J. Langdon and J. Masschaele, 'Commercial Activity and Population Growth in Medieval England,' *Past and Present*, 190 (2006), pp. 35–81.

38. P. Goodfellow, 'Medieval Markets in Northamptonshire,' *Northamptonshire Past and Present*, 7 (1987–8), p. 307.

39. K. Kilmurry, *The Pottery Industry of Stamford, Lincolnshire, c. AD 850–1250* (Oxford, 1980); L.A. Symonds, *Landscape and Social Practice: The Production and Consumption of Pottery in 10th-Century Lincolnshire* (Oxford, 2003).

40. J. Blair (ed.), *Waterways and Canal-Building in Medieval England* (Oxford, 2007), p. 15–18; J. Langdon, 'Inland Water Transport in Medieval England' and 'Inland Water Transport in Medieval England – the View from the Mills: A Response to Jones,' *Journal of Historical Geography*, 19 (1993), pp. 1–11, 26 (2000), pp. 75–82; E. Jones, 'River Navigation in Medieval England,' *Ibid.*, 26 (2000), pp. 60–75; E. Oksanen, 'Inland Waterways and Commerce in Medieval England,' *European Journal of Post-Classical Archaeologies*, 7 (2017), pp. 35-60 and *Inland Navigation in England and Wales before 1348 GIS Database* (2019).

41. J.F. Edwards and B.P. Hindle, 'The transportation system of medieval England and Wales,' *Journal of Historical Geography*, 17 (1991), pp. 123–34; R.H. Britnell, 'The proliferation of markets in England, 1200–1349,' *Economic History Review*, 34 (1981), pp. 209–21.

42. Oksanen, 'Trade and Travel in England during the Long Twelfth Century,' *Anglo-Norman Studies*, 37 (2015), pp. 181-204; H. Grieve, *The Sleepers and the Shadows in Chelmsford: A Town, its People and its Past. I. The Medieval and Tudor Story* (Chelmsford, 1988).

43. P. Clark and L. Murfin, *The History of Maidstone. The Making of a Modern County Town* (Stroud, 1995).

44. M. Bonney, *Lordship and the Urban Community: Durham and its Overlords, 1250–1540* (Cambridge, 1990).

45. N. Yates and J.M. Gibson (eds), *Traffic and Politics, the construction and management of Rochester Bridge, AD 43–1993* (Woodbridge, 1994).

46. V. Harding and L. Wright (eds), *London Bridge: Selected Accounts and Rentals, 1382–1538* (London, 1995).

47. P. Stell (ed.), *York Bridgemasters' Accounts* (York, 2003).

48. D. Thomas, 'The Long Bridges of Devon' and 'Medieval Tamar Bridges,' *Devon Historian*, 63 (2001) and 64 (2002); Oksan and S. Brookes 'Bridges of Medieval England to c.1250', *Early Medieval Atlas Projects*, 2019.

49. R.M. Haines, 'Three Christchurch (Twynham) Indulgences for the Repair of Bridges,' *Archives*, 26 (2001), pp. 30–5.

50. D. Harrison, *The Bridges of Medieval England. Transport and Society 400–1800* (Oxford, 2004) and 'Medieval Yorkshire roads, bridges and York merchants,' in S. Brown, S. Jones and T. Ayers (eds), *York. Art, Architecture and Archaeology* (Abingdon, 2021).

51. C. Martin, 'London: the hub of an English river transport network, 1250–1550,' in V. Allen and R. Evans (eds), *Roadworks*, pp. 249–76.

52. H. Jenkins, 'Medieval Barge Traffic and the Building of Peterborough Cathedral,' *Northamptonshire Past and Present*, 8 (1992–3), pp. 255–62.

53. *Ex. Inf.* Henry Summerson.

54. D.H. Kennett, 'Caister Castle, Norfolk, and the Transport of Brick and Other Building materials in the Middle Ages,' in R. Bork and A. Kann (eds), *The Art, Science, and Technology of Medieval Travel* (Aldershot, 2008), pp. 55–68.

55. C. Dyer, *Making a Living in the Middle Ages: The People of Britain, 850–1520* (2002), p. 215.

56. V. Allen and R. Evans (eds), *Roadworks: Medieval Britain, Medieval Roads* (Manchester, 2016).

57. C.T. Flower, *Public Works in Medieval Law* (2 vols, London, 1915, 1921).

58. *Ex. Inf.* Henry Summerson.

59. B.P. Hindle, 'The road network of medieval England and Wales,' *Journal of Historical Geography*, 2 (1976), pp. 207–21.

60. J. Masschaele, 'Transport costs in medieval England,' *Economic History Review*, 46 (1993), pp. 266–79.

61. A. Bell, C. Brooks and P. Dryburgh, *The English Wool Market, c. 1230–1327* (Cambridge, 2007).

62. J. Munby, 'From Whirlecole to the World on Wheels: Episodes in the Early History of London Transport,' in J. Cotton et al (eds), *Hidden Histories and Records of Antiquity: Essays on Saxon and Medieval London, London and Middlesex Archaeological Society. Special Paper*, 17 (2014), pp. 152–9.

63. Taylor, *Roads and Tracks*. The traditional work on the system is F.M. Stenton, 'The Road System of Medieval England,' *Economic History Review*, 7 (1936), pp. 1–20.

64. W. Harwood, 'Trade and consumption patterns in central Southern England: the supply of iron and wax to Winchester College, c.1400–1560,' *Southern History*, 29

(2007), pp. 1–28; M. Hicks (ed.), *Revolution and Consumption in Late Medieval England* (Woodbridge, 2001).

65. J. Blair (ed.), *Waterways and Canal-Building in Medieval England* (Oxford, 2007).
66. N. Allen, 'Built on Wool, the Medieval Wool Trade in England,' *Cake and Cockhorse*, 15 (2003).
67. H.S. Cobb (ed.), *The Overseas Trade of London. Exchequer Customs Accounts, 1480–1* (London, 1990).
68. M. Kowaleski, *Local Markets and Regional Trade in Medieval Exeter* (Cambridge, 1995).
69. D. Burwash, *English Merchant Shipping, 1460–1540* (Toronto, 1947); I. Friel, *The Good Ship: Ships, Shipbuilding and Technology in England, 1200—1520* (London, 1995).
70. J.H. Barrett and D.C. Orton (eds), *Cod and Herring: The Archaeology and History of Medieval Sea Fishing* (Oxford, 2016).
71. J. Langdon and J. Claridge, 'Transport in Medieval England,' *History Compass*, 9 (2011), pp. 864–75.
72. E. Hartrich, 'Charters and Inter-Urban Networks: England, 1439–1449,' *English Historical Review*, 132 (2017), pp. 219–49.
73. Eg. D. Dymond and E. Martin (eds), *An Historical Atlas of Suffolk* (2nd edn, Ipswich, 1989).
74. E.C. Woods, *Transactions of the Historic Society of Lancashire and Cheshire*, 87 (1935), pp. 1–21.

Chapter 2

1. J. Chandler (ed.), *John Leland's Itinerary: Travels in Tudor England* (Stroud, 1993).
2. P. Rogers, *Defoe's 'Tour' and Early Modern Britain* (Cambridge, 2022), p. 211.
3. A. Maczak, *Travel in Early Modern Europe* (Oxford, 1995).
4. J. Lee, *Cambridge and its Economic Region, 1450–1560* (Hatfield, 2005).
5. D. Rollison, *The Local Origins of Modern Society, Gloucestershire 1500–1800* (London, 1992).
6. G. Scammell, 'British North East Coast Fisheries, 1500–1750,' *Durham County Local History Society Bulletin*, 65 (2002).
7. S. Flavin, *Consumption and Culture in Sixteenth-Century Ireland: Saffron, Stockings and Silk* (Woodbridge, 2014).
8. J. Webb, *The Town Finances of Elizabethan Ipswich, Select Treasurers' and Chamberlains' Accounts* (Bury St Edmunds, 1996).
9. J. Mumby, 'From Carriage to Coach: What happened?,' in R. Bork and A. Kann (eds), *The Art, Science, and Technology of Medieval Travel* (Aldershot, 2008), pp. 41–54 and Evelyn journal, BL, Evelyn papers, vol. 49 fol. 21.
10. J. Munby, 'Queen Elizabeth's Coaches: The Wardrobe on Wheels,' *Antiquaries Journal*, 83 (2003), pp. 311–67, and 'Men in the Saddle and Women on Wheels: The Transport Revolution in the Tudor and Stuart Courts,' *The Court Historian*, 24,3 (2019), pp. 205–20.
11. J. Goodare, 'Witches' Flight in Scottish Demonology,' in Goodare (ed.), *Demonology and Witch-hunting* (2020).

Chapter 3

1. D.J. Taylor, *England from a Side-Saddle: The Great Journeys of Celia Fiennes* (Cheltenham, 2021).
2. C. Morris (ed.), *The Illustrated Journeys of Celia Fiennes c. 1682–c. 1712* (1982), pp. 157–9.
3. B. Tyson, 'The Cattle Trading Activities of Sir Daniel Fleming of Rydal Hall, 1656–1700,' *Cumberland and Westmorland Antiquarian and Archaeological Society*, 3rd ser., 2 (2002).
4. J. Parkes, *Travel in England in the Seventeenth Century* (Oxford, 1925), pp. 6–7, 10–11, 12.

5. Morris (ed), *Fiennes*, p. 250.

6. C. Phythian-Adams (ed.), *Societies, Cultures and Kinship, 1580–1850. Cultural Provinces and English Local History* (Leicester, 1992).

7. M. Bennett (ed.), *A Nottinghamshire Village in War and Peace. The Accounts of the Constables of Upton, 1640–1666* (Nottingham, 1995).

8. C.F. Foster, *Seven Households. Life in Cheshire and Lancashire 1582 to 1774* (Northwich, 2002).

9. G.A. Metters (ed.), *The Kings Lynn Port Books 1610–1614* (Norwich, 2009).

10. K.R. Clew, *The Kennet and Avon Canal* (Newton Abbot, 1985), pp. 15–18.

11. T.S. Willen, 'The Justices of the Peace and the Rates of Land Carriage, 1692–1827,' *Journal of Transport History*, 5 (1962), pp. 197–204; W. Albert, 'The Justices' Rates for Land Carriage 1748–1827, Reconsidered,' *Transport History*, 1 (1968), pp. 105–29.

12. A.G. Veysey (ed.), *A Handlist of the Denbighshire Quarter Sessions Records* (Hawarden, 1991).

13. M.C. Lowe, 'Notes on Archival Sources for Local Carriers in Devon,' *Archives*, 23, no. 98 (1998), p. 51.

14. D. Gerhold, *Carriers and Coachmasters, Trade and Travel before the Turnpikes* (Chichester, 2005).

15. P. Halliday, *Dismembering the Body Politic: Partisan Politics in English Towns, 1650–1730* (Cambridge, 1998).

16. R. Szostak, *The Role of Transportation in the Industrial Revolution: A Comparison of England and France* (Montreal, 1991).

17. J. Stobart, 'Regional Structure and the Urban System: North West England, 1600–1760,' *Transactions of the Historic Society of Lancashire and Cheshire*, 145 (1996), pp. 45–73.

18. A. Poole, *A Market Town and its Surrounding Villages: Cranbrook, Kent in the Later Seventeenth Century* (Chichester, 2005).

Chapter 4

1. Le Coq, Saxon envoy, to Marquis de Fleury, Saxon minister, 1 Feb. 1726, Dresden, Staatsarchiv, Geheimes Kabinett, Gesandschaften, vol. 2674 f. 2.

2. *York Courant*, 15 Jan. 1740.

3. *Mist's Weekly Journal*, 16 Dec. 1721; *St James's Evening Post*, 27 Jan. 1722.

4. Arthur Hart, Master of Merchant Venturers, to Edward Southwell and Robert Hoblyn, MPs, 10 Feb., Southwell to Hart, 15 Feb. 1746, Bristol, Public Library, Southwell Papers vol. 9.

5. Albemarle to Thomas, Duke of Newcastle, 17 Mar. 1746, London, British Library, Department of Manuscripts, Stowe MS. 158 f. 202.

6. Sir Everard Fawkener, secretary to Duke of Cumberland, to Andrew Fletcher, Lord Milton, 10 Feb. 1746, Edinburgh, National Library of Scotland, Dept. of Manuscripts, vol. 16621 f. 3.

7. Carmarthen, Record Office, Stackpole papers, vol. 138.

8. *Tom Jones*, VII, ix.

9. *Amelia*, II, i.

10. *Weekly Medley*, 3 Oct. 1719.

11. D. Gerhold, *Carriers and Coachmasters, Trade and Travel before the Turnpikes* (Chichester, 2005).

12. John to Richard Tucker, 17 Dec. 1743, Oxford, Bodleian Library, MS Don c. 106 f. 122.

13. P. Borsay, 'Gentry Papers: A Key Source for Urban Cultural History,' *Archives*, 19 (1991), pp. 374–83.

14. Roger to Sophy Newdigate, 22 Dec. 1745, A.W.A. White (ed.), *The Correspondence of Sir Roger Newdigate of Arbury* (Stratford-upon-Avon, 1995), p. 22. Chilvers Coton was near to Newdigate's Warwickshire estate at Arbury.

15. Brigadier-General James Cholmondeley MP to his brother George, 3rd Earl of Cholmondeley, 19 Nov. 1745, Chester, Cheshire Record Office, DCH/X/9a/11.

16. Field Marshal George Wade to Henry, 3rd Viscount Lonsdale, 13 Dec. 1745, Carlisle, Cumbria Record Office, D/Pen Acc 2689.

17. D. Thomas, 'Fenny Bridges in Feniton and Gittisham', *Devon Historian*, 50 (Apr. 1995), pp. 5–10.

18. D. Woolley, 'Thomas Hill of Tern, 1693–1782,' *Archives*, 21 (1994), pp. 167–8, 170.

19. Bristol, Archives, Southwell Papers, vol. 3.

20. B. Boyce, *The Benevolent Man: A Life of Ralph Allen of Bath* (Cambridge, Mass., 1967).

21. S. Miller, 'The Establishment of the River Wear Commissioners,' *Durham County Local History Society*, 26 (May 1981), pp. 11–25.

22. T.S. Willan, *River Navigation in England, 1600–1750* (London, 1936); T. Jones, 'Shipbuilding at Northwich,' *Cheshire History*, 30 (1992), p. 16.

23. S.W. Baskerville, 'The Establishment of the Grosvenor Interest in Chester 1710–48,' *Journal of the Chester Archaeological Society*, 63 (1980), p. 73.

24. Alderbury and Whaddon Local History Research Group, *Alderbury and Whaddon* (2000), p. 110.

25. *London Evening Post*, 22 Jan., *General Evening Post*, 26 Jan. 1734.

26. P. Rogers, 'Road-testing the First Turnpikes: The Enduring Value of Daniel Defoe's Account of English Highways,' *Journal of Transport History*, 40 (2019), pp. 211–31.

27. *York Courant*, 16 Jan. 1739.

28. M.C. Lowe, 'The Turnpike Trusts in Devon and Their Roads: 1753–1889,' *Transactions of the Devonshire Association*, 122 (1990), pp. 47–69.

29. *Tom Jones*, VII, iv.

30. *Tom Jones*, IX, vii.

31. *Tom Jones*, II, iii.

32. *Tom Jones*, XII, ix.

33. *Joseph Andrews*, IV, xvi.

34. *Joseph Andrews*, II, v.

35. See, for example, John Wells to Lydia Grey, 29 July 1723, S.M. Hardy, 'An Eighteenth-Century Love Affair,' *Buckinghamshire Record Office. Annual Report and List of Accessions* (1994), p. 22.

36. *Joseph Andrews*, II,ii.

37. *Tom Jones*, IX, vii.

38. *Tom Jones*, IX, iii.

39. *Tom Jones*, IX, iv.

40. *Tom Jones*, XII, iii.

41. *Jonathan Wild*, I, xiv.

42. *Sussex Weekly Advertiser*, 19 February 1749.

43. *The Weekly Courant*, 9 June 1737; Northumberland CRO ZRI 27/8.

44. Wood to Sir Charles Hotham, 19 Feb. 1749, Hull, University Library, DDHo 4/13; *Union Journal*, 19 June 1759. See also, on the Duke of Grafton 'from a peevish obstinacy of having a nearer road into Suffolk…' Richard Rigby to Sir Charles Hanbury Williams, 10 Ap. 1756, Farmington, Lewis Walpole Library, Hanbury Williams papers vol. 64.

45. Durham, CRO, Strathmore papers, D/St/C1/3/201–2.

46. Sir Henry Liddell to Matthew Ridley, 26 April 1744, 14 February 1745, Ashington, Northumberland CRO, Ridley of Blagdon papers, ZRI 25, 2.
47. M. and D. Honeybone (eds), *The Correspondence of the Spaulding Gentlemen's Society 1710–1761* (Lincoln, 2010).
48. G.J. Robertson, *The Origins of the Scottish Railway System, 1722–1844* (Edinburgh, 1983).
49. I. Christie, *British Non-elite MPs, 1715–1820* (Oxford, 1995); P. Gauci, *The Politics of Trade: The Overseas Merchant in State and Society, 1660–1720* (Oxford, 2001).
50. C. Whatley, *Scottish Society 1707–1830. Beyond Jacobitism, towards industrialisation* (Manchester, 2000).
51. D. Headrick, *When Information Came of Age. Technologies of Knowledge in the Age of Reason and Revolution, 1700–1850* (Oxford, 2001).
52. R. Price, *British Society 1680–1880* (Cambridge, 1999).

Chapter 5
1. Newcastle to Robert Keith, envoy in Vienna, 20 Ap. 1753, National Archives, State Papers 80/191.
2. W. Albert, *The Turnpike Road System in England 1663–1840* (Cambridge, 1972).
3. Halifax, Calderdale Archives, SH7/JL/25.
4. J. Stovold, *Minute Book of the Pavement Commissioners of Southampton* (Southampton, 1990).
5. B. Nurse (ed.), *Town Prints and Drawings of Britain before 1800* (Oxford, 2020), p. 212–13.
6. D. Starkei, *The Motorway Age: Road and Traffic Policies in Post-War Britain* (Oxford, 1982); J. Kelly (ed.), *The Letters of Lord Chief Baron Edward Willes to the Earl of Warwick, 1757–1762. An account of Ireland in the mid-eighteenth century* (Aberystwyth, 1990). See also, covering 1747–60, J. McVeagh (ed.), *Richard Pococke's Irish Tours* (Dublin, 1995).
7. M. Lowe, 'Archival Sources for Road Improvement in eighteenth-century Devon,' *Archives*, 20 (1992), p. 10.
8. N. Watson, *The Literary Tourist* (Basingstoke, 2008).
9. Nurse, *Town Prints*, pp. 212–13.
10. D. Sekers, *A Lady of Cotton. Hannah Greg, Mistress of Quarry Bank Mill* (Stroud, 2013).
11. N. Cossons and B. Trinder, *The Iron Bridge: Symbol of the Industrial Revolution* (Chichester, 2002).
12. D. Harrison, *Bridges and Communications in Pre-Industrial England* (DPhil. Oxford, 1996).
13. B. Riley, *The Bridges of Robert Adam* (London, 2023), esp. p. 33.
14. B. Cozens-Hardy (ed.), *The Diary of Sylas Neville* (Oxford, 1950), p. 277; D. Souden (ed.), *Byng's Tours* (London, 1991), p. 184.
15. J. Sharp, *Rolling Carts and Waggons*, descriptive advertisement, *c.*1770.
16. C. Hadfield, *The Canals of the West Midlands* (Newton Abbot, 1966).
17. A.W.A. White (ed.), *The Correspondence of Sir Roger Newdigate of Arbury, Warwickshire*, Dugdale Society, Vol. XXXVII (1995), p. 145.
18. J. Bourne (ed.), *Georgian Tiverton. The Political Memoranda of Beavis Wood 1768–98* (Torquay, 1986), p. 5.
19. D. Gerhold, 'Productivity Change in Road Transport before and after Turnpiking,' *Economic History Review*, 49 (1996), pp. 491–515; D. Bogart, 'Turnpike Trusts and the Transportation Revolution in 18th Century England,' *Explorations in Economic History*, 42 (2005), pp. 479–508, 'Did Turnpike Trusts Increase Transportation Investment in Eighteenth-Century England?', 65, and 'Turnpike Trusts, Infrastructure Investment, and the Road Transportation Revolution in Eighteenth-Century England,' *Journal of Economic History*, 65 (2005), pp. 439–68, 540–3.

20. D. Gerhold, 'The Development of Stage Coaching and the Impact of Turnpike Roads, 1653–1840,' *Economic History Review*, 67 (2014), pp. 818–45.
21. G. Clark (ed.), *Correspondence of the Foundling Hospital Inspectors in Berkshire 1757–68* (Reading, 1994).
22. Nurse, *Town Prints*, p. 22.
23. A. Young, *A Six Weeks Tour Through the Southern Counties of England and Wales* (London, 1772), pp. 323–4.
24. A. Currie, *Henleys of Wapping – A London Shipowning Family 1770–1830* (London, 1988).
25. Nurse, *Town Prints*, p. 81.
26. *Oxford Gazette*, 9 May 1757.
27. M. Elder, *The Slave Trade and the Economic Development of Eighteenth-Century Lancaster* (Edinburgh, 1992).
28. For praise of Liverpool, Anonymous, *A Tour Through Ireland* (Dublin, 1746) p. 33.
29. G. Place, *The Rise and Fall of Parkgate. Passenger Port for Ireland, 1686–1815* (Preston, 1994).
30. H. Rawlings, 'Extracts from the Sussex Quarter Session Records, 1626–1800,' *Sussex History*, 31 (1991), p. 33.
31. B. Frith (ed.), *Ralph Bigland's Historical, Monumental and Genealogical Collections relative to the County of Gloucester I* (Gloucester, 1989).
32. Sir Robert Murray Keith to Frances Murray, 18 Oct, 1788, San Marino, Calf, Huntington Library, HM. 18940, p.298. S. Bhanji, 'The Early Balloon Craze of Exeter,' *Devon Historian*, 63 (2001).
33. Hamilton to Francis, Marquess of Carmarthen, Foreign Secretary, 20 Nov. 1786, National Archives, Foreign Office papers 70/3.

Chapter 6

1. G. Wilson, 'Public Hire Chairs in Weymouth,' *Notes and Queries for Somerset and Dorset*, 33 (1994), pp. 289–94.
2. K. Davidson, *Improbable Pioneers of the Romantic Age* (London, 2022), p. 458.
3. A. Brontë, *The Tenant of Wildfell Hall* (London, 1848; 1979 edn), p. 474.
4. J. Barron, *A History of the Ribble Navigation from Preston to the Sea* (Preston, 1938; J. Sheail, 'Local Legislation: Its Scope and Context,' *Archives*, 30 (2005), pp. 39–43.
5. P. May, T. Wyke and A. Kidd, 'Water Transport in the Industrial Age: Commodities and Carriers on the Rochdale Canal, 1804–1855,' *Journal of Transport History*, 30 (2009), pp. 200–28.
6. S. Law, *Dark Side of the Cut. A History of Crime on Britain's Canals* (Stroud, 2023).
7. G. Place, *The Rise and Fall of Parkgate. Passenger Port for Ireland, 1686–1815* (Manchester, 1994).
8. P. Carter, 'Devon's Place in the Development of Tourism,' *Devon Historian*, 66 (2003), p. 19.
9. C. Ponsford (ed.), *Shipbuilding on the Exe: the Memoranda Book of Daniel Davy of Topsham* (Exeter, 1988).
10. P. Gulland, *Making the Road from Princes Risborough to Thame: a nineteenth century turnpike trust at work* (Aylesbury, 2006).
11. D. Gerhold, *Road Transport before the Railways: Russell's London Flying Wagons* (Cambridge, 1993).
12. W.J. Reader, *Macadam: the McAdam family and the turnpike roads, 1798–1861* (1980).
13. D. Howell, 'The Rebecca Riots,' in T. Herbert and G.E. Herbert (eds), *People and Protest in Wales* (Cardiff, 1988), pp. 113–38.

14. A. Bryne (ed.), *A Scientific, Antiquarian and Picturesque Tour: John (Fiott) Lee in Ireland, England and Wales, 1806–1807* (London, 2018), pp. 35, 42.

15. N. Rosenberg and W.G. Vincenti, *The Britannia Bridge: the generation and diffusion of technological knowledge* (Boston, Mass., 1978).

16. T. Meynell, *A Report Relative to the Opening of a Communication by a Canal or a Rail or Tramway from Stockton by Darlington to the Collieries* (Stockton, 1818).

17. L. Gooch, 'Papists and Profits: The Catholics of Durham and Industrial Development,' *Durham County Local History Society Bulletin*, 42 (May 1989), pp. 54–6.

18. D. Gwyn, *The Coming of the Railway. A New Global History 1750–1850* (New Haven, Conn., 2023).

19. M. Wheeler, *The Year that Shaped the Victorian Age. Lives, Loves and Letters of 1845* (Cambridge, 2023), p. 50.

20. R. Tibble, 'Brighton's First Railway Link With London,' *Sussex History*, 32 (1991), pp. 16–17.

21. E. Course (ed.), *Minutes of the Board of Directors of the Reading, Guildford and Reigate Railway Company* (Guildford, 1987).

22. L. Hawksley, *Dickens and Travel* (Barnsley, 2022).

23. J. Barney, *The Norfolk Railway. Railway Mania in East Anglia 1834–1862* (Norwich, 2007).

24. F. Cockman, *The Railways of Buckinghamshire from the 1830s. An account of those that were not built as well as those that were* (Aylesbury, 2006).

25. J.K. Walton and J. Wood (eds), *The Making of a Cultural Landscape: The English Lake District as Tourist Destination, 1750–2010* (Farnham, 2013).

Chapter 7

1. Graham to Raglan, 10 Jan. 1854, BL. Add. 79696, f. 87.

2. C. Brontë, *Villette* (London, 1853; Nelson edition), p. 47.

3. V.J. Bradley, *Industrial Locomotives of North Wales* (London, 1992).

4. H. Harris, *Devon's Railways* (Launceston, 2001).

5. B. Howard, 'Richard Wolston: Brixham Entrepreneur Extraordinary,' *Devon History*, 61 (2000), pp. 26–7.

6. R.J. Barrow, 'Rape on the Railway: Women, Safety, and Moral Panic in Victorian Newspapers,' A. Milne-Smith, 'Shattered Minds: Madmen on the Railways, 1860–80,' *Journal of Victorian Culture*, 20 (2015), pp. 341–56, 21 (2016), pp. 21–39.

7. C. Otter, *Diet for a Large Planet: Industrial Britain, Food Systems, and World Economy* (Chicago, Ill., 2020).

8. P. Parry, 'The Dorset Ports and the Coming of the Railways,' *Mariner's Mirror*, 53 (1967), pp. 243–9.

9. H. Compton, 'Staffing Oxford Canal – Around 1851,' *Cake and Cockhorse*, 14 (2000).

10. H. Compton, 'Oxford Canal and the Ironstone Business,' *Cake and Cockhorse*, 14 (1998).

11. W. Collins, *No Name* (London, 1862; 1994 edn), p. 82.

12. I. Ferris, P. Leach and S. Litherland, 'A Survey of Bridge Street and Mill Lane, Banbury,' *Cake and Cockhorse*, 12 (1992), pp. 54–65.

13. A. Crosby, 'Where was Banburyshire? Tracing the extent of an imagined county,' annual lecture of the Oxfordshire Record Society, 14 Oct. 2023.

14. J. Ruskin, *Praeterita* (1885–9), III, iv.

15. 'Railway Navvy to Farmer: The Memoirs of Thomas Henry Masters of Catesby (1878–1973),' *Northamptonshire Past and Present*, 8 (1990–1), p. 162.

16. J. Barry, 'The Streets and Traffic of London,' *Journal of the Royal Society of Arts*, 47 (1898–9), p. 9.

17. S. Mosley, *The Chimney of the World: A History of Smoke Pollution in Victorian and Elizabethan Manchester* (Cambridge, 2001).
18. P. Riden, *How to Trace the History of Your Car. A Guide to Motor Transport Registration* (London, 1991).

Chapter 8

1. 'My Early Years: Reminiscences of County Durham in the Early Twentieth Century by Ella MacLean,' *Durham County Local History Society Bulletin*, 39 (Dec. 1987), pp. 25–8.
2. *Daily Telegraph*, 15 Aug. 1947.
3. K. Graeme, *The Wind in the Willows* (London, 1908; 1994 edn), p. 49.
4. *Ibid.*, pp. 121, 133.
5. *Ibid.*, p. 42.
6. *Ibid.*, p. 46.
7. *Ibid.*, pp. 166–7.
8. *Ibid.*, p. 171.
9. *Ibid.*, p. 208.
10. G. Finch, 'Railways and the Balance of Trade in Victorian Devon,' *Devon and Cornwall Notes and Queries*, 36 (1988), pp. 86–7.
11. D. Bathurst, *The Selsey Tram* (Chichester, 1992).
12. T. Hopper, 'The Boilermakers Strike in Brighton Railway Works, 1909–1910,' *Sussex History*, 31 (1991), pp. 16–22.
13. R. Storey, 'Motor Vehicle Registration in Warwickshire, 1914–1918,' *Warwickshire History*, 8 (1992), pp. 159–62.
14. S.C. Gwynne, *His Majesty's Airship: The Life and Tragic Death of the World's Largest Flying Machine* (London, 2023).
15. *Leeds Mercury*, 11 May 1926.
16. E. Rose, *The Southern Railway 1923–1947* (Stroud, 1996).
17. T. Iresom, 'The Beginning of Motoring in Kettering,' *Northamptonshire Past and Present*, 8 (1987–8), p. 361.
18. Who had built railways in Scotland in the eighteenth century.
19. E.C.R. Lorac, *Death on the Oxford Road* (London, 1931; 2000 edn), p. 5.
20. J.B. Priestley, *The Good Companions* (London, 1929; 1962 edn), p. 12.
21. J.B. Priestley, *The Good Companions* (London, 1929; 1962 edn), pp. 11, 370.
22. P. Larkham and K. Dilley, *Planning the 'City of Tomorrow': British Reconstruction Planning, 1939–1952: An Annotated Bibliography* (Pickering, 2001).
23. J. Sheail, 'Environmental History: A Challenge for the Local Historian,' *Archives*, 22 (1997), pp. 160, 162.
24. S. Heffer, *Sing As We Go. Britain Between the Wars* (London, 2023), p. 343.
25. P.G. Wodehouse, *The Inimitable Jeeves* (London, 1923; 1991 edn), p. 148.
26. P.G. Wodehouse, *Right Ho, Jeeves* (London, 1934; 1953 edn), p. 11.
27. P.G. Wodehouse, *Stiff Upper Lip Jeeves* (1963; 1966 edn), p. 79.
28. R. Samways (ed.), *We Think You Ought To Go; An Account of the Evacuation of Children from London during the Second World War based on the original records of the London County Council* (London, 1995).
29. R. Postgate, *Somebody at the Door* (London, 1943; London, 2016 edn), pp. 15–16.
30. E.C.R. Lorac, *The Theft of the Iron Dogs* (London, 1946; London, 2023 edn), p. 22.
31. G. Crompton, '"Good Business for the Nation": The Railway Nationalisation Issue, 1921–47,' *Journal of Transport History*, 20 (1999), pp. 141–59; R. Toye, *Age of Hope*.

Labour, 1945, and the Birth of Modern Britain (London, 2023), p. 12; D.R. Devereux, 'State Versus Private Ownership: The Conservative Governments and Civil Aviation, 1951–62,' *Albion*, 27 (1995), pp. 65–85.

32. J.D. Carr, *He Who Whispers* (London, 1946; London, 2023 edn), p. 15, 66, 74–5, 108, 173.

Chapter 9

1. G. Crompton, '"Good business for the nation." The railway nationalisation issue, 1921–47,' *Journal of Transport History*, 20/2, pp. 153, 156.
2. C. Loft, *British Government and the Railways, 1951–1964: Beeching's Last Trains* (London, 2004).
3. *Observer*, 26 July 1998.
4. A. Brew, *The History of Black Country Aviation* (Stroud, 1993).
5. L. Johnman and H. Murphy, *British Shipbuilding and the State since 1918: A Political Economy of Decline* (Exeter, 2002).
6. G. Greene, *The end of the Affair* (London, 1951; 1975 edn), p. 30.
7. K. Amis, *Jake's Thing* (1978; London, 1979 edn), p. 34.
8. On cars as a democratic invention but isolating, C. Gorman, 'The Search for Intelligent Life in the Late 20th Century,' *Community* (Sept. 1994), https://pages.jh.edu/jhumag/994web/commun1.html
9. P. and R. Baldwin (eds), *The Motorway Achievement* (London, 2004).
10. R. Vinen, *Second City. Birmingham and the Forging of Modern Britain* (London, 2022), pp. 255–8.
11. T. Barker and D. Gerhold, *The Rise and Rise of Road Transport, 1700–1990* (London, 1993).
12. E. Schenker, 'Nationalisation and Denationalisation of Motor Carriers in Great Britain,' *Land Economics*, 39 (1963), pp. 219–30.
13. *Norwich Mercury*, 13 Mar. 1731, item from *Daily Courant*.

Chapter 10

1. Smollett *Travels through France and Italy* (London, 1766), letter 29.
2. T. Breen, A. Flint, C. Hickman and G. O'Hara, 'Whose right to roam? Contesting access to England's countryside,' *Journal of Transport History*, 44 (2023), pp. 276–307.
3. Scotland's Railway, *Strategic Business Plan* (Edinburgh, 2023), p. 37.

Chapter 11

1. J.G. Bishop, *'A Peep into the Past': Brighton in the Olden Times, with Glances at the Present* (Brighton, 1880), p. 272.
2. Dept. of Transport, https://roadtraffic.dft.gov.uk/summary/
3. Sustainability by numbers, 15 Sept. 223: https://sustainabilitybynumbers.com/P/uk-ev-electricity-demand
4. See for example, P. Bagwell and P. Lyth, *Transport in Britain. From Canal Lock to Gridlock* (London, 2002).
5. *Leeds Intelligencer*, 8, 15 July, 5 Aug., 23 Sept. 1766.
6. *Oxford Gazette*, 14 Feb. 1757, 18 May 1767; *Reading Mercury*, 15 Jan., 23, 30 Ap., 7 May, 3 Sept., 5 Nov., 31 Dec. 1770, 25 Feb., 11 Mar. 1771.

Index